I AM A STAR

"The author is one of 100 children who survived Czechoslovakia's Terezin concentration camp. . . . Auerbacher's family went to Terezin in 1942 when she was seven. Luck was seemingly the chief factor in their survival [but] it was only Allied liberation that spared the lives of the Auerbacher family. While the author's story is personal, there is recognition of the Nazi toll on non-Jews as well as of non-Jewish resistance to the ongoing horrors. . . . This account will be a revelation of manageable proportions to middle-grade readers, especially those who already know Anne Frank's story." —*Booklist*

"A small treasure in the current deluge of personal stories about the Holocaust." —*The Jewish Week*

I AM A STAR

Only "special" children wear a star,
I am noticed from near and far.
They have placed a mark over my heart,
I'll wear it proudly from the start.

A star's a reward, so I've been told,
This custom passed on from days of old.
I know all that the star is revealing,
But, I'll try to have a better feeling.
                                    I am a star!

Papa told me to avoid trouble,
Come home from school on the double.
To me the star's yellow is gold,
I'll try not to act so bold.

I stand tall and proud,
My voice shouts in silence loud:
"I am a real person still,
No one can break my spirit or will!"
                                    I am a star!

I AM A STAR

✡

Child
of the Holocaust
INGE AUERBACHER

WITH ILLUSTRATIONS BY
ISRAEL BERNBAUM

Puffin Books

PUFFIN BOOKS

Published by the Penguin Group

Penguin Books USA Inc., 375 Hudson Street, New York, New York 10014, U.S.A.

Penguin Books Ltd, 27 Wrights Lane, London W8 5TZ, England

Penguin Books Australia Ltd, Ringwood, Victoria, Australia

Penguin Books Canada Ltd, 10 Alcorn Avenue, Toronto, Ontario, Canada M4V 3B2

Penguin Books (N.Z.) Ltd, 182–190 Wairau Road, Auckland 10, New Zealand

Penguin Books Ltd, Registered Offices: Harmondsworth, Middlesex, England

First published in the United States of America by Prentice-Hall Books for
Young Readers, a division of Simon & Schuster, Inc., 1986
Published in Puffin Books, 1993

10 9 8 7 6 5 4 3 2 1

LIBRARY OF CONGRESS CATALOGING-IN-PUBLICATION DATA

Auerbacher, Inge, 1934–
I am a star: child of the Holocaust / Inge Auerbacher; with
illustrations by Israel Bernbaum.   p.   cm.
Summary: The author's reminiscences about her childhood in
Germany, years of which were spent in a Nazi concentration camp.
Includes several of her original poems.
ISBN 0-14-036401-3
1. Jews—Germany—Kippenheim—Persecutions—Juvenile literature.
2. Holocaust, Jewish (1939–1945)—Germany—Kippenheim—Personal
narratives—Juvenile literature.   3. Terezín (Czechoslovakia:
Concentration camp)—Juvenile literature.   4. Auerbacher, Inge,
1934–   —Juvenile literature. 5. Kippenheim (Germany)—Ethnic
relations—Juvenile literature. [1. Auerbacher, Inge, 1934–
2. Jews—Germany—Biography. 3. Holocaust, Jewish (1939–1945)—
Germany—Kippenheim—Personal narratives. 4. Terezín
(Czechoslovakia: Concentration camp) 5. Concentration camps—
Czechoslovakia.] I. Bernbaum, Israel, ill. II. Title.
[DS135.G4K553   1993]   940.53′18′094371—dc20   92-31444

Printed in the United States of America
Set in Garamond No. 3

Reprinted by arrangement with Viking Penguin, a division of Penguin Books USA, Inc.

I dedicate this book to

My parents, the guardian angels, who in the presence of great odds tried to shelter me from the blows, ease my pain, and still my hunger and fears.

Ruth and Tommy and the more than one and a half million Jewish children of the Holocaust, who now are stars of the night.

All the children of the universe, who are the new stars that shine brightly today and illuminate the world with their love.

CONTENTS

CHAPTER 1

✡

Beginnings

I remember as a little girl waiting impatiently for my birthday to arrive. My childhood birthdays were always very happy and special. That is, until my eighth birthday. I was seven years old in 1942 when I was sent with my parents to a concentration camp in Czechoslovakia. My next three birthdays marked the years of a nightmare.

Of fifteen thousand children imprisoned in the Terezin concentration camp in Czechoslovakia between 1941 and 1945, about one hundred survived. I am one of them. At least one and a half million children were killed in the Nazi Holocaust. The reason most of those children died is that they were Jewish.

Why should one remember these dreadful events? The death of one innocent child is a catastrophe; the loss of such numbers is unimaginable. Their silent voices must be heard today. This is why I feel compelled to trace the historical events that made this great evil possible and to tell my own story.

Many years have passed since these events. Sometimes particular things such as a uniform, high black boots, or the sound of a whistle and train, shock me into the past. On a vacation in Quebec City, Canada, the sight of the old fortification brought the memories flooding back. The high red brick walls seemed to close in on me. I felt frightened. It was as if I were back there in Czechoslovakia. Yesterday became today. This was not Quebec City anymore; it became Terezin. It brought back to me the time when the nightmare began.

I was born on December 31, 1934, in Kippenheim, a village in southern Germany. Kippenheim is situated at the foot of the Black Forest, close to the borders of France and Switzerland. The population of around two thousand was composed of about sixty Jewish families and approximately four hundred and fifty Catholic and Protestant families. My family belonged to the middle class. Papa had his own textile business. Jews had lived in Kippenheim for at least two hundred years. I was the last Jewish child born

there. The synagogue was the center of our lives. I remember well the interior of our beautiful synagogue. The bright chandeliers always caught my eye. It was very strange and special for me to hear Cantor Schwab chant our Hebrew prayers. Most of the Jewish people of Kippenheim attended the Sabbath service on Saturday morning. There was always a special festive spirit during our holidays, and the worshipers came dressed in their best clothes. It was common practice to visit one another after the synagogue service and to invite a stranger into one's home for dinner.

There was a very strong bond among the Jewish people of Kippenheim. We felt as if we were all members of an extended family. Many of the Christians of Kippenheim were farmers, while the Jews owned small shops and sold textiles or cattle. We were a friendly community, and both Christians and Jews assumed responsibility for their German citizenship, in peace and in war.

5

I AM A STAR

Papa was a soldier in the German army in World War I. He was only eighteen years old when an enemy bullet tore through his right shoulder and wounded him badly. He was decorated with the Iron Cross for his bravery in the service of his country.

I was the only child of Berthold and Regina Auerbacher. Papa's family had settled in Kippenheim some two hundred years earlier.

Most of his family made their living by buying and selling cattle, an occupation practiced by many Jews in southern Germany. Papa's grandfather bought the large house in which Papa and I were born. Many Auerbachers lived in Kippenheim, and all of us were related. Mama was born in Jebenhausen, an even smaller village some two hundred miles away. Her father was also a cattle dealer. Papa's parents had died a few years before his marriage to Mama. Three of Papa's married sisters lived in different parts of

I AM A STAR

It was a cold morning in November,
A day that I will always remember.
We were awakened from a peaceful sleep,
The flames of terror had begun to leap.
"Open the door, police, let us in;
Don't run or hide, you cannot win!"
We had avoided the truth and closed our eyes,
The knock on our door had caught us by surprise.
"All Jewish men are now under arrest,
Report to City Hall and join the rest!"
Grandpa attended services each day,
Now, from his prayers he was torn away.
The train rolled on toward incarceration,
Dachau, barrack number sixteen, their destination.
ARBEIT MACHT FREI* was their only greeting,
To hide the reality they would be meeting.
They wore blue and white striped uniform,
Beaten and hungry they faced the storm.
In the village only women and children were left,
Followed by rampage of tremendous ruin and theft.
Our temple became the prime target of hate,
Mama saw tablets ripped from their normal state.
The Commandments lay broken on the ground,
Heralding darkness with their crushing sound.
Broken glass crashing, echoed all day,
Our house was no place for us to stay.
In our living room, a stone grazed my head,
We ran for shelter in a backyard shed.
The volcano had exploded and begun to spew,
In its path lay the destiny of every Jew.

*work means freedom

BEGINNINGS

Germany, and the fourth lived in France. Two sisters had two children each. They were my older cousins Hella, Werner, Heinz, and Lore. Mama's only brother was married and lived a few hours away.

Berthold Auerbach (Moses Baruch Auerbacher), a member of my family, was one of Germany's most beloved folk writers. He lived from 1812 to 1882, and his stories of the Black Forest made him world famous. Berthold Auerbach was born and lived in Nordstetten in southern Germany, which was where my family came from.

We were a happy community in Kippenheim until the sound of marching boots shattered the peace of our tranquil village. A massive riot took place on November 9, 1938. That event is called Kristallnacht, or Night of Broken Glass. It marked the beginning of terror that would continue for seven years. I was then only three years old.

CHAPTER 2

✡

The Roots of Hatred

Anti-Semitism, or hatred of the Jews, has existed throughout the history of the Jewish religion. Many people disliked Jews because they had different customs and because they refused to become Christians. During the second half of the nineteenth century, however, a new type of anti-Semitism began to emerge. Some people began to say that Jews belonged to a different race and that Jews were racially inferior to Christians.

But who are the Jews and why did they inspire such feelings? Their origins can be traced to the patriarch Abraham, the father of a Semitic tribe of shepherds and farmers, whose revolutionary belief in the existence of one supreme God became the foundation of three great religions. The history of the Jews goes back almost four thousand years to their arrival in the biblical land of Canaan that was later called Palestine and today is called Israel. The Ten Commandments given by God to Moses serve as the basis for their religion, Judaism. Today there are people who follow this religion in almost every country in the world.

The Jews arrived in Germany about sixteen hundred years ago, around A.D. 400. They came from the Mediterranean region as traders following the Roman armies. From about A.D. 1096, during the time of the Crusades, which were Christian military expeditions that set out to recover the Holy Land from the Moslems, life became very difficult for the Jews living in Germany and other parts of Central Europe. The Crusaders offered the Jews the choice of baptism or death. "To sanctify the Name of God," they slaughtered thousands of Jews who refused to betray their religion. The church branded the Jews "Christ-killers," and Jews were thought of as evil people.

During most of the Middle Ages, the only occupations open to Jews were small trade and moneylending. The church regarded moneylending as sinful and did not permit Christians to charge interest. In this way, Jews were also associated with an evil practice.

In the Middle Ages, the Jews in Germany and other parts of Europe were sometimes forced to live in a restricted part of the city called a ghetto. In some places the Jews were isolated from other people behind walls. In the ghetto the streets were narrow and dark. Many people were poor and lived in overcrowded, crumbling houses, although some people became successful merchants. Everyone in the ghetto was forced to pay high taxes. No Jew was allowed to leave the ghetto from nightfall to daybreak and on Christian holidays. A locked gate sealed them off from the outside world. Harsh penalties were enforced if Jews were found outside of the walls during the curfew.

Conditions grew even worse when the Black Death struck. History records several outbreaks of this widespread plague and there was a particular epidemic that killed thousands of people in Europe between 1348 and 1351. The terrible sickness was blamed on the Jews, whom the Christians accused of practicing black

I AM A STAR

magic and of poisoning the wells from which the Christians drew
their water. Many Jews were expelled and fled eastward from
Germany to Poland, Lithuania, Czechoslovakia, Hungary,
Rumania, and Russia, where they established thriving Jewish
communities. They were always a small minority in the total
population in any country, however, and were regarded as
outsiders because of their different religion and customs.

For those Jews who remained in Germany, conditions finally
improved. In the early 1800s they were permitted to leave the
ghetto, and they were gradually accepted by some of the Christian
community. During the 1870s, they became full and equal citizens
under the law throughout the country. They felt part of the
German family, differing from other Germans only in religion.

A large number of Germans, however, never fully accepted
their Jewish fellow citizens because of their different traditions.
Jews were still not permitted to reach the highest ranks in law,
government, the armed forces, or the universities. At the same
time, a new wave of hostility based on a racist theory emerged in
many parts of Europe. People began to believe that the Jews were
a separate, inferior race. Jews tried hard to become accepted by
society, some of them proudly proclaiming that their religion was
secondary to their nationality.

At first, in Germany as elsewhere, most people did not believe
this racist anti-Semitism. This attitude changed however as
Germans looked for a scapegoat after their disastrous defeat at the
end of World War I in 1918. During the war both Jews and non-
Jews had fought side by side and died together for their
fatherland, but with Germany's spiritual and economic defeat, this
period of unity and patriotism ended. Germany was forced to sign
the Treaty of Versailles in 1919 and to admit that she had started
the war. She had to accept the severe measures that the Allies
imposed, and to drastically reduce the army. She also had to pay
large amounts of money to compensate for the suffering caused
during the war, and to reduce the German Empire. A new
democratic government was elected and the Weimar Republic was
formed.

THE ROOTS OF HATRED

The Weimar government was troubled from the start. The post-war years saw inflation, unemployment and finally, in 1929, a world depression. Jewish people were blamed for the ailing economy and extremists called for them to be pushed out of German society. Racist anti-Semitism gathered support. In this climate of hostility and depression the stage was set for Hitler's Nazi party to emerge.

CHAPTER 3

✡

Adolf Hitler's Rise to Power

Adolf Hitler was born on April 20, 1889, in Braunau, a village in Austria near the German border. He was not a gifted student, and he failed as an artist. In 1907, he moved to Vienna where his political aspirations were born. At the age of twenty-four he arrived in Munich, Germany, and soon was in the midst of World War I. He volunteered for service in the German army, fought in many battles and reached the rank of corporal.

In 1919 in Munich, Hitler joined a small nationalist group called the German Workers' Party, which changed its name a year later to the National Socialist German Workers' Party. This group later became known as the Nazi Party.

On November 8, 1923, Hitler held a rally in a Munich beer hall and called for a Nazi revolution against the Bavarian government. The following day he attempted to seize power. This event became known as the Beer Hall Putsch, which means revolution. Hitler was arrested for treason and sentenced to five years in prison. He only served nine months of his prison term. During his time in prison, he put his ideas into a book called *Mein Kampf*, or *My Struggle*.

Many Germans were enchanted by Hitler's magnetism and regarded him as their savior. He made it clear in *Mein Kampf* what he would do to create a new Germany. He intended to establish a New Order (the Third Reich) that would last a thousand years. Hitler said that Germany must rid itself of all Communists and Jews, whom he considered enemies of the state. He held a special hatred for the Jews and singled them out to bear the blame for all of Germany's troubles. Hitler believed the Jews as a race were inferior to the Aryan (German) "Master Race." Pure Aryans, he contended, were large-boned, blond, and blue-eyed, although Hitler himself was short and dark-haired. He believed that all Jews had to be eliminated because their blood was inferior to that of the German Aryans. He said Jewish blood would pollute the "master race." The truth is all blood types occur in all races and all nations. Hitler's brand of anti-Semitism would be the worst ever seen anywhere.

After Hitler was released from prison, he convinced the government that his party would respect the law. He rose steadily to power and gained support from labor unions, business, industry, and agriculture. In the New Order the swastika, or twisted cross, became the symbol of the Nazi Party.

In 1930 Hitler's brown-shirted storm troopers, or Sturmabteilung (SA), marched through the streets with the Nazi swastika flag, singing, "Today we rule Germany, tomorrow the world!"

On January 30, 1933, Hitler was appointed Chancellor of Germany by the ailing President von Hindenburg, who died eighteen months later. After von Hindenburg's death, Hitler abolished the presidency and made himself the absolute ruler, or Fuehrer, of the nation. Crowds cheered him with cries of "Heil, Hitler," which means Hail, Hitler. The Weimar Republic, which had lasted from 1918 to 1933, was over.

From the start, Hitler's government was based on lies and deception. Hitler had a secret police called the Gestapo and a special security force known as the SS, for Schutzstaffel, also called the Blackshirts. He named Josef Goebbels chief of propaganda, assigning him to spread his doctrine, but Hitler himself was an excellent speaker and influenced both young and old. Hermann Goering became second in command to Hitler. Rudolf Hess was Hitler's secretary, and Heinrich Himmler became the party's chief executioner.

Two themes dominated Hitler's dictatorship from beginning to end: *Lebensraum*, the belief that Germany needed more land and was entitled to invade her neighbors in order to get it; and *Judenfrage*, the theory that the entire Jewish race had to be eliminated. During the Hitler regime, the Nazis did their best to carry these ideas to their murderous extremes. Anti-Semitism became official government policy.

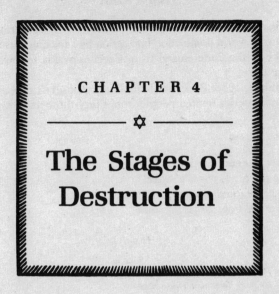

CHAPTER 4

✡

The Stages of Destruction

The first stage in Hitler's planned destruction of the Jews, from 1933 to 1938, was to deprive Jews in Germany of all rights. Decrees followed one another in rapid succession. The first decree was for a one-day boycott of Jewish shops and businesses. Then the ritual slaughter of animals in accordance with Jewish dietary laws was forbidden. There were public burnings of books written by Jews. The first German concentration camp—Dachau, located near Munich—was established in 1933.

Between 1933 and 1935 most Jewish teachers, public servants, and professionals lost their jobs. On August 2, 1934, Hitler was named president and commander-in-chief of the armed forces. The Third Reich had become a reality. On September 15, 1935, the so-called Nuremberg Laws, which were anti-Jewish racial laws, came into effect. Jews could no longer be German citizens. Those of mixed Jewish and Aryan backgrounds were called *Mischlinge*, or half-breeds, and were subjected to the same harsh laws. Jews were

17

no longer permitted to fly the German flag. In 1938, Germany put its dream of world domination into action by annexing Austria. The takeover of the Sudetenland from Czechoslovakia followed soon afterward.

On July 6, 1938, President Franklin D. Roosevelt of the United States of America invited people from thirty-three nations to meet

IF ONLY

They met at Evian on Geneva's shore,
Holding the key to freedom's door.
Thirty-two nations claimed open mind,
They saw the light; yet acted blind.

If only!

Talking for days; finding excuse,
Leaving us prey to mounting abuse.
In humanity's sea we were adrift,
Our doom would be violent and swift.

If only!

How many lives could have been spared,
Had one FREE nation really cared?
Human beings offered for sale,
Our cries rose up to no avail.

If only!

We still feel the pain and we weep,
This nightmare will not let us sleep.
A page in history; one must learn,
Yesterday us, tomorrow your turn?

If only, if only!

at Evian, France. Thirty-two nations sent representatives to this conference to discuss how they could aid political refugees who wanted to emigrate from Germany and Austria. These refugees were mainly Jews, whose lives were becoming unbearable in those countries. The Evian Conference failed. A German newspaper ran this headline: "Jews for Sale—Who Wants Them? No One!"

On November 7, 1938, Herschel Grynszpan, a seventeen-year-old Polish Jewish student, walked into the German embassy in Paris and shot Ernst vom Rath, a minor German official. Grynszpan had been angered by the forced deportation of his parents from Germany to Poland. The Grynszpans, like many other Polish Jews, had lived in Germany for a long time without seeking citizenship and now were mercilessly thrown out of the country. Vom Rath died two days later on November 9, 1938.

This incident triggered a nationwide riot in Germany and Austria on the night of November 9, 1938. Kristallnacht, or the Night of Broken Glass, continued for two days. Almost all Jewish houses of worship were put to the torch. Jewish homes and businesses were looted and destroyed. Many Jewish men were arrested and sent to concentration camps. Those who resisted were shot.

Soon afterward, Jews were forbidden to attend German schools and to own property or businesses. The Nazi scheme was to make conditions for the Jews impossible by keeping them from making a living. This tactic, they hoped, would drive the Jews out of Germany.

Many Jews managed to leave Germany and Austria, but most of those who lived in Eastern Europe were stranded. Those Jews who remained in Germany, in spite of all humiliation, were still attached to the country they had lived in for so many years. Most of them thought this, too, would pass, not recognizing the danger they were facing. When they finally were ready to leave, they found that the doors of the outside world would not open. Escape routes were blocked because of immigration quota systems, unemployment, and general apathy in the countries of the free world.

I AM A STAR

On September 1, 1939, Germany invaded Poland. World War II had begun. Hitler, drunk with power, told his soldiers: "Close your eyes to pity! Act brutally!" His armies would conquer many countries in Europe before his defeat by the Allies in 1945. The fate of the remaining Jews in Europe was sealed. The Nazis were planning total extermination. The term Holocaust, which means complete destruction by fire, is often used when speaking of this period of slaughter and brutality.

The extermination of the Jews took place in stages. At first the Nazis resettled the Jews into ghettos and concentration camps, where many died of starvation and disease. The able-bodied were

Map of Europe showing how far Nazi power extended.

Map of Europe showing the position of some of the concentration and extermination camps.

often forced to perform slave labor. The largest ghettos were in Poland, where many of Europe's Jews lived. On November 15, 1940, the Warsaw Ghetto, containing approximately 500,000 Jews, was sealed off from the outside world.

In March 1941, Adolf Eichmann was appointed head of the Gestapo section for Jewish affairs. His job was to speed up the extermination. After September 1941, all German Jews over the age of six were required to sew a large yellow Star of David on the left breast of their clothing, and were forbidden to walk in public without it.

As the Nazi hordes marched farther east, more Jews came under their control. Special death squads called Einsatzgruppen rounded up the Jews, forced them to dig their own graves, and then shot them. By the beginning of 1942, these squads had killed close to 1.4 million people.

The elimination of the Jews was not going fast enough for Hitler, however. Cheaper and quicker methods of killing were needed. At the Wannsee Conference of January 20, 1942, the Nazi leaders worked on the details of the Final Solution, the plan to kill all of Europe's Jews. The concentration camps and ghettos were eventually to be liquidated. Their surviving population would be sent to extermination camps. The largest of these was Auschwitz in Poland. This camp was equipped with poison-gas chambers and crematoria, ovens in which the bodies were burned. Four million people died in Auschwitz. Most of them were Jews.

The Germans tried to hide their intention of murder. They used terms like umgesiedelt (resettled) instead of deported, and they hung signs saying "Arbeit macht Frei" (work means freedom), over the gates of the camps. When prisoners entered an extermination camp, a flick of a finger by a Nazi doctor selected an individual for a life of hard labor and starvation or for immediate death. Those who were sentenced to die were forced to enter the "showers," which actually were gas chambers. They were given a piece of soap and an SS officer told them to breathe deeply. He said it would help their lungs to stay healthy by disinfecting them and would keep them from getting sick. Within a short time only their ashes would remain.

CHAPTER 5

✡

My Story

I remember well that November day when Papa and Grandpa were sent to the Dachau concentration camp. It was Kristallnacht. Grandma and Grandpa had come to visit us in Kippenheim and were caught with us in the unforgettable terror. How thankful we were to welcome my father and grandfather home again a few weeks later. They spoke quietly about having been beaten and mistreated in that awful place, saying, "The child must not hear these things." Soon afterward, Papa lost his textile business.

It was time to leave Germany, but where could we go? Most nations of the free world were closing their doors. In May 1939, we packed our belongings and sold our house. We left our village and moved in with my grandparents in Jebenhausen. This was meant to be a short stay, since we still hoped to find a way of leaving Germany. Grandpa soon succumbed to a broken heart. He died from a combination of illness and a disappointment in the country he loved.

Even so, some of my happiest memories of my childhood go back to the two years we spent in Jebenhausen. My grandparents were the only remaining Jewish family in this village of one thousand inhabitants. The other children were friendly and had no bad feelings toward me. I became their leader as we marched up and down the street singing the popular songs of this time, which often contained Nazi propaganda. The frenzy of the day was infectious. We did not understand the implications of these songs in our childhood innocence.

Even though there was little anti-Jewish feeling in Jebenhausen, my grandparents had always practiced religion with caution. According to the Jewish religion, the forty year period during which Moses and his flock wandered in the desert is commemorated through the Feast of the Tabernacles, or Succos. This festival calls for a symbolic hut (a succo) to be built of reeds, tree branches, and grass. The interior is decorated with colorful ornaments and the fruits, vegetables, and flowers of fall. The roof of the attic room in my grandparents' house was lifted off and the room converted into a succo. Although the room could not be seen, after my grandpa died, we did not dare to celebrate even in this secret way.

Every day new restrictive decrees were announced. Jews were compelled to give up all their gold and silver. They had to take Israel or Sara as a middle name to make them recognizable as Jews. My name became Inge Sara Auerbacher. Some of the villagers of Jebenhausen were not alarmed by these anti-Semitic laws and continued their friendship with us, even though Christians were forbidden to associate with Jews. A few of the farmers continued to give us food.

Our beloved Christian friend, Therese, who had worked as a servant in my grandparents' house for over twenty years, placed food behind my grandfather's gravestone at night for us to pick up in the morning. She was able to save a few of our things until after the war, including two family photo albums and some of our prayer books. The pictures shown in this book were among the items she kept for us. By associating with us, the people who helped us risked their lives. They were very brave.

Jewish children were no longer permitted to attend regular schools. I had to walk two miles to Goeppingen, a larger neighboring town, and then travel one hour by train to attend classes in Stuttgart. This was the only Jewish school in the province. I needed special travel permission papers for this trip, since Jews were no longer allowed to move freely.

This trip became even more hazardous, when, on September 1, 1941, Jews were made to sew the yellow Star of David on their clothes as a distinguishing mark. On the star the word *Jude*, which means Jew in German, was written in Hebrew-like letters. Papa told me to sit in such a position on the train so as to "naturally" cover my yellow badge, even though it was strictly forbidden to hide that "mark of shame." This was not always possible, and other children taunted and heckled me. Some people took pity on me, though. One day a Christian woman left a bag of rolls next to my seat. She must have felt sorry for the little Jewish six-year-old child traveling such a long distance by herself.

The "Final Solution," the Nazi plan to liquidate all the Jews in Europe, began for us in 1941. Rumors of our "resettlement" were the talk of the day. Many people made frantic attempts to leave Germany, but to no avail. All borders were closed to us.

Deportations to the "East" began in late 1941. One morning, my grandmother, my parents, and I received our orders for transport. Papa was a disabled veteran of World War I and used this as a plea for us to be spared. He succeeded, but we were not able to help my grandmother. She and most of my classmates were sent to Riga, Latvia. I shall never forget our tearful good-byes as we watched her descend the stairs in the Stuttgart railroad station until she was out of view. I would never see her again. Almost all of these unfortunate people became victims of the Einsatzgruppen, in a forest near Riga. They had to dig their own graves before they were shot.

BEZIRKSSTELLE WÜRTTEMBERG
der Reichsvereinigung der Juden in Deutschland

Rdschr.Nr. 107
Mx/L

Stuttgart, den 14. August 1942
Hospitalstr. 36
242 41

Herrn/Frau/Fräulein
Berthold Auerbacher
Göppingen, Metzgerstr. 16

und Kinder   Inge Auerbacher *408*

Ihre Transportnummer: *407*
Bitte genau beachten!

Anlagen:

Betrifft: Abwanderung

1.) Auf Anordnung der Geheimen Staatspolizei, Staatspolizeileit-
    ... davon zu verständigen, dass
    ...inder zu einem Abwanderungs-
    ...nd.

2.) D... ...ndet voraussichtlich am
    S... ...tt.
    J... ...rung zu widersetzen oder sich
    z... ...ieht schwerwiegende staatspo-
    l...

    K... ...hen, ganz gleich welcher Art,
    k... ...bwanderung nicht bewirken. Von
    d... ...isse bitten wir daher abzu-
    s...

3.) A...

We were forced out of my grandparents' home in Jebenhausen
and relocated in one of the "Jewish houses" in Goeppingen. My
parents were sent to work for very little money in a women's
undergarment factory. My school in Stuttgart was closed before I
completed the first grade.

The war was in full gear in 1941. We were awakened many
nights by the screaming air raid sirens, which always badly
frightened me. Most of the Allied bombs at this time were
dropped far from where we were living, however.

DEPORTATION

It was a morning like no other,
The deadly letter was opened by Mother.
She screamed out with a loud cry:
"It is true, we can no more deny,
We are no longer citizens with a name,
Now a transport number replaces the same."
Too long we had closed danger's door,
Hoping for life as it was before.
The document showed no cause or reason,
Mama packed up clothes for every season.
No statement of where we were going,
Rumors of shipment to a camp were growing.
We were herded to a gathering place,
For resettlement designated for our "race."
Packed together on the sealed train,
Would we ever see our home again?
We passed through an unfamiliar countryside,
Two days later loud shouts ended our ride.
We had arrived at the Bohušovice station,
"Drop everything—march—no confrontation!"
Guards surrounded us with whip and gun,
Fatigue and fear plagued everyone.
The old and infirm fell to the ground,
And pierced the air with a shrieking sound.
Two miles later Terezin was in sight,
Its high walls would soon shut out the light.
Searched and left with only one dress,
We were sent to the Dresden Fortress.
Here we bedded down on the bare floor,
Wondering what else was for us in store.
Night had come with its enveloping curtain,
Our situation was hopelessly uncertain.
We had arrived in Satan's new city,
Where was the world? There was no pity!

I AM A STAR

Finally, our turn to be deported came on August 22, 1942. There was no longer any way to avoid a transport. I was now number XIII-1-408, a person without any citizenship. We packed our meager belongings according to the very specific instructions we were given. All our money was taken from us. The police came to our apartment. Mama was told to place our keys on the dining room table. The official then said, "Now you can go!"

We were herded into a school gymnasium in Goeppingen and searched. My greatest fear was that the SS would take away my doll, Marlene. She had been a gift from my grandmother, the only token of remembrance I had of her. The officials removed Marlene's head to see if any valuables were hidden inside her hollow body, but they finally decided to let me keep my doll. I was not so fortunate, however, with a wooden decorative pin. An SS officer took a liking to it and tore it off my dress.

A DUTCH BOY PIN

A Dutch boy pin nestled on my dress,
Standing strong with pride and happiness.
Greedy fingers tore him from me,
Did those hands know my destiny?
My last ornament before I'd depart,
These claws ripped him off and broke my heart.

"You won't need this where you are going!"

A gift from my mother, lovingly attached,
All my struggles hopelessly outmatched.
I ponder, Whom was that pin given to?
Could another girl find joy if she knew?
Was it discarded, is it part of the past?
Does he still hope to find me at last?

©Israel Bernbaum
1986

From Goeppingen we were taken to Stuttgart, which was the main gathering place for Jews who were being transported. I was the youngest of almost twelve hundred people in the group. We were housed in a large hall at Killesberg which was usually used for flower shows. We bedded down for two days on the bare floor.

CHAPTER 6

✡

A Place of Darkness

Our destination was Terezin, or Theresienstadt as it was called in German, a concentration camp in Czechoslovakia about forty miles north of Prague. It was built in 1780 by Hapsburg Emperor Joseph II in memory of his mother Empress Maria Theresa. The garrison was abandoned by the military in the 1880s and was settled by civilians. By the late 1930s, Terezin was in a state of bad deterioration.

On October 10, 1941, Reinhard Heydrich, Adolf Eichmann, and other high-ranking Nazi officials selected Terezin as a transit camp for Jewish deportees before their extermination in the East. The Nazis masked the camp as a "model ghetto" for propaganda purposes. The first Jews sent there in November 1941 were from Czechoslovakia. They were followed next by the elderly from Germany and Austria who were not expected to live long anyway. Many prominent doctors and lawyers, decorated war veterans, and distinguished Jewish leaders, like Rabbi Leo Baeck from

I AM A STAR

Germany, were sent to Terezin. Their immediate deportation East to the killing centers would have aroused suspicion. Eventually, Jews from all walks of life arrived at Terezin from Austria, the Netherlands, Denmark, and other European countries, including people whose parents were of mixed Jewish and Christian origin.

I remember a particular transport of at least one thousand children from Poland in the summer of 1943. They came dressed in rags and were all very thin and dirty; many were sick. All were ordered by the SS to remain in quarantine in a special area. Rumors spread that they came from Bialystok, Poland, and had seen their parents shot before their eyes. A short time later they were sent to the gas chambers in Auschwitz.

WALLS

Walls, walls, walls are eyeing us all around,
Silently absorbing each wailing sound.
Unlike Zion's, where they are our soul,
Here even our thoughts are under control.

Walls covered by a grassy knoll,
Death-defying leapers take their toll.
The red brick demons stand very firm,
Quiet objects demanding their term.

Soldiers march on them to and fro,
Guarding people with no place to go.
These walls are closing in on me,
Dare I dream to climb them and flee?

© Israel Bernbaum
1986

I AM A STAR

Terezin consisted of huge brick barracks, underground cells and old broken-down houses. It was sealed off from the outside world by high walls, deep water-filled trenches, wooden fences, and barbed wire. Radio, telephone, and newspaper communication with the outside was strictly forbidden. On rare occasions, however, bits of war information leaked into the camp. These rumors were called "latrine talks," because the prisoners exchanged news in the public bathrooms. Stories often changed in content as they spread through the camp.

It was also forbidden for women to give birth, but a few hundred children were born during the years I was there. Breaking this rule usually meant immediate shipment to the East for both mother and child. Yet, miraculously a handful of these babies survived the war in Terezin.

A PLACE OF DARKNESS

I AM A STAR

Terezin was originally built to house 7,000 people, but at times the camp was crowded with 60,000 prisoners. A Jewish Council of Elders was set up to regulate internal affairs. This group was chaired by the Judenaeltester, or chief of elders. The council's most important duty was to draw up lists of inmates for deportation to the East, following SS instructions. Terezin was under the absolute rule of a Nazi SS commandant. Between 1941 and 1945, a total of 140,000 people were sent to Terezin; 88,000 of them were shipped to the killing centers of the East; and 35,000 died of malnutrition or disease in Terezin.

A short distance from the large fortress, where I was, across the Ohře River was a smaller fortress called Kleine Festung. This also belonged to the Terezin complex, but it was a military prison and had its own SS commandant. It also served as a place of extra punishment for any misconduct we in the large fortress might commit. Our crimes were things like stealing potatoes, or being caught drawing a picture of the "real" conditions of the camp. The small fortress had solitary confinement cells and an area for firing squads. It was a brutal place that was feared as much as being sent to the East.

A PLACE OF DARKNESS

Terezin was a gruesome place. The inhuman conditions brought out the best and worst behavior in people. Hunger makes people selfish and irritable. After our arrival at Terezin we went through the Schleuse, a body-and-belongings search area in an underground cell. After the search for valuables we were sent to the attic of the Dresden Fortress, which was a particularly large brick army barrack containing exercise courtyards and gaping archways. This is where the "Angel in Hell"—Mrs. Rinder, a Czech woman—found us lying on the bare stone floor. She asked someone whether there was a child in the newly arrived transport. Fingers pointed towards me.

AN ANGEL IN HELL

We searched the dump for each potato peeling,
Stole from the dead without guilt or feeling.
Nothing seemed to change; time stood still,
Was there anyone left with good will?

To this planet of shadow and despair,
An angel came to give help and care.
One hand was clutched by her little son,
She wanted to mother everyone.

Through time she moved on unseen wings,
Bearing food and other needed things.
This stranger reached out with heart and hands,
Asking no thanks, or making demands.

Both would never leave the abyss,
Or be touched again by life's kiss.
I search my heart for an answer, Why, why?
Where was justice, why their sentence to die?

41

I AM A STAR

Hundreds of people were moving hopelessly in this dark, airless, hot area. They stumbled over the covered dead bodies and got lost in the mass of new arrivals. Mrs. Rinder had arrived earlier in Terezin with her husband and young son Tommy. This good lady, whom we had never met before, gave me a mattress by dividing her son's mattress in half. Mr. Rinder was fortunate to work in one of the community kitchens and therefore was able to share some extra food with us at times. A deep friendship developed between us until the fall of 1944, when the entire Rinder family was deported to Auschwitz and death in the gas chambers.

Under these terrible conditions, some people lost the will to live and took their own lives. A few days after our arrival in Terezin, my father saw a man starting to jump from an attic opening of the Dresden Fortress. Papa managed to grab the man's legs and pull him back inside. To his amazement, it was an old man from our transport. Papa spoke encouraging words to him and made him promise not to repeat this act. The next morning a broken body lay lifeless in the fortress courtyard. Papa identified him. It was the same old man.

Soon after our arrival we were moved to a different area. Most men, women, and children were housed in separate quarters. I had the good fortune to stay with my parents in the disabled war veterans' section. Life was especially harsh and strange for children. We slept on the floor or, if lucky, on straw-filled mattresses, packed like sardines on double and triple-deck bunk beds. The rooms were smelly and steamy in summer and freezing in winter. We grew up fast and became self-reliant. The most important words in our vocabulary were *bread, potatoes,* and *soup*. I used to look out from the room where some birds had made a nest high up on a ridge. How I envied them. They could fly away from all this misery, while we stayed walled in.

Three times a day we stood in line, our metal dishes in hand, to receive our daily food rations from the community kitchens.

GAMES

We were not like other children at play,
The future becoming more uncertain every day.
Our playground was a garbage heap,
And the treasures from it we'd reap.
There our curiosity was stilled,
Finding remnants from dreams unfulfilled.
We put our imagination to the test:
Who could describe a sumptuous meal best?

"Don't run around and waste your energy,
Save your shoes, don't use them foolishly!"
We played checkers on a hand-drawn board,
With black and white buttons we scored.
"What was your day's flea and bedbug catch?
Let's have a bunk bed running match."
We saw carts piled with bodies roll along,
And turned our heads away to sing a song.

A PLACE OF DARKNESS

Most of the kitchens were located in the open courtyards of the huge barracks. The lines were always very long. It was especially hard in the winter, waiting in the bitter cold. Breakfast consisted of coffee, a muddy-looking liquid, which always had a horrible taste. Lunch was a watery soup, a potato, and a small portion of turnips or so-called meat sauce; and dinner was soup. By the time the people reached the barrels from which the food was ladled out, they were so hungry and exhausted that they immediately gulped their portion down.

SOUP

Three times a day we stand on line,
Pretending that on delicacies we dine.
It spills over clothes and makes a spot,
People fight, push and shove a lot.
                    Soup, soup drink it down!

Today's dinner is water with caraway seed,
Food unacceptable even as animal feed.
I don't have a choice and gulp it down,
A little disgruntled wearing a frown.
                    Soup, soup run for seconds!

It is poured into a metal can,
Ladled out by an impatient man.
Thin or thick, with or without taste,
Not a bit of it will go to waste.
                    Soup, soup means life!

I must get more and get my fill,
To keep the cries of hunger still.
With a spoon we scrape out the last drop,
Not until barrel is empty do we stop.
                    Soup, soup, soup, soup!

I AM A STAR

I remember Mama marking off each day on our rationed loaf of bread to make certain that we would have enough left to last us a week. This was often difficult. When the hunger pains became too strong, she regretfully cut slightly into the next day's portion of bread.

Birthdays presented a special challenge. One year I received a potato cake the size of my palm, prepared from a mashed boiled potato with just a hint of sugar in it. Another year Marlene, my doll, was given a new outfit sewn from rags. On my tenth birthday my gift was a poem my mother had written especially for me.

The smell of death was everywhere. Many old people had been sent to Terezin. They could not withstand the terrible conditions and died of starvation or disease. Two-wheeled hand-drawn carts

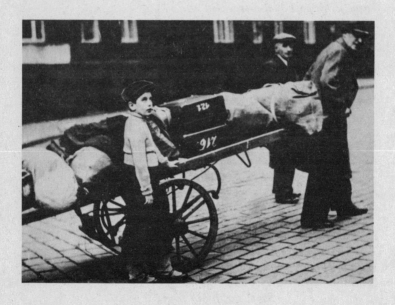

were used alternately to transport our food and to take away the sick and the dead. We hand-pumped most of our water from polluted wells.

There were constant epidemics due to overcrowding and lack of hygiene. Rats, mice, fleas, and bedbugs were a constant menace to us. I contracted scarlet fever soon after we arrived in Terezin and spent four months in the so-called hospital. All the patients were isolated from the rest of the camp. I feared the worst—my parents' deportation to the East without me. My condition grew worse every day as more complications arose. I was not expected to live. Measles, mumps, and a double middle ear infection followed the scarlet fever in rapid succession. I was infested with worms, I lost my voice, and my body was covered with boils.

IN THE HOSPITAL

We are two in a bed; the paint is peeling,
Flies cover the walls from floor to the ceiling.
I share my place with a younger child,
Most of the time our bed is defiled.

We speak in different tongues; yet we are one,
Two small windows let in rays of the sun.
At least fifty share our chamber here,
There is a feeling of death stalking near.

How thin our fever-ravaged bodies have become.
I have lost my voice; my senses feel numb.
We must leave this dungeon and recuperate,
What is our future, what will be our fate?

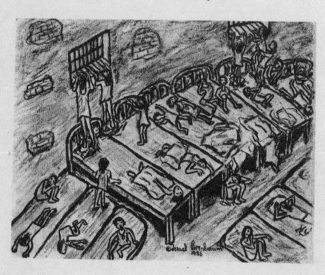

A PLACE OF DARKNESS

I made a new friend in the hospital. Ada was of German Jewish origin. She taught me a new song about Palestine, which is now Israel. Its words spoke of a perpetual paradise where the cedars of Lebanon kiss the sky. She promised me we would soon go to this place. "Just hold on a little longer," she used to say. Ada's dream never came true. She died at the age of nine in Auschwitz.

Just before my eighth birthday I was released from the hospital. Before I joined my parents, I was washed in a large bucket containing a disinfecting solution to help remove some of my lice. My hair had been cut very short, and Mama used a small comb with narrow teeth that dug into my scalp to try to rid me of the remaining lice. I still can feel the awful stomach cramps from dysentery, and the long walk to the public toilets, which were always overcrowded and without any privacy.

Most of the adults in the camp were forced to work. Some women were selected to work as slave laborers splicing mica, a product used by the Nazis in their war effort. This was considered a good job, since it sometimes kept a person from being sent to the East. Mama's first job in the camp was washing laundry from typhus patients. One day she found a very high stack of what appeared to be soiled sheets. As she tried to gather them up, she found to her dismay that they were dead bodies covered with sheets. People died like flies in Terezin.

Mama's fortune improved when she became a nurse in the old people's hospital. Often she chose the night shift so as to get an extra ration of bread. I recall those deathly sick people holding sticks to ward off the rats, which sometimes jumped into their beds. Every night someone died, and the staff divided the leftover rations and clothes among themselves.

Papa became a scavenger, rummaging every day in the garbage dump in search of potato peelings and rotten turnips. If he was extra lucky he might find boiled horse bones that we could cook again to extract any leftover fat and grizzle.

I made a bed for my doll in a cardboard box at the head of my upper-level bunk bed. One day I discovered a dead mouse in it, another victim of starvation. Not even a mouse could find enough leftover crumbs of bread to survive.

DIAMONDS ON THE SNOW

Winter had come; the earth lay frozen,
To be in Terezin, we had not chosen.
Snow covered up blight with a veil,
Bad times for hardy; worse for the frail.
Mama had gotten some valuable jewels,
Endangered her life by breaking the rules.
She entered the cellars during camp's curfew,
A certain death sentence, if anyone knew.
Oh, what great wealth and secret we kept,
While on those precious diamonds we slept.
Rumors abounded of our block's inspection,
We must conceal them before their detection.
In the rubbish Papa found an old suitcase,
There wasn't one minute to waste in this race.
His ingenuity produced a master plan,
A spot under rag heap that no one would scan.
He threw them all into the cavernous box,
To keep them safe, despite broken locks.
He peered out the door—the time was right—
And ran with the treasure through the night.
One must not hestitate, be fearful, or stall,
Running on icy snow soon made him fall.
The suitcase opened, its contents all around,
Cushioned by the snow, not making a sound.
They lay like gems in a store on display,
Their contrasting hue made them easy prey.
Papa carefully picked up every one,
In a few minutes, his job would be done.
Placing the valuables in the chosen spot,
A deserted place that everyone forgot.
Nervously, we awaited Papa's quick return,
His safety our chief worry and concern.

The door opened, his mission a success,
Next day's search would bring much distress.
In a few days the coast was clear,
We would again have our valuables near.
Each and every "diamond" on the snow,
To us a treasure—a precious potato.

I WISH

I wish I were a little bird
up in the bright blue sky,
& that sings and flies just
where he will and no one
sks asks him why.

I wish I could run free,
And play to my heart's desire.
Climb mountains, walk on soft grass,
Never would I tire.

I wish these strange conditions,
Were no more than a nightmare.
That there are still people somewhere,
Who understand and care.

I wish I could sleep on a soft bed,
And eat a good meal.
Never again to hunger,
To barter, and to steal.

I wish I would wake up
To a new and brighter morn.
In another time, a different land,
And be reborn.

I AM A STAR

Some attempts were made to teach us in *Beschaeftigung*, or keeping-busy classes. School was absolutely forbidden, but some heroic teachers gathered us children in attics and other places where there was a little space. They taught us from memory, since very few schoolbooks were smuggled into the camp. In an English class I learned "I Wish I Were," which I wrote into a worn notebook and hid from view on one of Eichmann's visits. It was only recently that I completed this poem with my own thoughts.

I remember vividly the Bohušovice Ravine roll call on November 11, 1943. It was the only time I ever got outside the camp walls. We were told that some inmates were missing and a complete count had to take place outside the camp. At least forty thousand of us were herded very early in the morning onto a large muddy field. It was a cold and rainy day. We did not know what was going to happen to us. Our future seemed uncertain. We were surrounded by soldiers and guns. No food was given to us the entire day. No toilets were available to us. I watched in horror as an SS man smashed the butt of his rifle into my mother's back. Some people had actually escaped and may have got away. News of our outing leaked out and was broadcast on the English radio. Consequently, direct orders from Berlin halted any further action on that day. We returned to the camp after midnight. Many people died on the field from exhaustion, cold, and severe beatings.

By the end of 1943, rumors of mass murder in the East had begun to circulate. The International Red Cross requested permission to inspect a camp to find out if these accusations were true. The Nazis chose Terezin for this purpose. Many months passed before this request was granted on June 23, 1944. In the meantime Terezin went through a "beautification" program. Certain parts of the camp were cleaned up. Some people were given new clothing and good food to eat. A few children received chocolates and sardine sandwiches just as the commission walked past them. I was not one of the lucky ones. In the center of town an orchestra played in a newly erected band shell. The areas filled with the things that had been stolen from us were carefully locked up. Blind, crippled, and sick people were warned to stay out of sight. Even the most brutal SS officer, Rudolf Haindl, acted friendly on that day. Transport lists to the East were carefully hidden. The International Red Cross inspections team left the camp believing the immense deception that Terezin was a "model" place for Jews to live in. A film was made at this time to document the "good" conditions in Terezin.

I AM A STAR

DECEPTION

All is readied for a Red Cross inspection,
Our very existence is based on deception.
Could the world be lulled to believe,
The camouflage only a devil can conceive?
Numbered blocks are renamed with a street sign.
It is paradise here; we are doing fine.
In the park a band shell is erected,
Special lines are taught us and perfected.
"Uncle Rahm,[1] again we have sardines today?
We are really sick of them, we want to play."
A children's pavilion set up to impress and show,
Life is normal here; a "fact" for everyone to know.
In the square there is a new café house,
Only the selected are allowed to browse.
We have our own bank and money here,
On which Moses and the tablets appear.
With it nothing but mustard can be bought,
And a new school, in which we are not taught.
Markers to theater and playground,
All will soon be no longer around.
Only special areas are shown with pride,
Most of us are ordered to remain inside.
As fast as commission is out of sight,
We have to bear again tyrannical might.
Soon there will be another selection,
No change; the world believed the deception.

[1] SS camp commandant.

Terezin was the antechamber to Auschwitz. Eichmann personally saw to it that there was a constant flow of transports from Terezin to feed the gas chambers at Auschwitz. He and the SS commandant of Terezin determined which groups of people were to be sent East and then ordered the Jewish Council of Elders to draw up a list of one thousand people from the designated groups for each transport. At one time only old people were called up; at another, the most highly decorated war veterans. The selection process depended entirely on the whims of the SS. We lived day and night with the fear of being sent to the East. There were times when transports left every week. The unfortunate people who had been selected were given a number which was tied around their necks, and were told to assemble at a specific barrack. From there they were forced to enter the cattle cars. The doors were bolted and not opened until their arrival in Auschwitz. Most of the camp Elders eventually suffered the same fate: they, too, were killed in the gas chambers in Auschwitz. When the last selection to the East was made in 1944, all remaining disabled war veterans had to appear at SS headquarters. A red circle was drawn around our names. We had been spared from certain death.

SOMETHING TO REMEMBER ME BY

He was a stranger; we had never met,
He wanted me to recall him, not to forget.
Obviously sensing his awful situation,
Nervous and persuasive in his presentation.

He handed me a box filled with treasure,
And hoped it would give me much pleasure.
Odds and ends up to the brim,
For dreams of any child's whim.
        "Something to remember me by!"

I was startled and full of surprise,
A rainbow of color before my eyes.
Things made of threads attached to eternity,
Knitted by loving hands without identity.

His eyes looked hopeless; in a daze,
He walked restless, as if in a maze.
He was a humble man—without fame,
Staying unknown—never stating his name.
        "Something to remember me by!"

He rode away on the death train,
Filled with desperation and pain.
He rests with the ashes in sleep,
His memory I will forever keep.

The little girl now fully grown,
Remembers him, though still unknown.
To this day his words sound loud and clear,
His presence assured from year to year.
        "Something to remember me by!"

Israel Bernbaum
1936

Israel Bernbaum
1986

HOLD ME TIGHT

Come with me, my child, hold my hand,
Be calm, my child, do not try to understand.
Don't be afraid, my child, walk with pride,
You know your mother is here at your side.
>Hold me tight,
>Day has turned to night,
>Soon we'll see the light.

No, no, don't look at the chimneys—see the blue sky,
My arm is around you to protect you; don't cry.
Come close—let the blows fall on me,
There'll be a day when again we'll be free.
>Hold me tight,
>Day has turned to night,
>Soon we'll see the light.

Give all your belongings to them, quickly undress,
One day soon we will again have happiness.
Sleep my child—I have no more to give,
Oh, God, Oh, God—we are not going to live!
>Hold me tight,
>Day has turned to night,
>Hold me tight.

My best friend Ruth and her parents, who had shared our bunks in a tiny room for two years, were in these last transports to the death camp. She was also an only child, just two months older than I. We were like sisters and shared our daydreams and secrets with each other. She had beautiful blond hair. Her greatest pleasure was to draw pictures on scraps of paper with colored pencils that she had smuggled into the camp. She had hopes of becoming an artist. Ruth and her parents came from Berlin. Her father walked with a limp caused by a World War I injury. We both found it strange to live with and see around us so many disabled men with missing arms, legs, and other war injuries. Ruth and I owned identical dolls. Before she embarked on her final journey, she entrusted me with all of her doll's clothing, which her mother had carefully sewn from rags. Ruth's father was half Christian and half Jewish, and Ruth was raised as a Christian.

Ruth died because of her Jewish heritage, even though she never considered herself Jewish. She would never live to see her tenth birthday. In "Hold Me Tight," my heart still cries out to her and so many other children as they marched with their mothers to the gas chambers in Auschwitz and the other extermination camps.

CHAPTER 7

✡

Liberation

I learned an old Czech folk song in Terezin. It speaks of the hope and the changes that come with spring. Would we ever be allowed to leave the winter that was Terezin, see the smile of spring, and feel the touch of May again?

Přijde jaro přijde	Spring is in the coming
Bude zase Máj	May is near again
Usmívá se slunce	Sun is warmly smiling
Zelená se háj	Green is meadow's plain
Rozpuknou se ledy	Ice will melt and vanish
Volný bude proud	Streams will freely flow
Po vodach šumících	On silvery waters
Lodě budou plout	Boats will come and go

The spring of 1945 was different from the other two I had spent in Terezin. Unknown to us, Hitler's Third Reich was collapsing and the German armies were facing certain defeat. The Allied forces were closing in on Europe. Meanwhile the Nazis made their last attempts to kill all the remaining survivors in the death camps of the East.

As the Allies advanced, the soldiers forced their prisoners on death marches to places still under complete Nazi rule. I remember when these miserable people arrived at Terezin. They were barefoot, or their feet were covered with rags or torn sandals. Some wore blue and white striped uniforms, others only rags. Their heads were shaved. Many were no more than walking skeletons suffering from typhus and other diseases. In vain I searched the long lines, hoping to find Grandma among them.

During these last days of World War II, orders were given to build gas chambers at Terezin. The plan was to kill us either by poison gas or by drowning in a specially prepared area. Not one Jew in Europe was to stay alive. By the time we were freed, the gas chambers at Terezin were almost completed. It was only the rush of events that spared our lives.

LIBERATION

Guards fearing capture by the Allies began to burn the camp's records. Bits of partially burned paper floated through the air. The evidence of death and suffering had to be destroyed. Then, at the beginning of May, most of the guards living outside the barricades ran away. They made some last efforts to slaughter us as they left, by shooting wildly and throwing hand grenades into the camp.

We were finally liberated on the eve of May 8, 1945 by the Soviet army. The first thing we did was rip off the yellow star from our clothes. I had spent three years in this human hell. I can still see the boisterous Russian soldiers singing and dancing on their tanks. All of us felt joy, pain, and relief. Many questions remained. Who was left of our families? What would our future hold?

After liberation, the barricades were left up for a while, because a severe typhus epidemic was spreading quickly through the camp. Having survived the war, many prisoners died of the disease even after liberation. I remember climbing one of the barricades to accept a piece of black bread with what seemed a mountain of butter from a Russian soldier. I chewed it gently, allowing the butter to melt slowly in my mouth. Was I awake or dreaming?

Despite the typhus quarantine, my father and I went outside the camp walls in search of food. We walked to the fields and picked rhubarb, and in the surrounding towns we begged for food. Back in the camp we bartered the rhubarb for bread and potatoes.

I joined a few other children, and together we stole into the former Nazi living quarters just outside the camp compound. We found bullets lying on the floor and strips of movie film showing sea battles. To our surprise, we saw a swimming pool inside a beautiful park next to these quarters. How different life must have been on the other side of the walls! While we were starving, suffering, and living in fear for our lives, these people just a few yards away lived a life of luxury.

When the typhus epidemic subsided, a few of the survivors began to leave the camp on foot. Most of them did not know where to go or who would help them. Finally, in early July 1945, a bus appeared from Stuttgart, Germany, to pick up the small group of survivors from the state of Württemberg. Out of our original transport of about twelve hundred people, there were thirteen survivors. Three of them were from my family.

LIBERATION

Our camp's population began to swell,
Remnants of other places sent to our hell.
Time was running out; the tyrants began to retreat,
It was clear their armies were facing certain defeat.
One by one each guard was abandoning his post,
The uncertainty what next, we feared the most.
Urgency and anticipation filled the air,
Each minute we were torn between hope and despair.

I climbed the barricade and stole a forbidden glance,
A hand grenade flew close, but missed me by chance.
The sudden explosion gave me a scare,
I touched my head to make sure it was there.
Quickly I sought my parents' side,
In a dark cellar we would hide.
A stream of people joined us as we did descend,
"Could we survive, would this tomb become our end?"
One small candle emitted a ray of light,
A beacon of hope against this darkest might.

Minutes became hours; time was impassively fleeting,
Deadly silence; only the sound of my heart beating.
I found solace in reading my prayer book,
Would someone dare go upstairs and take a look?
Evening had come; the hour was close to nine,
One man chose to go forward and lead the line,
We waited with trepidation; his absence was brief.
"The Allies are here, we are free, we have relief!"

I AM A STAR

MY OMA'S[1] LULLABY

In some strange and distant land,
A life snuffed out by flick of hand.
I hear the shot; I feel the pain,
My Oma did not die in vain.

I read her last postcard now and then,
"With God's help we'll be together again."
Her birthday has become our Yahrzeit[2] date,
To remind us of love and man's hate.

She sang me to sleep with a lullaby,
My child, be happy, do not cry.

Her Shabbos[3] candles had a special glow,
I hope she knew that I loved her so.
Only she held the secret to prepare,
The challes[4] and cakes without compare.

I will always recall her last gaze,
Her eyes, soft smile, and beautiful face.
Her spirit still radiates with undying love,
I know she is looking down at me from above.

She sang me to sleep with a lullaby,
My child, be happy, do not cry.

[1] *Grandma*
[2] *Memorial*
[3] *Sabbath*
[4] *Holiday bread*

We set off from the camp and soon found ourselves passing through badly bombed German cities. The once majestic city of Dresden had been turned completely to rubble. Wherever we stopped, curious Germans gathered outside our bus. One little girl pressed a small doll into my hands and insisted that I keep it and remember her.

After a few days on the road we arrived at the displaced persons' camp in Stuttgart. Here we received our first good meal. I

70

remember the beautifully set table and the white tablecloth. I can still taste the noodle soup, which I ate slowly to relish every spoonful. Never in my life would soup taste as good again. We stayed only one week in this temporary facility, which had been especially prepared to house returning Jewish refugees. Our aim was to return to my grandmother's home. We hoped she would still be alive and greet us there.

When we arrived in Jebenhausen, we faced the awful truth. Grandma had not survived. A total of thirteen people from our family had lost their lives during those awful years. Our only hope was to find our beloved Christian friend Therese. To our dismay, the war had claimed her life also. When the American soldiers entered the village, they searched many houses for ammunition. Therese heard the knock on her door, but did not open it, fearing for her life. She remained standing behind the closed door. Eventually, an impatient American soldier shot through the door. She died instantly.

THERESE

To honor her I placed a flower on the grave,
Recalling a woman who generously gave.
Her life in danger; she came in the night,
Bringing food and helping us in our plight.

She did not heed the GI's knock on the door,
A shot rang out; she fell lifeless to the floor.
As before in a distant and strange land,
My grandma's life snuffed out by an SS hand.

I had prayed for their safety every night,
Now they walk together in an unseen light.
The two were inseparable, each a good friend,
A Christian and a Jew united in the end.

I AM A STAR

The new owners of Grandma's house prepared a room for us. When Grandma was deported to Riga in 1941, her house was taken away from us and we were ordered to move into the Jewish houses in Goeppingen. A Christian family received permission to occupy Grandma's house.

Our return after so many years was greeted by a vase filled with field flowers which stood on the table. The Christian family tried to ease our pain. One day someone brought us a big bowl of whipped sweet cream. Mama and I gorged ourselves until we were sick from it. The years of hunger had taken their toll; our stomachs were not ready to digest this rich food.

We soon found more permanent living quarters in the neighboring town of Goeppingen. The mayor invited us to visit him at City Hall. As soon as we stepped into the Mayor's Chamber, Mama noticed the Oriental carpet: it was ours. The mantel clock had a familiar chime; it, too, had once been our property. After our deportation to Terezin, all our belongings had been distributed to different Christian families. Some items had found their way to City Hall.

The townspeople, fearing reprisal from us, insisted that they knew nothing of the horrors we had suffered. They said they had never hated the Jews and were therefore not guilty of any crime. Why then did they not question the fate of so many innocent people taken away so brutally at the time?

Our home became a famililar place for the American soldiers. They showered us with personal goods and candy. Some ran with their melting ice cream rations to our home so that I could have a special treat.

To my knowledge, I was the only Jewish child survivor in the state of Württemberg. My eleventh birthday was a sensation. I was invited to the local UNRRA (United Nations Relief and Rehabilitation Administration) Commission Headquarters. I had but one wish—to receive a new doll carriage, even though I seemed too old for it. I remembered just before my deportation to Terezin how heartbreaking it had been to wheel my light green carriage for two miles to town and give it to another child.

How thrilled I was with my first new outfit, a black and white checked dress sewn especially for me. I felt like an animal let out of a cage. I just wanted to run free and play, instead of studying at school. Papa resumed his textile business and once more began to be successful.

Israel Bernbaum
1986

WE HAVE BOTH SURVIVED

As we wandered through the night,
We held on to each other in fright.
Both of us carried on our back,
Few belongings packed in a sack.

While the whips snapped all around,
Only I heard her crying sound.
I held her gently in my arm.
To protect her from any harm.

We both lived through a violent time,
Prisoners, guiltless of any crime.
Even during the greatest despair,
I always knew that she was there.

We calmed and soothed each other,
She was the child, I was the mother.
I felt safe when she was near,
Losing her became my greatest fear.

Now she is brittle, her limbs are worn,
Her clothes are faded with age and torn.
But she still looks at me with loving eyes,
With a warmth that time can't compromise.

She has been carefully stored away,
With memories of many a yesterday.
I thank her for playtime hours spent,
Hoping she knows how much she's meant.

I AM A STAR

Life slowly returned to normal again, but it was still lonely. We took the first opportunity we could to immigrate to America in May 1946. We rode in the boxcars of a freight train to the seaport of Bremen. The cars had been decorated with tree branches, and on their sides was written with chalk: "God bless President Truman and America." It was a stormy ten days at sea on the Marine Perch, an American troop transport ship. We arrived in New York Harbor at night. I stood in awe of the blinking lights of Manhattan, which seemed like a wonderland to me. Lady Liberty was especially bright as her lamp's light welcomed and guided us to a new life. The next morning we disembarked just as the sun rose on a new day.

CHAPTER 8

✡

Afterthoughts

Where were the church and all the good and decent people of the world while this barbarism was going on? The heads of the Christian churches and the leaders of Islam and Buddhism made no protest against this inhumanity. The leaders and intellectuals of the free world did not scream out in protest. Some of the clergy in Belgium and France helped to save Jewish children by hiding them in nunneries and safe houses. Very few of the clergy, however, became involved in this tragedy. Pastor Niemöller of Germany did provide this daring example of the way some people acted during the Nazi era:

> In Germany, the Nazis first came for the Communists, and I didn't speak up because I wasn't a Communist. Then they came for the Jews, and I did not speak up because I was not a Jew. Then they came for the trade unionists, and I didn't speak up because I wasn't a trade unionist. Then they came for the Catholics, and I was a Protestant so I didn't speak up. Then they came for me . . . by that time there was no one to speak up for anyone.

Murder on such a scale could not be hidden. The stench of burning flesh from the crematoria reached houses miles away. Many people outside the camps knew of these evil happenings, but did nothing to help. There were some exceptions. The people of Denmark, led by King Christian X, saved seven thousand Jews by helping them escape to Sweden. Raoul Wallenberg, a Swedish diplomat, saved thousands of lives in Hungary. He devised the protective passport, or *Schutzpass*, with the Swedish colors and embassy stamp that placed many Jews in Budapest under Swedish government control. Some of the people of Bulgaria and a few heroic individuals in Germany and the occupied countries risked their lives to aid the Jews.

One might ask, did the Jews go like sheep to slaughter? Yes, they were slaughtered, but not without resistance. Most of them were completely helpless. They had few weapons, were broken in body and spirit; tortured and starved to death. Some were branded like cattle with a tattoo on their left arm. Soap was made from fat of their dead bodies, and human skin was used to make lampshades. Children, especially twins, were used for painful and gruesome medical experiments by Nazi doctors.

There were some heroic acts of resistance by the Jews in the ghettos and camps. One of them was the superhuman effort of the Warsaw Ghetto uprising in April 1943. A small group of poorly armed young Jewish fighters held off the German army for over a month. They did not give up until the Nazis burned the whole ghetto down. Jews were among the first to become partisans (resistance fighters) against the Nazis. There was also resistance of the spirit. Some children in the ghettos and camps were taught against great odds in illegal classes. Just to stay alive one more day was an immense struggle for the human spirit.

What was the toll of these dreadful years? World War II consumed fifty million lives. A total of eleven million people were murdered by starvation, gassing, phenol injection, shooting, electrocution, torture, experimentation, and disease. Six million of them were Jews: two-thirds of the entire Jewish population of Europe had been slaughtered. The other five million humans so

AFTERTHOUGHTS

PEACE

An acorn gives life to a thousand trees,
Many tiny raindrops form the greatest seas.
Nothing is impossible; if only we try,
The smallest tree can reach the sky.

We may differ in thought and ideas,
Every mother cries some salty tears.
If flowers can grow in desert sand,
Hate can turn to love in any land.
                    All wars must cease
                    There will be peace

Pick a rose with its thorn,
A world of peace for each newborn.
Let's share the milk and honey today,
Where there is will, there is a way.

Beat each sword into a plowshare,
We must search our hearts and care.
Together we can survive and win,
The time is now; let us begin.
                    All wars must cease
                    There will be peace

brutally slain were Gypsies, Slavs, and people who had been branded enemies of the Nazi state. Germany—one of the greatest, most civilized, cultured, and scientifically advanced countries of the world—became the most barbaric nation in history.

Hitler killed himself in his protected bunker in Berlin as the Allies were closing in on him. Some of his aides were tried by an international military tribunal for crimes against humanity. They were sentenced to die or to serve long prison terms. Many escaped to other countries and were never punished for their crimes.

I AM A STAR

The philosopher George Santayana wrote that "those who cannot remember the past are condemned to repeat it." It is our responsibility to be watchful of all our leaders in government. We must speak out against evil and injustice. Let us build bridges of understanding and love to join mankind in every land. My hope, my wish, and prayer is for every child to grow up in peace without hunger and prejudice.

WE SHALL NEVER FORGET

Out of ashes our spirits rise,
Tears rain down from the weeping skies,
We have suffered and endured the fire,
Immense horrors and miles of barbed wire.

History's greatest evil and hell,
We all bear witness, we are here to tell.
The world was deaf, where was the light?
There seemed no end to the long, long night.

CHORUS: *We will always remember, WE SHALL NEVER*
FORGET!
Trumpets of joy sound freedom's call,
Love for God and man, above all,
WE SHALL NEVER FORGET!

Minds were dulled by bombs of hate,
Only the hero cared about our fate,
We saw the truth, it began to unfold,
You may kill the body but never the soul.

Here we are with honor and pride,
A new generation at our side,
The silent voices join us today,
Never, never again, we hope and pray.

(Repeat CHORUS at will.)

Words by Inge Auerbacher
Music by Rosalie Commentucci

Timetable

1919	Adolf Hitler joins the German Workers' Party, which a year later becomes known as the National Socialist German Workers' Party—the Nazi Party.
November 8, 1923	Adolf Hitler leads Beer Hall Putsch in Munich, Germany. He is arrested and sent to jail, where he writes *Mein Kampf*.
January 30, 1933	Adolf Hitler is appointed chancellor of Germany.
March 23, 1933	First concentration camp is established in Dachau, Germany.
April 1, 1933	Boycott of Jewish shops and businesses begins.
April 21, 1933	Ritual slaughter of animals in accordance with Jewish dietary laws is forbidden in Germany.
May 10, 1933	Public burnings of books written by Jews begin.
August 2, 1934	Adolf Hitler is named president and commander-in-chief of the armed forces of Germany.
September 15, 1935	The Nuremberg Laws, anti-Jewish racial laws, come into effect.
March 13, 1938	Austria is added to Germany.
July 6, 1938	Conference to aid political refugees is opened in Evian, France.
September 1938	The Sudetenland, a part of Czechoslovakia, is taken over by Germany.
November 9–10, 1938	On Kristallnacht, or Night of Broken Glass, the anti-Jewish riots erupt in Ger-

	many and Austria. Synagogues are burned, and Jewish houses and businesses are looted and destroyed.
September 1, 1939	Germany invades Poland, and World War II begins.
November 15, 1940	Warsaw Ghetto is sealed off.
March 1941	Adolf Eichmann is appointed head of Gestapo section for Jewish affairs.
September 1, 1941	Jews in Germany must wear the yellow Star of David.
Fall 1941	Auschwitz-Birkenau mass extermination camp in Poland is established. Terezin in Czechoslovakia is selected as a transit camp.
January 20, 1942	Nazis at Wannsee Conference work out plans to murder all the Jews in Europe.
April 19, 1943	Warsaw Ghetto uprising begins.
November 1944	Last Jews are transported from Terezin to Auschwitz.
May 8, 1945	Terezin is liberated by the Soviet army. Germany surrenders to the Allies.

Suggested Further Readings

Altshuler, David A. *Hitler's War against the Jews*. New York: Behrman House, 1978.

Baer, Edith. *A Frost in the Night: A Girlhood on the Eve of the Third Reich*. New York: Pantheon, 1980.

Baldwin, Margaret. *The Boys Who Saved the Children*. New York: Julian Messner, 1981.

Bernbaum, Israel. *My Brother's Keeper—The Holocaust through the Eyes of an Artist*. New York: Putnam, 1985.

Frank, Anne. *Diary of a Young Girl*. New York: Pocket Books (reprint), 1971.

Green, Gerald. *The Artists of Terezin*. New York: Schocken, 1978.

Kantor, Alfred. *The Book of Alfred Kantor*. New York: McGraw-Hill, 1971.

Katz, William Loren. *An Album of Nazism*. New York: Franklin Watts, 1979.

Meltzer, Milton. *Never to Forget*. New York: Harper & Row, 1976.

Orgel, Doris. *The Devil in Vienna*. New York: Dial Press, 1978.

Reiss, Johanna. *The Upstairs Room*. New York: Crowell, 1972.

Richter, Hans Peter. *Friedrich*. New York: Dell, 1973.

Rossel, Seymour. *The Holocaust*. New York: Franklin Watts, 1981.

Rubin, Arnold P. *The Evil That Men Do*. New York: Julian Messner, 1977.

Schoenberner, Gerhard. *The Yellow Star: The Persecution of the Jews in Europe, 1933–1945*. New York: Bantam, 1973.

Volavková, H., ed. *I Never Saw Another Butterfly*. New York: McGraw-Hill, 1964.

Wiesel, Elie. *Night*. New York: Avon, 1972.

Ziemian, Joseph. *The Cigarette Sellers of Three Crosses Square*. New York: Avon, 1977.

Acknowledgements

My most heartfelt thanks go to my beloved parents, who cheered me on and gave me much valuable advice and support in completing my manuscript.

I am immensely grateful to my editor, Denise Johnstone-Burt, whose expert guidance, intellect, talent, and love for humanity are shown in this book.

My most ardent thanks go to Distinguished Professor Randolph L. Braham of the City University of New York for sharing his scholarship and for his encouragement. Without his inspiration, friendship, and support, this book would never have been written.

I am indebted to Sharyn November, Nancy Paulsen, Ron Buehl, Iris Rosoff, and Diane Arico for believing in me and opening the doors to the publishing field.

I would like to express my sincere thanks to my dear friends Else Bakke, Orest Dutka, and Mollie Kramer of the New York City Public Library, who helped me so much in spirit and research in completing this book.

Many thanks go to authors Judy Blume and Herman Wouk for lending a helping hand.

I am deeply grateful for and will never forget the help given me by Art Raymond, of radio station WEVD, who was the first to bring my writing to the attention of a large audience.

My thanks go to composers Rosalie Commentucci-O'Hara, with whom my dream began, and to Barney Bragin, James Donenfeld, and Sol Zim, who added so much talent to my words.

I am grateful for the permission to reproduce photographs from the Kulturamt-Stadtarchiv, Landeshauptstadt Stuttgart, State Jewish

Museum in Prague, and the YIVO Institute for Jewish Research.

Appreciation goes to Dr. Karel Jindrak for his English translation of the Czech folk song "Spring Is in the Coming."

I would like to thank the following for their help: Dr. Kurt Maier, The Simon Wiesenthal Center, the Anti-Defamation League of B'nai Brith, the American Jewish Committee, Benjamin and Vladka Meed of the American Gathering of Jewish Holocaust Survivors, the United States Holocaust Memorial Museum, and filmmaker Emanuel Rund.

I am thankful to many people, too numerous to mention, whose omission is no measure of the help they gave me in achieving an important point in my life.

About the Author

Inge Auerbacher was born in Kippenheim, Germany. She was imprisoned from 1942 to 1945 in the Terezin concentration camp in Czechoslovakia when she was seven to ten years of age. In 1946 she emigrated to the United States of America and has lived since then in New York City.

She graduated from Queens College with a B.S. degree in chemistry and has done postgraduate work in biochemistry at Hunter College. She has been associated with many renowned researchers in the field of medicine. Today she is a chemist for Mount Sinai Services at City Hospital Center in Elmhurst.

Ms. Auerbacher is a world traveler, travel writer, and avid photographer. More than fifty of her poems on various themes have been published. She wrote the lyrics to "We Shall Never Forget," the only original song presented at the World Gathering of Jewish Holocaust Survivors, 1981, in Jerusalem. The lyrics are set to music written by Rosalie Commentucci-O'Hara. The record album, *Jewish Memories,* contains four of Ms. Auerbacher's lyrics, sung by the cantor and entertainer Sol Zim. Other lyrics have been set to music by James Donenfeld and Barney Bragin.

Inge Auerbacher appeared in *Childhood Memories of the Holocaust,* a television documentary produced in 1985 by the New York City Board of Education.

She was the subject of the documentary films *Inge and the Yellow Star* and *All Jews Out,* produced in Germany. Both films were shown on German television. *All Jews Out* has been presented in many countries and has won prizes at major film festivals, both here and abroad.

Inge spends much of her free time lecturing on the Holocaust.

HIGH PRAISE FOR
JACK KETCHUM AND *OFF SEASON*!

"If you read *Off Season* at Thanksgiving, you probably won't sleep until Christmas."

—Stephen King

"[*Off Season*] still influence[s] horror today. Only a novel of expert articulation and emotional truth can cast such a long shadow, and Ketchum's is both."

—*Publishers Weekly*

"Ketchum [is] one of America's best and most consistent writers of contemporary horror fiction."

—Bentley Little

"Just when you think the worst has already happened… Jack Ketchum goes yet another shock further."

—*Fangoria*

"Ketchum's prose is tight and spare, without a single misplaced word."

—Cinescape.com

"For two decades now, Jack Ketchum has been one of our best, brightest, and most reliable."

—*Hellnotes*

"Welcome to Jack Ketchum's ferocious and unforgettable first novel."

—Douglas E. Winter

"A major voice in contemporary suspense."

—Ed Gorman

"Jack Ketchum is a master of suspense and horror of the human variety."

—*The Midwest Book Review*

JACK
KETCHUM

OFF SEASON

LEISURE BOOKS   NEW YORK CITY

A LEISURE BOOK®

June 2006

Published by

Dorchester Publishing Co., Inc.
200 Madison Avenue
New York, NY 10016

ISBN 0-8439-5696-8

The name "Leisure Books" and the stylized "L" with design are
trademarks of Dorchester Publishing Co., Inc.

Printed in the United States of America.

Visit us on the web at www.dorchesterpub.com.

Two writers have made it their business over the years to make sure I didn't simply disappear into the woodwork career-wise—the late and dearly missed Robert Bloch, to whom I dedicated *Hide and Seek*, and Stephen King. This one's for Steve, with much gratitude. Who it turns out read the original Way Back When.

OFF SEASON

"My God! My God!
Must I die like this?"
—Jack Slade

"Sodom and Gomorrah,
they run the roadhouse."
—John Cougar

PART I

SEPT. 12, 1981

12:26 A.M.

They watched her cross the meadow and step over the low stone wall, into the woods beyond. She looked awkward. She would be easy to catch.

They took their time. Breaking off the white birch switches, peeling the bark away. They could hear her moving through the underbrush. They looked at one another and smiled, but said nothing. They peeled the switches, and then they started after her.

She thanked God for the moonlight. She had nearly missed seeing the old cellar hole, and it was deep. Now she moved carefully around it and kept running, through the long grass and cattails, past white pine, black pine, birch, and poplar. Beneath her feet moss and lichen. The scent of rot and evergreen. She heard them tumble through the slashing behind her, their voices light and musical; children playing in the dark. She remembered their hands on her; coarse strong little hands with long sharp dirty nails that raked her

3

skin as they clutched at her. She shuddered. She heard them laughing close behind. In front of her, the forest thickened.

She had to go more slowly now. It was terribly hard to see. Long branches tugged at her hair and poked cruelly at her eyes. She crossed her bare arms in front of her to protect her face; the woods scraped them and they bled. Behind her the children paused and listened. She began to cry.

Stupid, she thought, stupid to start crying now. She heard them move again nearby. Could they see her? She plunged ahead through the thick scrub. Old brittle branches stabbed through her thin cotton dress as if she were naked, raking new troughs of blood along her arms and legs and stomach. The pain did not stop her; it drove her on. She gave up trying to protect her face and beat back the branches with her arms, thrashing her way through the scrub to the clearing.

She took a deep breath and immediately she smelled the sea. It could not be far. She broke into a run. There might be houses there, fishermen's cottages. *Someone.* The meadow was long and wide. Soon she heard the sound of surf ahead and she kicked off her shoes and raced barefoot toward the sound; while eleven small pale bodies broke through the last stands of brush and watched her in the moonlight.

She could see nothing ahead of her, no houses, no lights. Only the wide plain of tall grass. What if there was only the sea ahead of her? She would be cornered, trapped. But she would not think of that. *Hurry,* she told herself, *faster.* Her lungs felt cold and ached

4

inside her. The sound was louder now. The sea was very near, somewhere just beyond the meadow.

She heard them running behind her and knew that they were close, too. She ran with a power that surprised her. She heard them laughing. Their laughter was horrible; cold, evil. She saw some of them moving up alongside her, running without effort, watching her and grinning, their bared teeth and eyes gleaming in the moonlight.

They knew she was defenseless. They were playing with her. All she could do was run and hope against hope that they tired of the game. She could see no house nearby. *She was going to die alone*. She heard one of them yipping like a dog behind her and suddenly she felt something slash across the backs of her legs. The pain was sharp and intense and it nearly made her fall. She was not going to make it. They were all around her; it was impossible. She felt her bowels give way, and knew she was giving in to panic.

For the thousandth time she cursed herself for stopping the car, for playing the Good Samaritan. But it had shocked her to see the little girl stumbling alone along the dark, lonely road. She had swung around a corner and suddenly there she was, her dress torn almost to the waist, and in the headlights she could see that the girl had her hands to her face and seemed to be crying. She could not have been more than six years old.

So she'd stopped the car and approached her, thinking, *Accident, rape;* and the girl had looked up at her with those intense black eyes that had not the slightest trace of tears in them, and grinned at her. Something made her turn around, then, to glance back at the car and she saw them standing in front of it, blocking her return. Suddenly she was afraid. She screamed at them to get away from the car, knowing they would not. "Get the hell out of here," she'd yelled, feeling helpless and foolish, and that was when they first began to laugh at her and first began advancing. That was when she felt their hands on her and knew they meant to kill her.

Now the runners beside her started to close in. She permitted herself a look at them. *Filthy. Awful.* There were four of them, three to the left of her and one to the right. The group of three were all boys and the single runner was a young girl. She veered toward the girl and rammed her. Her momentum flung the girl away and she heard a cry of pain. There were whoops of laughter from the others. She felt a quick burning pain cross her back and shoulders, then two lashes in quick succession across her buttocks. Her legs felt weak and rubbery. She knew her strength was waning. Yet her fear of falling was worse than the pain, much worse. If she fell they would beat her to death. Her thighs and shoulders felt wet and she knew they had bloodied her. And now the sea was so close she could taste it, feel the spray upon her body. She kept running.

She saw that the runners to her left had been joined by a new boy, a big boy moving fast. My God, she thought, what is he wearing? Some skin, some *animal*. Who in God's name are these people? There were two more children to the right of her now. She could not tell if they were boys or girls. They moved easily through the tall grass. *Stop playing with me,* she thought, oh please stop. The big boy broke out ahead of her, darting directly into her path. So now she was surrounded. He glanced back over his shoulder and in the moonlight, she saw that his face was a solid mass of scabs and pimples.

The fear was cold and hollow inside her now. Their switches cut deep into her back and legs. There was nothing to do but keep running. There was only running, running and the sea.

She stared hard at the boy's back, trying to focus, trying to keep up her strength and courage. Then suddenly he whirled and she saw the blur of his switch and all at once her face exploded with pain. Her nose was bleeding and her face felt raw from cheek to cheek. The taste of blood in her mouth. It was hard to breathe. She knew she would have to stop soon. She felt as if something were already dead inside her. She almost ran into the boy as he halted in front of her. Her eyes darted to the right and left of him, looking for a way out. She could not look at him. Not until she had to.

She saw something glint in the moonlight behind him. There it was. The sea. It made her feel terribly weary. There was nowhere left to go, no help at all. There were no houses. Only a sheer drop down the sudden granite cliffs into unknown depths of ocean. The fall alone would probably kill her. There was no hope, none. She stopped running and turned slowly to face the pursuers gathered around her.

For a moment they were only children again, and she stared bewildered at the tattered rags and sackcloth, at the incredibly filthy faces, at the eyes bright with the chase, and the small tight bodies, and she thought that this could not possibly be happening, that no children could be this way. That she was lost in a dream of blood and agony. Then she saw their bodies crouch and tense, the birch switches poise and rise again, the eyes narrow and the lips press tight together. She closed her eyes against them.

And then an instant later they were upon her. The foul claws tearing her clothing, the switches falling hard on her head and shoulders. She screamed. It only caused more laughter. She felt their drooling mouths press against her, and her flesh began to crawl with the feel of blood and saliva. She screamed again and felt a fear like none she had ever known well up and burst desperately against them. Suddenly she felt immense and strong compared to them, a huge wounded monster. She opened her eyes and struck out wildly, struck foreheads and mouths with her small fists and pushed hard against their vile, filthy bodies. For a moment she seemed to burst through them toward the big boy in front of her. Then they surged back at her again, and she pushed against them and whirled twice, spinning them off her, and then she was through, the way was clear, and the big boy saw her intent and stepped quickly out of her way.

There was never anything to consider, no time to think or fear. She had no options. She ran past the boy into the thin night air. And her leap drew her far away over the rockface and breathlessly down into the wild, churning waves, into immense and frigid darkness, and washed her blood in the cold salt sea.

1:15 A.M.

There wasn't much in the small blue suitcase to interest them. Three cotton blouses, slightly soiled. A green pullover sweater. Otherwise only bras, panties, stockings, and a tweed skirt. In the front seat was a sweater that buttoned down the front, white cashmere. The girl put that on over her tattered army shirt and ran her rough hands over the soft material, rubbing dirt into the sleeves, vaguely distracted by the two ten-year-olds attacking the glove compartment with their penknives. The car smelled of the woman's perfume and cigarette smoke.

Except for some papers—maps, a license and registration—the glove compartment was empty. The boy with the bad skin emptied the pocketbook on the front seat and ran his long bony hands through its contents: plastic comb and brush, hairpins, a red silk scarf, lipstick, rouge, eyebrow pencil and a bottle of eyeliner, an old cloudy pocket mirror, address book, sunglasses, passport, pocket calculator, a paperback thriller, emery board, another lipstick, a wallet. Inside the wallet was a total of eighty-five dollars in tens, fives, and singles, a Bloomingdale's charge card and credit cards from Master Charge and American Express. He flipped through the pictures in the plastic frames—a man and a woman in bathing suits, smiling into the camera; a small, strange-looking dog; an old woman cleaning a chicken in a porcelain sink, her hair in curlers. There was nothing here he wanted.

He moved his gawky adolescent body out of the car and motioned to the little boy and girl who waited behind him. The children crawled up on the seat. The boy child selected the darker of the two shades of lipstick and began scrawling circles on the rearview mirror. The girl liked the snapshot of the slightly ratlike dog and the pocket mirror and slipped them inside the grimy leather bag she wore around her neck. Meantime the big boy found a can of de-icer wedged under the seat. He shook it. Nearly empty.

He could not open the trunk because he had no crowbar. That the keys to the trunk still dangled from the ignition meant nothing to him. He did not understand keys. Only that there might be something good in there.

On their way back through the woods, they spotted an owl and waited silently while it made its kill, a large bullfrog barely visible to them above the waterline. They watched the owl return to its tree with the frog and begin to tear it apart. Then the boy with the bad skin pelted it with a rock. The rock caught the bird square in the chest and tumbled it into a patch of blackberries. The smaller children cried out in pleasure. But the boy did not bother with its carcass. The thorns were too much trouble. Some animal would come along who would not mind the thorns. At night everything hunted.

11:30 A.M.

The kitchen was beginning to please her. It would be a great kitchen, once she got it clean again. Long double-leaf table; plenty of counter space; plenty of light from the big window over the sink facing east down the mountain over the field of dying goldenrod that passed for a backyard now, and two smaller windows west and south. Best of all, a big old potbellied stove near the center of the room, big enough to heat it and probably both bedrooms as well.

The kitchen was the largest room in the house and obviously intended to be the focal point of life there. Both doors led directly into it: the back door just to the left of the sink and the front door just beyond the table, next to a huge leather sofa. It was going to be very comfortable. Carla stood back from the sink for a moment and took a look around. It looked good now. She picked up the brown paper bag filled with toweling and ashes from the stove and brought it out back to the garbage cans on the porch.

A lovely day, she thought. The sun was bright and there was just enough of a nip in the air to give her an excuse to get the stove going. In the distance she could hear the waves against the shoreline. It was too bad you couldn't see the ocean. Just an albatross drifting high a half-mile away.

She opened the door to the woodshed and found it piled high with split oak and poplar. There was kindling in a box on the floor. Someone had done a pretty good job getting the place ready for her. Oh, it was dirty. But you had to expect that, and Carla didn't mind a little cleaning. She appreciated the wood, though—chopping wood was not one of the things she had learned to do well in life. And she appreciated the little touches, like the emergency numbers over the telephone in case she should need a doctor or—miserable idea—the police, and like the extension cord for her typewriter left on the kitchen table and the fact that somebody had thought to plug in the refrigerator. Someone had even done a cursory job with a broom. Considering that the agent said the place hadn't been rented in over a year now, it wasn't even all that dirty. Bad season last summer, he'd told her. Too many jellyfish on the beaches. She'd expected an awful mess, and it was nice to find that wasn't the case at all. All told, they'd left her in pretty good shape. There was a good sharp axe in the woodshed should she need some more kindling. But from the look of the shed she was confident that unless it was a hell of an autumn, she wasn't going to have to do any more splitting.

She made a few trips to the stove and back and laid in some wood, enough to do for the time being. Then she poured herself a cup of coffee and sat down at the table to consider what still remained unfinished. The bathroom was clean, the bedrooms were clean, and now the kitchen was done, too. That left the living room and, if she wanted to bother, the attic. Were she not expecting Jim and Marjie and the others tomorrow she'd have let the living room go for a few days, but with six of them in the house she figured she'd need the space.

Dumb idea, she thought, to have them here so soon, before I'm even settled in. But she had invited them on impulse and what was done was done. Jim's shooting was over now and who could know when he'd have to run off to L.A. for another idiot TV commercial or something. So the timing was convenient for him at least. How in hell had she gotten involved with an *actor,* anyway? By and large they were not her favorite people. They tended to be very single-minded, very egocentric. But she knew how she'd gotten involved with him, all right. It was simple—she'd never seen anything prettier in her life. The admission made her smile.

After Nick it had seemed so much simpler just to have a man around who was attractive, who made love to her and took her places and left it at that. Nick had been much too complex. She had put entirely too much energy into that one. Now it was work that interested her, not men. She had always given too much of her life over to relationships, and they'd never quite worked out. Now she was simplifying her life in favor of her career. It gave her a sense of control to watch herself succeeding, and a great deal of satisfaction. As for Jim, he was very handsome, and very nice to touch. And that was that.

She sipped distractedly at the coffee, her eyes fixed on a bright patch of sunlight on the kitchen counter. Even her relationship with Nick was simpler now, she thought. They were friends. At the moment she was looking forward to seeing him. She remembered how jealous he'd been when she first began seeing other men. She was glad that was over now, glad they'd had that little talk, which was really a marathon lasting till dawn. Otherwise it might have been messy having Jim and Nick in the same house together. Friendship and sex were really all she wanted from men these days. Nick gave her one, Jim the other—and life wasn't bad at all.

She considered the sleeping arrangements. Nick and Laura could have the first bedroom, she thought, Marjie and Dan the second. She and Jim could use the old pullout couch in front of the window in the living room. That meant she'd better get off her butt and clean it. She downed the coffee like a shot of whiskey and went to work.

In a way, the layout of the house was strange. The living room seemed almost an afterthought. It lay along the wall of the first and largest bedroom almost as if it, too, were a bedroom—so that all you had was a kitchen on one side of the house and three similar-sized rooms, plus a bathroom, on the other. There was a small fireplace in the living room, and Carla figured she'd better lay in a stack of wood there as well. Because of the placement of the potbellied stove in the kitchen, it didn't seem likely to heat the living room too well. There was a vaguely musty smell about the room that was present nowhere else in the house. It wasn't terribly comfortable. The furniture was old and had never been top quality. One by one she carried the chairs outside for a good airing and beat the dust out of the cushions.

One thing the room did have was those hand-hewn beams across the ceiling. According to the agent, the house was over a hundred years old, and it was in the beams that it really showed. They were massive, made out of some beautiful dark wood, really lovely. Made you want to carve your initials in them, so they'd be around another hundred years too, except you'd feel rotten if you spoiled them that way. They'd be nice to stare up at in the firelight, she thought, with a certain young actor on top of her. For a moment she could almost see and feel it. Log fantasy #620A, she thought, subsection Pioneer Spirit.

Very bawdy, Carla. All the same, she hoped the fireplace was in working order. Otherwise, Jim or no Jim it was going to get very cold in there. Of course she could leave the attic door open, and the heat that collected during the day would moderate the temperature somewhat. But she didn't like to do that. There was something sort of spooky about an old attic, and she'd just as soon leave it closed. As soon as the place was clean, she'd try the fireplace.

By two o'clock the living room was clean enough, and Carla had most of its furniture back inside. She was tired. It had been a very good day's work and she was glad she'd thought to leave the motel early enough to finish up today. Otherwise she'd probably still have been cleaning when her guests arrived.

In a way she wished they were already gone. She was beginning to have a sense that all this was really hers—now that she'd rescued it from its patina of dust and grime. She felt sure the editing would go well. The kitchen table was going to make a perfect desk. In fact, with both leaves open, it would be the biggest desk she'd ever had. Not like that tiny hunk of three-quarter-inch plywood in her apartment in New York. Or the one crammed full of letters and contracts at the office. She could spread out here. And one month's work in a place like this would be worth two back home. Plenty of quiet, plenty of time to think. No bars to distract her nights and no hangovers in the morning and no men around to complicate her life once Jim's visit was over.

Though she just might miss getting laid now and then. She wondered what the guys around here were like. Farmers and fishermen, probably. That might be interesting. She wondered if there was a bar in town. If there was, she supposed she'd have to climb into the rented Pinto and check it out. But only once, she thought. And nothing involving. Please God, nothing even remotely involving. I'm here to haul my way through a book on fifties rock 'n' roll that I have signed and which is a good book and is going to make me a star, or at least a full editor. Good money and reasonable deadlines. And that's all. That's what it's about.

In five days the company would be gone and she could get started. Long lonely walks by the sea and eight hours a day at the typer. Sounded like heaven. The book was solid, thoroughly professional and exciting. An editor's dream. Her boss had given her two extra weeks added to her vacation time on the understanding that when she returned to the city the editing would be finished. It would be. But what he didn't need to know was that she'd be finished in one week flat, working at a nice easy pace, and after that she could just relax and be alone awhile. It was cheating a little, she knew, but she'd been working very hard. She deserved the vacation and needed the extra time. Maybe she'd do a little writing of her own. Maybe just lay back and do nothing for a change. Whatever. And for this she was on full salary. The important thing was that she deliver a good book. She would. And the rest was gravy. She thought, *Good work, Carla*.

Now, about that attic.

She'd been up there earlier and it was pretty messy. Her sense of order urged her to give it at least a perfunctory cleaning. She supposed she ought to. But first things first. First she'd see if the fireplace was working. She went outside to gather some kindling and a few logs from the woodshed. She took some sheets from the sports section of the Sunday *Times* and rolled them into long tight bundles and then crisscrossed the kindling on top of them. Finally she placed three logs on the grate and checked to see that the flue was open. She lit a match and put it to the newspaper. The smoke began to draw, and soon there was a good hot fire going.

Poker, tongs, and shovel lay in a stand beside her. She used the poker to adjust the logs, placed two more on top of them, and then sat back awhile, enjoying the warmth from the fire. It was throwing heat quite well. So the room would be fine tonight. She brought in the last old overstuffed armchair and decided she could procrastinate no longer. It was the attic now or never.

She opened the door and started up the stairs.

They creaked, naturally, but seemed safe enough. There was a second door at the top of the stairs. She opened it and stepped onto the landing and reached overhead to turn on the light.

There was not much point to cleaning. The place was a mess. The floor testified to whole flourishing colonies of mice there. Shit city. And she wondered about bats. Everything she remembered about country living told her that when you had mice in the attic you had bats, too. Maybe she'd look for them come nightfall. And maybe not. But she decided to forget about the cleaning.

OFF SEASON

The pitch of the roof was so sharp that the job would be hell on her back. And there was nothing much up there, anyway. A few hangers scattered around on the floor. An old mattress, water-stained and weathered. A heavy old dresser, most of its drawers missing. A rusty scythe.

That was about it. There was only one window and that was small and completely clouded over with dust and dirt. Next to the chimney there was a pile of old magazines, an almanac from 1967, and a few old comic books—*Detective Comics* and *Plastic Man*. The comics looked good. She gathered them up and the smell of them, the old musty paper, pleased her. It was a smell she was very fond of. It stirred adolescent memories of a dime store in upstate New York, circa '64. Mown hay in the summertime. Malteds. Good things.

She put the comics aside next to the landing and walked to the window, stooping slightly from the waist.

I'll give it an airing, anyway, she thought. She found the latch and swung the window open toward her, stepping back slightly in order to accommodate it; and in so doing she realized she'd kicked something. It was difficult to see very well in that far corner of the room, but she had . . . *scattered* something. She'd heard something roll across the floor. With the window open now the light was a little better, but she still had to kneel in order to see. She peered at the floor. Now what the hell was *that*?

She was looking at a pile of bones; a small, neat

pile. Exactly what kind of bones she couldn't really tell, though she guessed they belonged to some sort of bird—or birds, because there were some long tail feathers and some smaller, white ones mixed into the pile. She recognized a few of the bones—a tiny humerus, a few sections of vertebra. She saw that they seemed to have been picked clean. Probably insects. They looked pretty old. The real question was how they'd gotten there. She'd only disturbed a few of them when she'd kicked them; the rest were stacked into a small pyramid a foot or so in diameter. As if they'd been swept there in front of the window and then forgotten. Someone had swept the floor and then neglected to finish the job. She guessed that was it.

But why only bones and feathers? The floor was covered with droppings. Yet somehow none of them had found their way into the little pile. Was there some sort of animal that habitually did this? An owl or something? She tried to sort through her college biology. It was hard for her to picture some bird or— God forbid—some rat stacking up the remains of its prey that way, though she supposed it was fully possible. But it looked more like the kind of thing a human being would do. A kid, maybe. She remembered the comic books by the chimney. She pictured some poor, lonely, half-demented kid stacking up chicken bones here in the attic while his parents bickered down below, and wondered who the previous tenants had been.

She returned to the landing and picked up the

comics. I hope I'm not robbing your secret stash, kid, she thought. She went downstairs and got herself a dustpan and broom. There was something she didn't like about that pile. She'd pick up that much, anyway.

4:35 P.M.

Peters looked up at the old Pabst clock on the wall and ordered a second Bud. Aside from the Pincus boys down at the end of the bar, he was alone. The Caribou was nice and dark and quiet, just the way he liked it.

Hank drew him the beer and set it down beside a half-eaten turkey club. There were advantages to eating this late, he thought, even if he wouldn't want to do it every day. For one thing you worked up an appetite—not that his own had ever failed him. But also you got to relax a bit. Around lunchtime the place was too busy to relax. That was the trouble with being a state cop; life was too damned public. Whenever there were people around they always had stories or complaints or just plain gab for you, or else they expected you to have a yarn or two for them.

You got no peace. In a small town everybody knew everybody else's business and a cop was watchdog over all of it. That was his job; at least the way they saw it. Peters saw it differently. His job was to keep the peace—his own peace, first of all. So he tried to avoid the questions and comments, but what could you do? A small town got very short on public figures, and folks made shift with what they had.

Now that accident today. That had caused quite a stir. Mostly because it was the Boston people, but also because Dead River was short on accidents, too. Peters would have bet, way back in June when they'd first arrived, that the Landers woman was going to get into some sort of trouble sooner or later. She'd managed to hold off, though, until the day they were supposed to leave. Well, he thought, better late than never.

Quite a cookie, she was. The kind of woman that all these open spaces naturally made uncomfortable. He'd met them plenty of times before. Belonged in the city, where a woman would have all the conveniences, plenty to keep her busy and plenty of people to take her troubles to. Out here if the plumbing broke down—as hers had in July—you maybe had to wait a day or two. Folks got busy. Things moved slow. Back where she came from, all you had to do was call the maintenance crew in the basement of your big old high-rise and they were up there in an hour, and two hours later you had your hot water. That was what you were used to. But this was not the city.

So what had she done? *Called the police*. Called him up to complain that it had been a day and a half and the plumber still hadn't shown. What was he supposed to do, ma'am, he asked her, drag John Fraser out there at gunpoint? *If you have to,* she'd said. Even knowing the tourists, he could hardly believe it. And now, secretly, he was glad the accident today had been her fault, that she had plowed into the Williams kid's rear fender at Maine and Maple and not the other way around. Williams had a good boy there. And like most tourists, Mrs. Landers was trouble start to finish.

Well, not exactly to finish, he thought. She was responsible, after all, for this nice late lunch today.

He took a too-large bite out of the sandwich—as he usually did—and had some trouble chewing—also as usual. Teeth going, back going—I'm a mess, he thought. Too much weight on me and too many years. Give the job to Shearing, he wants it. It was an old, old song with him and he knew who he was kidding. There was the retirement money to think of, and if he was honest, he wouldn't have given up the work if you begged him. Maybe because he'd been at it so long. Maybe he liked the law. And maybe he just liked the people, liked his position among them, and found it pleasant to give them a hand now and then. When he thought that way he suspected he'd be giving orders from his deathbed, and the idea didn't seem half bad.

He took a long swallow of the Bud and heard the Pincus boys holler down the end of the bar, looking in his direction. He turned and saw Lydia Davis glide in, with Shearing holding the door behind her. There was a big dumb grin on Shearing's long thin face, but Peters guessed he couldn't help it. Lydia Davis was quite something.

"Hey, boys," she said, "who's gonna buy?" The accustomed greeting. She walked by Peters without so much as a glance. Peters was married and a cop and there were no free beers coming from that quarter. All the same, she gave him a good close look at those pretty young breasts under the blue halter as she passed him, and again as usual, looking at Lydia made him wish he was twenty years younger and not quite so happy with his wife. Then the Pincus boys seemed to swallow her up in the dim light of the bar, and Shearing sat down on the stool beside him.

"Ain't that something?" he said to Peters, shaking his head like a wet yellow dog.

"Happens every year," said Peters. "The tourist girls go home and Lydia comes out struttin'. You could tear off a page of the calendar. Always nice to see it, though."

"That it is."

"Good shorts."

"Very nice."

"The Queen Bee of Dead River," said Peters. He smiled, mostly for Shearing's sake. He was thinking that when he was in the army there had been a girl like Lydia in every town he'd seen that made its living on the tourist trade; shy girls or unhappy girls, usually, who were pretty enough when there was not much competition, girls who would eventually marry badly for fear of growing old alone. He wondered if Shearing, who had never gotten out of Dead River, could see that. He doubted it. You had to get away for a while and hear the same foolish bar talk, the same strutting and flashing over and over again in every town, to know how sad it was. And most of these kids, Shearing included, had never been farther away than Portland.

For a moment he and Shearing stared into the bleak artificial twilight of the bar while Lydia and young Jim Pincus went to the juke to feed it quarters and push the familiar series of buttons. The juke hardly ever changed at the Caribou—only when Hank would get drunk nights and, fed up with some tune or another, pull his old battered record case out of the cellar and find a substitute. Two weeks ago he'd gotten angry at a Marty Robbins tune, and now at A41 you had Elvis singing "Are You Lonesome Tonight." The record was a little warped, but Hank was the only one he'd ever heard play it anyhow.

> *I'm lookin' for a feelin'*
> *That I once had with you . . .*

A Waylon Jennings song. That meant Pincus had picked it. Lydia would come up with something a lot more raucous, like Jerry Lee Lewis; and Peters reflected once again on the odd fact that in some ways a man was a much more romantic creature than a woman. Even if the man was a tough young weasel like Jim Pincus. In some ways much more romantic.

"How drunk are those boys?" asked Shearing. It was as if he were reading Peters' thoughts, but that was nothing new. You work with a man for six years or so and it was bound to happen now and then.

"I'd say moderate."

"Lydia goes for the rough ones, don't she?"

"You see anybody else around?"

"Us."

"Officers of the law, Sam. You want the ladies, you'll do better fixing Port-a-Sans."

Shearing took him seriously. He hadn't meant to be taken seriously. "Now, George . . ." There was a whining tone in his voice that Peters had learned to put up with over the years. "You know I never . . ."

Peters gave him a broad wink. You had to be broad with Shearing.

"Don't worry, Sam," he said. "Helen knows how you fool around nights. Pinball, shuffleboard, eightball, and lager. Some life. Some ladykiller." Shearing smiled. He had himself a good woman in Helen. He'd be crazy to pull anything on her. You never knew how these things would turn out in the long run, but as of now Shearing played it straight and narrow. The day he didn't, thought Peters, would be the day you could begin to write a postmortem on Sam Shearing, because in a town like this, without the wife and kids it was all decline.

"You get the Landers people on their way all right?" he asked.

Shearing motioned to Hank and ordered a beer. "Sure did," he said. "And happy to see it, too."

"You got yourself some company there," said Peters. "I swear that there is something about a stupid woman with a problem that makes me want to hand her seventeen more." He waved his hand in a gesture of dismissal. "And sometimes I do," he said.

They drank their beers. Nobody was playing the

jukebox now and the bar was quiet; Hank a few feet away from them staring out the window to the street in that dreamy, sad-eyed way of his that was so strange to see in a man his size; Lydia leaning on the bar between Jim and Joey Pincus; Joey's arm slung over her shoulder, silent with something that Peters thought was very like romance, as close to that as their fear and fool bravado would probably ever take them. He began to feel the second beer swimming in his head and he pushed it away from him. He felt the old discomfort in his back that the doctor had told him came from carrying too much weight and which the beers did nothing to alleviate. The beers, in fact, did nothing much at all.

"Town's real quiet," he said to Shearing. "Everybody gone."

Shearing nodded.

"I got this feeling," Peters said. "It's not good."

"What kind of feeling?"

"Probably old age, Sam," he said. "I'm maybe tired of the sameness, that's all."

Shearing nodded again. There was nothing to say.

"In season you got the clowns. The tourists. Off season you've got only us, and sometimes I think we're clowns, too. Sitting in a little town waiting for summer to come, the fishing worse and worse every year. What's the point? I don't sleep good, Sam. I'm restless. Pushing fifty-five and I'm restless. Now that's a joke, I think. When things get easy this way it always seems like a joke to me. Oh, we keep busy but it's nothing really. And I think, This year something's gonna happen. Between now and June One something's gonna happen to me. Jackpot in the lottery. Some rich aunt dying I never heard of. Something. And then I take the money and the little lady and off we go to Paris. I was stationed there during the war, you know. You know about that. But in twenty-three years of work, in twenty years of marriage, nothing. That's a joke, isn't it?"

He pushed himself away from the bar. "Aw, to hell with it," he said. "Two beers and I got the blues. I can't even drink like I used to. When you gonna take this job away from me, Sam?"

"When hell freezes over," said Shearing. "When you give it to me."

Peters smiled. "Sounds like I got a little time, then," he said.

The bar door opened and Willis walked in. For a moment he squinted against the darkness and then he saw Peters and Shearing sitting in silence. He walked over to them in long, gawky strides. He's in a hurry, thought Peters. I guess that means that lunch is over.

Willis and Shearing were both in their late twenties, but where Shearing was studied and taciturn, Willis was exuberant and jumpy as a boy who'd just shot his first five-pointer. The man, thought Peters, was always in a hurry. But he didn't come looking for them often. And to Peters the proof that it was business was that he made no notice whatever of Lydia. Willis, unmarried and hungry, was usually at Lydia like a coonhound barking up a tree.

"So?" said Peters.

"So you're wanted back at the office right away," said Willis. "The both of you."

"What's up? Mrs. Landers blow a tire or something?"

Willis smiled. "We got a good one this time," said Willis, his face flushing red. "I mean a dilly. Fished a woman out of the ocean a little while ago."

"Alive?"

"Alive and beat all to hell. You never saw anything like this, George."

"You want to bet, son?" he said.

He grinned. "I'll bet."

"Okay," said Peters, moving off the bar stool. "If you win, Shearing here owes you a ten. If I win you lay off that girl Lydia down there the rest of the year."

"You got it," he said.

Peters opened the door and nodded to Hank the barman and the three of them filed out. Willis paused a moment in the doorway, the bright glow from the street flooding through the pale-yellow gloom of the bar. He turned and waved. "Hi there, Lydia," he said.

The Pincus brothers scowled. The girl turned briefly and smiled and returned his wave with her long delicate fingers. "Hi sweet," she said. By the time Willis was out the door the beer was raised to her lips, Hank was drawing her another, and the two brothers sitting beside her were happy again.

5:17 P.M.

Nothing but waste and self-indulgence, Carla thought. It was not very cold out. But she wanted to keep that fire going in the stove. It made her feel lazy and relaxed and vaguely sexy, and she loved the smell. She had let the fire in the living room die out. The dampness had never quite disappeared from that room, even with the fire. The musty odor lingered. She probably wouldn't be using it much, once her company left. The kitchen was much nicer. She folded up her *Press Herald* and put the bowl of fruit back in the refrigerator.

It was almost sundown. If she was going to have a fire all night she'd better get in some wood, she thought. She was enough of a city girl to balk at opening the door to a woodshed after dark. Tired as she was, it was better to do it now. She was also starving. The fruit was no help at all. She'd get in the wood and have a shower and then fix an early dinner. She had chicken and fresh vegetables in the refrigerator. There was pretty good produce in Dead River. She hadn't

37

had a meal since breakfast and that was fine for her figure but rotten for her disposition. As to the house, enough was enough, it was fine now.

She opened the back door and stepped out onto the porch. A wind had come up. Fallen leaves blew about the yard and swirled over the faded gray floorboards beneath her feet. She opened the woodshed and began loading logs into the crook of her arm. The logs were light and dry. She brought in one load and then went out for another. When this load seemed heavier she realized she was really very tired. That shower was going to feel wonderful. She made a third trip for some kindling; and as she closed the woodshed door, she saw him.

Rather, she saw the shirt. It was bright red, the kind of shirt hunters wear to protect themselves from other hunters. She saw it moving way across the field, and only a moment later did she realize it was a man threading his way along the brook at the base of the hill, not a redbird or a patch of leaves. God, she was exhausted! Had he not been wearing red she'd have missed him, but his own eyes were obviously better. He stopped a moment and turned in her direction. At that distance it was impossible to tell what he looked like, but something about the way he moved told her he was young and strong. He waved at her. Sociable, too, she thought. She smiled and waved back. She doubted he could see the smile.

He stood facing her for a second or two and then continued moving along upstream, crouching low as if he were looking for something. Crayfish? The agent had told her there were a lot of them down there. Or maybe it was frogs. Maybe she had a neighbor who was fond of frog's legs. There was no accounting for taste, she thought. In any case he was soon out of sight, disappearing behind the trees.

She decided it was a good idea to drag the entire box of kindling inside. That way she'd not have to make so many trips. She propped the back door open with a garbage can and went to work. She wondered where the man lived. According to her recollection of what the agent had said, her nearest neighbor was two miles away off the old dump road. She'd chosen the house for privacy—as well as price and charm. On all counts it was perfect.

By the time she'd hauled the kindling through the kitchen and set it down next to the stove she was utterly done in. Everything ached. If she allowed herself to lie down now it would be all over, and she'd wake some time next morning. At dawn, she thought, since her bedroom had an eastern exposure. It was lovely how all these little bits of information were coming back to her. Eastern exposure. How to build a good fire. Beating the dust out of the cushions.

In recent years her visits to the country had been infrequent. There was a friend in New Hampshire and another in northern Vermont. Once every two or three years she'd drive up to visit. It was a catch-as-catch-can way to learn but Carla was a good observer and remembered what she saw. She and Marjie had always had a fine time on those trips—in fact it was the visits to New Hampshire and Vermont that had prompted this trip, though the state of Maine was wholly new to her. They both had always liked the country. Any country. She sat down at the kitchen table for a moment.

She thought about her sister. Marjie was also a good observer—maybe too good. Sometimes Carla thought that watching was all she'd ever do. She was as good an illustrator as Carla had ever seen and a pretty decent painter too, but she'd refused to do anything with her talents. Instead there had been a dreary succession of part-time jobs; typing jobs, receptionist jobs, sales jobs—she remembered one particularly ludicrous one in the toy department of Bloomingdale's during the Christmas season, Marjie selling baseball bats and electronic games to East Side brats whose mothers all wore furs and carried monogrammed designer handbags and seemed to hate the kids they were buying for. Nothing else had been as bad as that.

Except, perhaps, her sex life. God knows that was a mess. Either she would fall in love at the drop of a hat with somebody who ought to have been a one-night stand, and this schoolgirl non-relationship would go on for months, or else she'd hibernate in her apartment for weeks at a time and see nobody at all, like a wounded animal licking its wounds and waiting for the snow to disappear.

At least there were signs that that much was changing. This guy Dan she was seeing loved her and was willing to say so. And though Marjorie was not so willing, she seemed to be staying with it for a change, seeing what she could make of it and what would develop. At least she wasn't hiding.

But she still wished she could see a little outright strength and resolve in her sister. Maybe because she herself had come by a good dose of it over the last few years. If anything, Carla worried now that she was getting a bit too tough for her own good, that she was making a bad trade off between emotions and her efficacy in the world, and she wondered if she were still capable of falling in love now and then—when she had time to wonder.

But she knew she was better off than her sister. Marjie was still too much the fragile flower for her own good; and though she'd always sensed a hidden toughness in her sister, in all these years she had yet to see it in action.

She opened the grate and threw two more logs on the fire. Time for that shower, she thought. The shower, a cup of coffee, and a meal—that would revive her. She still wanted to do some reading tonight.

She undressed in the bedroom and walked naked into the bathroom. She knew that the water took a while to warm up so she turned on the shower and waited for the steam to rise. In the meantime she had a look at herself. She had to laugh. She looked like two separate people. Her hands were filthy. Her face was streaked with dirt and her hair was filled with dust. It looked as if the hands and head were rubber Halloween gear slipped onto an otherwise neat and clean—and estimable—body. At thirty-two she looked nearly as good as she had at twenty. The ass had a bit

JACK KETCHUM

more sag to it, yes, but then again her skin was a whole lot better. Another tradeoff. She turned to the side. Her small breasts quivered. Nice lines, she thought.

The shower did what it was supposed to do. It soothed and refreshed her. It also made her a little horny. It was only when she was clean that she really liked to make love. She could never understand those people who liked to do it first thing in the morning. Obviously morning was your dirtiest time of day. You'd been wrapped in covers and maybe sweating all night, your mouth smelled like a sewer, your hair was limp and ratty. Really, it was a disgusting idea.

Not so after a shower. The flesh tingled. Too bad Jim wasn't around. She thought she was never so committed to Jim as when she considered never being able to ball him again. And by now it seemed as if it had been a long time. Tomorrow night, she thought. I can wait.

She dried herself off and then wrapped her long dark hair in the towel. She pulled on a bathrobe and made some coffee in the kitchen. She decided to keep dinner simple—just fry up some chicken and sauté a few vegetables. To hell with the cholesterol. Mushrooms, onions, and peppers would be nice. Add a little garlic and soy sauce, maybe. She felt much better after that shower. Ready to start cleaning all over again, if she'd had to. Praise God she didn't have to. She sipped the coffee.

She was washing the peppers when the mouse ran over her bare foot.

It made her jump. The bold little bastard! She watched it stop a moment, trembling, a few feet away.

She laughed. She guessed that a warm foot was probably just as big a surprise to the mouse as the mouse had been to her. It disappeared into a corner cupboard. Exactly where she was keeping the bread, flour, and sugar, naturally. She guessed that meant war. Too bad. It was kind of a cute little thing. But then you had the droppings. She remembered the condition of the attic. She had seen some traps under the sink. She'd set a few tonight in the drawers and cupboards. It was a shame there was no cat around. She hated traps. But you had to claim what you needed, she supposed. That was life. And she needed her flour and sugar. With a little luck, by morning it would all be over for the mouse.

9:30 P.M.

He watched a long time through the kitchen window. She sat at the table with her back to him, a book open in front of her. She didn't move much but he liked to watch anyway, knowing that in the dark she could not possibly suspect he was there. He was patient. He liked to see her when she shifted in the chair. He watched her hips move. He could almost tell by now when she was ready to turn the page. He liked it when she removed the towel from her head and shook the long, damp hair. She was pretty. He would have liked to make a noise and spook her, watch her jump. But no.

His broad hand slid down the axe handle and slid back up again.

Inside the house Carla heard a light snapping sound. The trap! she thought. She put down the book and went to the cabinet, opened it, and looked inside. But the trap had not been sprung. She closed the cabinet and opened the drawer. Not there, either. She opened the drawer next to it.

There it was. It was a clean kill, thank God. A small gray mouse, its back broken across the shoulders, its eyes open wide and mouth still crammed with Gouda cheese, one front paw extended and the other barely visible beneath its body, a tiny pool of dark piss below its haunches. She stood there a moment in front of the window, fascinated and uncomfortable. If she touched the body it would still be warm.

She did not touch it. Instead she picked up the trap and brought it to the back door. She opened the door and gazed into the moonless dark outside. What an amazing, profound darkness once you left the city, she thought. She could not even see the end of the porch or the woodshed door. Good she'd brought the logs in.

She paused a moment, enjoying the night, the sounds of frogs croaking in the distance, crickets nearby, the feel of the cool moist air. Overcast tonight, she thought. She tossed the trap as far as she could into the field of goldenrod, wondering what kind of animal would find it there. A raccoon, maybe. There was always a raccoon or two checking out the houses, she recalled. She went inside and closed the door.

He crouched in the field and waited for her to get ready for bed. It would not be long now. She had not gone back to the book. She was cleaning some dishes right in front of his window. He smiled. He was not ten feet away from her and yet she could not see him. The night had turned the red shirt black. So funny to be so helpless and stupid.

To throw the trap that way. He wanted to laugh. But he had perfect control of himself and he wouldn't. He had perfect control and only smiled at her in the dark.

She finished the dishes and walked into the bedroom and took the hairbrush off the night table. She bent over and tossed her hair forward and began to brush. One hundred strokes, she thought. What nonsense. But she did it anyway. The collar of her terrycloth robe got in her way slightly so she straightened up again, removed the robe, bent back over and continued brushing. The stove had warmed the house enough so that she was comfortable naked. She'd sleep that way.

She closed her eyes and brushed hard, enjoying the scrape of the bristles on her clean scalp. The wind was up again outside; she heard it move something against the house.

When she'd had enough she straightened up and brushed her hair back and side to side a bit, and then stopped. She walked into the kitchen and got herself a drink of water. She turned off the lights. She walked back into the bedroom and drank the water, put the glass on the night table, and got into bed. She was much too tired to read. She turned off the bedside lamp.

The sheets were cool against her naked body. Outside she heard the sound again and thought, I wonder if that wind means rain. In no time at all she was asleep.

11:20 P.M.

It was raining in Manhattan. Through the window of her second-floor apartment Marjorie could see the rain slanting down through the glow of a streetlight half a block away, could hear it drumming on the roof of the Checker cab parked below. She knew without having to feel it how cold the rain would be. A man in a too-thin jacket stood in a doorway across the street, waiting for a letup. For once the street looked bright and clean. She was glad she was going to the country.

There was a rule her mother had taught her about packing and she always adhered to it: begin at the feet and work up to your hat. She never wore hats but the rule was good, anyway. She ticked off the items in the suitcase in the appropriate order. Shoes: two pairs, one dressy and one comfortable. Sneakers. Socks and stockings. Five pairs of panties. Tampons (she was due by the end of the week—shit!). One slip, one skirt, and two pairs of jeans. A simple cotton dress. Blouses, tee shirts. One sweater, one jacket. Nightgown. Razor for the armpits. Her skin was delicate and prone to break out now and then even at this late date, so she packed a bar of Ivory and the stuff her dermatologist had given her. In the morning she'd throw in the toothbrush, shower cap, and hairbrush. And that would do it.

She closed the suitcase and put it at the foot of the bed, then walked to her desk and wrote herself a note so she'd remember to water the plants in the morning. She glanced outside. The cab was gone and so was the man in the doorway across the street. The rain looked thinner now, a drifting mist. According to the news the storm was supposed to break by morning, so that with luck they'd have a good day for traveling. She undressed in the bathroom and washed her face and hands, then pulled the old spare nightgown on over her head, the one with the hole in the shoulder. Actually she liked the hole there. She had good shoulders.

Was there anything she'd forgotten? She walked slowly through the apartment but could think of nothing. One more note, though. She went to the desk and wrote: *Unplug everything*. She'd do that the very last thing. She walked into the kitchen and poured herself a glass of water. She took a drink and then refilled the glass. Carrying the glass of water, she walked back into the bedroom, turning off the lights in the hall and living room along the way. She climbed into bed, an unread copy of the evening *Post* and Carla's book on Maine beside her.

The paper first. She sipped the water and scowled, wondering for the thousandth time why she bothered to buy such a miserable newspaper. She guessed just to see what the *Times* had left out. The scandal. The murder.

The murder always upset her though, slightly. She read about it, but knew it wasn't good for her. A cerebral poison. The headline was: 5 KILLED IN BLOODY RIKERS RIOT. She noted the alliteration. There was plenty of international news today, but that was the *Post*'s front-page story. She hardly ever bothered to actually read the stories. The headlines were usually quite enough. She flipped through the paper and the boldface type disgorged today's necrology. *Refugees Slain . . . Subway Rider Killed . . . 7 More Die in Iran . . . Youth, 17, Seized in Rape-Murder . . .*

There were two stories in particular that she did read, so odd that in spite of herself they commanded her attention. In one a 45-year-old laborer in Paramus had tried to set his wife afire, having gone out to the garage after a drunken squabble to fill his glass with gasoline. He'd doused her with the gas but then, police said, was too drunk to light a match properly. In the other story a man in Virginia had hanged his beagle puppy from a tree in the backyard because it wouldn't obey him.

Marjie read the stories through with a grim fascination. Her amazement at how desperate and crazed people could be simply never abated. These two stories were so strange they were almost comic. Yet if remembered that they were not just stories, but real events in the lives of strangers, the mind boggled and they were not funny at all. *The sudden lives of strangers:* where was that from? Something dark and very sad settled over her for a moment. An image of a man walking away from a struggling puppy. She tossed the paper to the floor.

In Maine, she would not have the *Post*. Fine.

She opened the book Carla had loaned her, a well-thumbed, broken-backed volume her sister had found in a flea market somewhere, *A Short History of the Maine Woods*. She read Indian legends about trout and elk and the story of the building of FDR's summer home at Campobello Island across the bridge from Lubec, near Carla's house at Dead River. Her sister had red-penciled local stories of particular interest. Marjie sipped her glass of water and awaited sleep. The book's style was quaint and a little stuffy. Sleep would not be far away. She read:

> *Lashed by gale-force winds and fierce seas, Barnet Light on Catbird Island is one of the most isolated lighthouses on the Atlantic seaboard, set high on a barren, jagged rock overlooking Dead River across the bay . . .*

There was a red slash-mark beneath the words, *"Dead River."* Marjie liked the feeling of her sister having read all this before her. For a moment it was as if they were reading side by side. She continued.

> *. . . today a federal wildlife sanctuary, Catbird Island is rarely visited by either tourists or residents due to its treacherous seas, and the Light*

has been unoccupied since 1892, when the Lighthouse at West Quoddy Head opened in its stead. The early history of the Island is, however, curious and worth mentioning.

Established on the southernmost tip of the Island in 1827, the Light was originally a wooden tower situated at the end of a stone dwelling that was habitable only in fair weather. Its fixed light was elevated 83 feet above high water. But in 1855 when the Lighthouse Board was informed the Barnet's visibility fell far short of the hoped-for fourteen miles (its lack of visibility worsened by the fact that the Light is fog-enshrouded a good thirty percent of the time) a new tower was constructed to an elevation of 95 feet. A reconstruction of the keeper's house was likewise undertaken and accomplished.

That same year Daniel Cook was appointed keeper of the Light and moved his entire family—his wife Catherine, his son Burgess, twelve, and his daughters Libby and Agnes, ages thirteen and ten respectively—into the stone dwelling on this inhospitable site, where they lived for three years without incident.

Then on January 19, 1858, a terrible gale struck the coast of New England, making a complete breach of the Island's sea-wall and, as the tide came in, flooding the keeper's house entirely, until finally the only habitable spot on the Island was the tower of the Light. Luckily, the Light itself held

throughout the gale, and Daniel Cook and his fam-
ily all were spared. They had gathered their hens
together in good time, managing to rescue all but
one. But for five weeks thereafter, owing to rough
weather, no landing could be effected on the Island.

At this point the story becomes slightly un-
clear. Apparently Cook and his son Burgess set
out from the Light at some time during the morn-
ing of either January 29th or 30th, feeling that
the storm had abated sufficiently so that it would
be possible to sail to the mainland to obtain pro-
visions, food and water. By this time the hens
were gone. Their skiff was small, its sail home-
made, and neither Cook nor his son were ever
heard from again. Meantime Mrs. Cook and her
daughters were reduced to daily rations of one
egg and a cup of corn meal per day, and that
supply soon went the way of the hens.

On the 23rd of February a landing on the rock
was finally effected by Captain Warren of Booth
Bay. He found only one survivor, the daughter
Libby, by that time quite hysterical and nearly
perished for want of food. Their ordeal had
lasted a full thirty-three days. Tragically, Mrs.
Cook had died only the day before. Libby had
buried her in a shallow grave some few yards to
the north of the Light; and had done so alone,
for her sister Agnes had disappeared some days
previously. Her own search had revealed no trace
of her, whether drowned or lost; nor did the Cap-
tain's subsequent efforts clarify the matter.

Mrs. Cook was exhumed and buried at Christ Church in Lubec a few days later. Libby Cook was taken to the home of her great-aunt Mrs. White, also of Lubec, and lived out the remainder of her life there alone after the aunt died in 1864, though apparently she never quite recovered from the incident. It was her contention that her sister was still alive somewhere on the island. But of Agnes Cook no trace was ever found.

A month following the incident a new keeper of Barnet Light was appointed, one James Richards of Dead River, who held the post until early the following year, 1859, when he relinquished it to Lowell S. Dow, who, like Daniel Cook before him, brought with him his entire family—wife, infant son, and daughter. Again tragedy struck the Island. In 1865 Dow's son, then seven years old, disappeared, believed to have been washed out to sea while playing too near the shoreline. Again an exhaustive search for the boy turned up nothing. Apart from this second tragedy, the lonely post remained occupied without incident until the Light was abandoned twenty-seven years later.

It is always amusing to note what the locals make of such drama. As noted previously, the Maine-iac is a born storyteller. In this case, the local intelligence has it that Libby Cook was quite right about her sister Agnes; that she did not die on the Island but instead turned mad and savage out of pure starvation, hiding from her *sister and her doomed mother in one of the many granite caves which dot the high northern Barnet cliffs. Likewise the disappearance of the Dow boy is also attributed to Agnes; a simple kidnap to assuage her great, consuming loneliness. To this day, the two ghost children are said to gambol through the ruins of the old Lighthouse, through the haunts of terns and eiders, in search of other youngsters; and children are threatened by stern and unkind mothers with the ghost of Agnes Cook . . .*

What better place, thought Marjie, to put away a book for the night than at the end of a ghost story. She turned off the light beside her bed. And very shortly she was asleep, the corner of her mouth turned upward in the hint of a smile. Outside the rain had stopped and a fog rolled in from the river. The clock wound slowly down to morning.

PART II

SEPT. 13, 1981

2:15 P.M.

Nick shifted into the front seat and took the wheel. His black '69 Dodge shuddered as the cars rolled swiftly by on the highway. It was a bright sunny day and nobody was paying the slightest attention to the speed limit. He reached into his pocket and took out his glasses. He heard the car door close on Jim's side.

"You wear glasses?" said Jim.

"It's cheaper than buying a dog," he said.

He turned the key in the ignition and pulled the car off the shoulder. He patted the steering wheel gently. Good old car, he thought. You've been no trouble at all. He hoped things would stay that way.

Beside him, Laura seemed engrossed in the latest issue of *Master Detective* magazine. Some reading matter this crew has got here, he thought. There was an old Zap comic going around in the back. He glanced at Laura's cover. NICE KID NEXT DOOR WAS A SEX-KILLER was one story. LURED TO HIS DEATH BY

A HOMICIDAL HOMO seemed to be the feature. But the best was in smaller letters at the bottom: *Question for Kentucky Homicide Detectives: Where Are the Nurse's Arms and Legs?* Where indeed? There was a posed picture on the cover of a brunette lying on some cheap wall-to-wall carpeting, trying to fend off some guy with a big saw.

Jesus! Laura loved that stuff. Well, he couldn't kick. He flipped through the rags when she was done with them. He smiled at her.

"How's the magazine?" he said.

"Tawdry."

"Which one you reading?"

" 'Who Spooked the Blonde's Butcher-Knife Killer'?"

"It's not on the cover," he observed.

"It's a sleeper." She popped a Bazooka bubble-gum bubble at him and made a face.

He smiled again, a little ruefully. It was that kind of stuff that got to him sometimes. Sometimes he thought she was about twelve years old. He had long since gathered that she didn't mind giving that impression. But at thirty-three he was just a little bit too old for kid stuff. She was a nice girl and he liked her, but it was not exactly his idea of fascinating to be clowning around all the time. He liked her in bed too, but bed was not all he wanted. He wondered what he did want and found no ready answer. Once it had been Carla. He wondered how it would end with Laura; and thought it would probably not end well at all.

He lit a cigarette. The old black Dodge slid heavily down the road.

*   *   *

They decided to take 95 straight on up and skip the
Mass. Pike altogether. It had been Marjorie's idea and
now she was glad she'd pressed them on it. It was obviously the nicer route, hugging the coast of Connecti-
cut as far as New London before heading north to skirt
Providence and Boston, then returning to the coastline
again around Brunswick, Maine. After that, Highway
1 would take them past Bar Harbor nearly all the way
to Dead River. There would be decent highways and
few truckers right on through. She could sit back and
enjoy the trees turning, all the bright reds and golds,
and maybe sketch them later when they got to Carla's,
if they didn't arrive too late in the day.

She'd seriously underestimated the length of the trip.
What looked like nine hours on the map was going to be
more like twelve. After eight hours on the road, Dead
River was still a long way up the coast. They'd probably
arrive just before nightfall. Well, thought Marjorie, that
would do. They had nearly a week once they got there.

She was beginning to get fidgety. She'd never liked
closed-in places or prolonged close proximity to others.

She was one of those people who always wanted an
aisle seat in a movie theater, a window seat on a bus, a
place at the end of the table. Carla called her eccentric
but she knew what she needed.

So far so good, though. Her mood was holding up
pretty well, and Carla would have been pleased with
her, she thought. Her sister always said Marjie was a
bitch to do any long-distance driving with, mostly because Carla liked to speed now and then and Marjie

hated that. Her idea was to get there nice and easy, but *get there*. In that way at least, she thought she was a lot more sensible than Carla. But today she was doing fine. She hadn't even complained when they'd lit the joint outside of Boston, though that was pretty dangerous, too. The beginnings of autumn were stirring in her. The day was just too lovely to bother with any serious complaining.

Less-than-serious complaining, though, the quiet kind, she couldn't help but doing. The company was not great, if she was to be honest about it. Nick was fine as always—pleasant, quiet, dependable. He hadn't even taken a hit of the joint when Dan offered it to him. But that girl of his, Laura, was a bit of a pain. If she was not silly she was posing, and if she wasn't posing she was distant. There was a lot of wisecracking. She wondered what Nick—a man who had once loved her sister (and not so long ago, either)—could see in a phony, rather abrasive record-company flak from L.A. Who with her close-cropped hair and bubble gum and tee shirt and beat-up leather jacket was acting about ten years younger than her age. It stumped her. There was just no telling about men.

She could live with Laura, though. She'd have to. Otherwise it was going to be a long week. Maybe the posing, like the outfit, was just protective coloring. Probably. Oh hell, she thought, you've only just met the girl. Let it ride.

Anyhow it was Jim who was the problem. There was something about that man that Marjie just didn't like.

Carla had talked about Jim and said it was mostly sex with them, and Marjie could understand that—he was awfully nice to look at. But what an ego! Everything was I, I, I. I auditioned for this. They said I was right for that.

She had never met an actor who wasn't utterly dim, and James Harney was no exception. He could talk theater, all right. But who in God's name was interested? Here was somebody who actually wanted to be in a musical comedy—and you got the feeling that almost any musical comedy would do. Just like any commercial would do. Or any soap opera. The whole thing struck her as a colossal waste of time. Was that the payoff for being beautiful? Ego and soap flakes? She was glad she was just attractive.

She was being a snob about it, she knew, but it was hard not to. The guy was involved with her sister. She felt very protective toward her sister and knew the feeling was mutual. If the situation were reversed, Carla would have had exactly the same reaction. *Why bother?*

She wondered if it would matter to Carla to know that Jim had been cruising her pretty hard all day, touching her whenever he could, smiling, flirting. Probably not. But it mattered to Marjie. She didn't like it at all. Laura she could put up with. But she wasn't even going to try to like Jim Harney.

She had to admit she'd been a lot more comfortable with Carla when she'd had a real relationship going with a man, like the one with Nick. It was sad to see that fail—though she guessed it was really very nice that they were still good friends. She wondered how they'd managed that. She wondered about many aspects of that relationship, but she'd never asked. There was something about Carla's self-sufficiency these days that scared Marjie off, that distanced her. As if Carla didn't want to be bothered. As if she was too busy for personal problems and personal questions. But if they could have talked about things like they used to, it might have helped Marjie in her own tentative move toward Dan, and she could have used the help.

She glanced at him sitting beside her, at the low, bushy eyebrows and the high forehead, the well-lined face that let you know he was a man who got outdoors now and then, the strong wide shoulders. He was a good-looking man and a nice one, too. And there were times she actually felt she wanted to hold onto him, to make the real commitment he had asked for. But it was hard for her. She needed somebody to talk to. She wished her sister were a little less closemouthed, a little less given to toughing things out these days. For her own reasons.

If Carla's problem was an excess of self-reliance, hers, she guessed, was that she had too little. Too little confidence to tackle a really rough job, too little sense of stability to commit herself to a man and one man only. And now she was bucking the habit of a lifetime, which told her that easy work and non-relationships were the only way to fly. It felt good to be bucking it, but it was not easy. For every step forward with Dan, she seemed to take two back. He had put up with all of it, every bit.

And now she wondered, *Just who the hell am I to be coming down on any of these people?*

She settled back next to Dan and thought and watched the tarmac roll by.

"Anybody else hungry?" Dan asked later.

"Me," said Jim. "It's after two and we haven't stopped since breakfast. God, find someplace!"

"There's fruit in the bag," said Marjie.

"Fruits everywhere," said Laura, turning a page.

" 'Lured to His Death by Homicidal Homo,' huh?" said Nick.

"Right," said Laura.

Dan flicked a cigarette butt out the window. "I need something substantial," he said. "How about stopping before too long?"

"Fine with me," said Nick. He could stand something too, he thought. Especially now that they were in Maine and you could get a good cheap lobster. He hoped nobody would insist on some fast-food joint in order to make time. They'd been riding long enough to take a good long break for lunch. Carla wasn't expecting them at any particular hour, anyway.

"How about a seafood place?" he suggested.

"Great idea," said Dan.

Nick passed one exit and then another until he saw the little knife-and-fork sign along the highway. He turned off at Kennebunk and prayed it would not turn out to be Howard Johnson's. It wasn't. The roadside was lined with seafood places on both sides. He braked and proceeded slowly.

"Take your pick," he said.

"Captain's Table looks okay."

"How about the Golden Anchor?"

"Shit, *anything*," said Dan.

Nick pointed off to the right. "How about that one?" he said. "The Norseman."

"Waiters in skins with horns on their heads," Laura said. "You drink out of gourds and helmets."

Marjie laughed. "Not out here," she said.

"Yeah," said Dan, "back in New York is where you find that shit."

"I forgot," said Laura. "This is the country. This place is fucking *civilized*."

He pulled in and cut the motor.

2:55 P.M.

"How is she?" Peters asked.

He nearly had to shout. As usual, the station was noisy as a kennel. He shifted his weight in the black swivel chair. He stared up at Sam Shearing and scowled. "Close the door," he said.

"Hospital says she's still under sedation," said Shearing. He stepped into the office and blew his nose into a handkerchief.

"Got a cold, Sam?" asked Peters.

"Little one." Shearing shrugged.

"What else do they say?"

"They think she'll come out of it okay," said Shearing. "Suffering mostly from exposure, I guess. And of course those crabs did quite a job on her."

Peters winced. The crabs were the part that disgusted him. Seems they had been at her legs for hours before the lobster boat had sighted her. Tough little woman, she was. Delirious and near unconscious and only half-alive, yet still holding onto those rocks, still mean-minded.

"Any word on the wounds on her face and back?

"Looks like she was running through the woods," said Shearing. "They picked particles of bark out of the wounds. Birch."

Peters grunted. "That must have been a hell of a run," he said. "I figure some of those cuts to be half an inch deep."

"Doctors say deeper than that. Nearly an inch, some of them."

"It don't scan," said Peters. "You don't get hurt like that and keep running long. Not unless you got a bear after you."

"Maybe she did."

"Sure. And maybe she was facing that bear too, staring right at him while she was running backward away from the sonofabitch. That how you explain those wounds on her back?"

"Guess not, George."

"Guess not. I figure somebody was running along right behind her, beatin' at her. Those wounds have the look of a whipping to me."

Shearing sniffled. "Not much we can do until she gets so she can tell us something."

"We should be able to find her car. Must be an empty car parked somewhere along in there. Maybe got some identification in it, too. She's not a local woman, we know that. Get Meyers and Willis on the radio and have them look around some. How long before we get to talk to her?"

"Doctors say she'll be out a few hours yet."

"Okay. Have them call in as soon as she gets her eyes open.

"And Shearing."

"Yeah?"

"Get some damned lunch, will you? State pays you a salary, I assume. Yesterday I counted you had one beer. That ain't enough, boy. You got to take care of that cold. And you look skinny as a cedar post. You want this chair, you got to fatten up to fill it, son."

"Who says I want the damn chair, George?"

"Who says Nixon was crooked? I say. Now get out-ahere."

Peters shifted again and pushed aside some of the clutter on his desk. He tore a leaf off his note pad and began drawing, sketching the marks he'd seen on his Jane Doe's back. He had a good memory and drew them well. That sure was a whipping, all right. Most of the marks were clustered in the area of the lower back. He stood up and went to the wall map.

They'd found her just to the north of Dead River. Not much around there off season. A mile offshore was Catbird Island, where that fishing party—four of them, he recalled—had disappeared summer before last. That had been a strange one. Came from Cooperstown, New York, as he remembered. They shared a summer place in Lubec. They'd rented a small fishing boat from a fellow named Short in Dead River and never came home.

They'd found the boat anchored just off the island's northern landing. No evidence of foul play, no evidence of trouble. So they'd searched the island for days, ten good men, and all they'd come up with was the surprising evidence that somebody had been living out there now and then—there was nothing on Catbird but an old, abandoned lighthouse and a lot of puffins. Probably kids, they'd thought at the time, partying with their girlfriends. But they searched it anyway, just in case. Nothing. They'd had to assume that, despite Short's warnings to the contrary, the men had gone swimming off the boat and, not reckoning with the current out there, drowned.

There was one other incident out that way, but he couldn't recall it right now. He knew it was a few years back. Maybe Shearing would remember. But apart from that, he could think of no other trouble in the area. No trouble at all.

He sighed. By now whoever had done this to her could be well into Canada. He hoped she'd talk soon. If not, may as well not bother talking at all. They'd never catch him.

He thought about those crabs again. One of the most ancient forms of life, the crab was. Right up there with sharks and cockroaches. In all those years, it hadn't needed to learn a thing about the way the world had changed; nothing had crossed its mind but its next meal. A simple, straightforward, brutal form of life. How anybody could make a meal of crab he couldn't figure. The tourists, naturally, thought fresh crab was a pretty big deal. But the tourists were dumb as dirt. Not Peters. He'd grown up in this country.

A crab was nothing but a carrion-eater. A feeder off the dead or—as in this case—the dying. Same thing as a vulture. The thought of those claws on her nearly made him shudder. But he was not the kind of man to shudder. He was more the kind of man to shrug and say life was life; and to suppose that, like anything else, the crab had found its evil little niche.

5:20 P.M.

There were finally in Washington County (the most depressed county in the nation, Carla had told her, even worse than Appalachia—and that looked about right to Marjie). They had turned off Highway 1 onto 89. Now they were to go past a lake, make a left at a blinker light onto Palermo Road, pass a couple of trailers and a big dilapidated barn, and get on the dump road for Dead River. Once they were on the dump road, Carla's road was the first right, and her house the first they would come to. Marjorie was glad there would still be some light when they arrived. She wouldn't relish searching for a turnoff on a dirt road in the dark, with nobody around for miles to ask for directions. As it was, they'd just about make it before dusk, if Nick and Jim didn't take too long getting the beer.

The sign over the front door said HARMON'S GENERAL STORE. The place was small, its white paint weathered badly and peeling. Through the door she could see Nick standing at the counter in front of a rack of Woodsman's Dope and mosquito repellent, talking with a fat, red-faced woman behind the counter in a faded cotton print dress. She supposed Jim was hunting down the beer in the back of the store.

The countryside had changed considerably over the past hour or so. Everything seemed smaller somehow—the houses, the barns, the gas stations—as she supposed was appropriate to a depressed area. Part of the problem, no doubt, was that there were so few people living out here. They'd driven for miles without seeing a soul, or for that matter a house or building of any sort. Of course it was off season. In the summertime it would doubtless fill up some. But were it not for the hills she'd have thought herself somewhere in the Midwest, it was so empty. Rough dirt roads, streams and marshes feeding right off the highway. And not only were the houses smaller, but so were the trees, as if the trade winds off the coast had smothered them, and the earth could give them little in the way of sustenance.

It was pretty, though, in its way. Long, roller-coaster hills that Nick was having a wonderful time driving, an occasional hawk flying overhead, great wide ferns and cedars and scrub pines, and a long beautiful stretch of newly reforested white birch along the roadside. This far north, most of the trees had already turned, and there was a distinct feeling in the air that winter wasn't far away now and might well overtake them during their stay here. It was that close. Already Laura was complaining that the leather jacket was her heaviest item of clothing.

The beer had been Dan's idea. He and Nick were really the only drinkers among them, though Marjie too thought it would be relaxing after the long drive. Dan had not been saying much since lunch, except to moan about how many steamers were lying cramped and sodden in his gut. Well, they had all overeaten.

As far as she was concerned, it had been a terrific meal. The lobsters had been big and sweet and the steamers cooked to just that point where they were perfect; a few seconds later, they'd have become stringy and tough. She'd sat back in her none-too-sturdy cane-back chair when it was over, knowing she'd overdone it, that she was just the slightest bit this side of comfortable. She looked at the table, cluttered with cracked claws, legs broken and sucked dry, broken backs and tails, empty clamshells, and a tablecloth spackled with butter. What you should do after this kind of meal, she thought, was to clear the table fast and get rid of it immediately.

She thought of a drawing by the German painter George Grosz. There was a big, fat, red-cheeked man sitting at a table in his living room, a table laden end to end with fish, chicken, a couple bottles of wine, a soup tureen—scraps of maybe five different dishes. He was gnawing a chicken bone greedily. At his feet was a mongrel dog working on another. The place was a shambles, everything in it given over entirely to the man's gluttony. The chairs were stained with grease, the pictures (of food, she remembered) askew on the cracked walls, the floor in front of him was strewn with garbage. Both man and dog looked avaricious and ugly. There was only one door to the room, and it was open. Through the door peered a leering skeleton—Death, come to fetch its victim.

Their own table had looked a little like that by the time they'd finished. Every so often life reminded you of how grimy and carnal a creature man could be if he set himself to it.

All the same, she'd get herself another fresh Maine lobster first chance she got. She wondered what Carla was planning for dinner. She half considered going into the shop with Jim and Nick to buy half a dozen lobsters to take with them for tomorrow. She decided against it. No, she thought, it was much better to buy them fresh, and Carla might already have something else in mind. Better let it go. The beer was a good idea, though. All this driving was making her weary. The more she considered it, the more she thought she might enjoy a few drinks tonight. She only wished they'd hurry.

The Pincus brothers pulled in at Harmon's and the first thing they noticed was the old black Dodge with the New York plates and the two women inside. They paid no attention to the man in the backseat, who seemed to be dozing. Joey pulled over beside them and the Chevy pickup groaned to a stop. He smiled at his brother and wiped his hands on his flannel shirt. "Look what we got here," he said.

They climbed slowly out of the pickup and shuffled to the passenger side of the car. Both its windows were open. Joey leaned over on the windowsill and grinned wolfishly at the short-haired blonde in the backseat. "Afternoon, ladies," he said. Jim bent low at the waist and peered in at the thin brunette and smiled. She moved away from him a little and nodded.

Marjorie did not like the look of them at all. They were going to hassle her. They were doing it already, just by being there. She didn't like their faces, the smiles that were really nothing more than leers. She didn't like the close-set eyes, the lean, unshaven cheeks, the wind-burned, sunburned high foreheads. Even at a glance you could tell they were brothers. They had the same brutal, inbred faces. Like the houses, like the trees, the people out here looked stunted, almost still-born, as if centuries of social immobility had thinned their seed, bled them dry. She had seen the look in people along the highway, in the face of the fat woman inside the store. To her eyes, used to diversity, there was a troubling uniformity about them all, something that spoke of isolation, and a dull and thoughtless cruelty.

"Please leave us alone," she said. They only smiled at her and did not move.

In the backseat Dan had taken their measure, and now he opened the door opposite them, closed it behind him, and strolled slowly into the store.

Jim Pincus laughed and glanced at his brother. "Whoops," he said. "You girls just lost your boyfriend!" That started Joey giggling.

"Your boyfriend just moved on, girls!" he said. Then they both were laughing and Joey began pound-

77

ing on the trunk of the car. Marjorie rolled up her window. Laura tried to do the same but Joey stopped laughing abruptly and put his hand over the windowsill, holding the window down. "We don't mean no harm," he said, smiling. "We're just friendly."

"Just a couple friendly local boys," said Jim. "Where you ladies from?"

"N-New York," said Laura. Her voice was very quiet.

Joey snapped his fingers. "We guessed that," he said. "Saw your plates. Me and my brother Jim here notice things like that. Like we noticed you was pretty right off. *We smelt it.*" That started them off on another riot of laughter. Joey began pounding on the trunk again with the flat of his hand and that gave Laura the opportunity to close her window. The Pincus boys saw that and didn't like it at all. They moved in closer. Joey slapped the window. "Damn!" he said.

"You fellas got some business here?"

The fat woman in the cotton print dress stood in the doorway, filling it completely, with Jim, Nick, and Dan standing on the porch beside her. Her voice was strangely high-pitched for a woman of her size. But it stopped the Pincus brothers, anyway. She stood there glaring at them in suppressed anger, beefy hands at her hips, and Marjie could see that under the armpits her dress had faded to a bleached white.

"Cigarettes," said Joey mildly.

"Well, come and get 'em," she said, the truce established, "and leave these nice folks alone."

With a glance at the girls inside the car, they did what they were told.

OFF SEASON

"It took you long enough," Marjie said to Dan as she rolled down the window.

He smiled at them and climbed into the car. "Had to pay for the beer," he said.

She swatted him and both girls laughed in relief.

Nick and Jim lugged the two cases of beer down the porch steps. "You guys planning a big party?" asked Marjie, leaning out the window.

"We thought that for a week in the country, this was pretty conservative," said Jim, smiling. Jim, thought Marjie, was too damned gorgeous when he smiled.

"I didn't know you were a drinker," she said.

"Only around your sister," he said.

"Throw us the keys, will you?" said Nick. "I want to get this stuff in the trunk."

Dan reached over to the ignition and tossed the keys through the window to Nick. The two men opened the trunk and piled the beer between the spare tire and their bags. The nice thing about the old Dodge, Nick thought, was the trunk space. Jim put his hand on Nick's shoulder and leaned in close to him. "Look here," he said. "I want to show you something."

He reached into a blue flight bag and took out a wooden box big enough to fill the bag almost entirely.

He opened the box. Inside was something covered by a cloth zippered bag. Even inside the bag Nick could make out the shape of a gun.

"Check this out," said Jim.

"Jesus," said Nick.

"I'm glad those guys didn't give us any real trouble.

I'd hate to have had to use this." He took it out of the box and pulled away the bag.

"Christ," said Nick. "What are you doing with that thing?" It was bigger than any pistol he'd ever seen.

Jim handed it to him. Heavier, too.

".44 Magnum," said Jim. "I bought it here a few years ago, when I was doing stock in Portland. Actually, this is the only state it's legal in. Just a little souvenir."

"Some souvenir."

"I took it to New York with me because, hell, you never know in New York. But I haven't really had a chance to shoot the thing in years. I thought that if Carla's house is as far away from everything as she says it is, we could do some target shooting. Maybe bag a quail or two."

"With a pistol?"

"We could get lucky."

Nick turned it in his hand. "Magnum, huh?"

"That's right. Just like Dirty Harry. Makes a hell of an explosion. Look." He dug around in the bottom of the flight bag and pulled out a box of cartridges and another, smaller plastic box.

"Earplugs," he said. "You shoot this thing without earplugs and you'll be deaf for a week. We can clean 'er up at the house and I'll show you how to shoot her."

"Sounds good to me. Carla know you've got this with you?

"Hell, no. Just you. You think any of these women would go for the idea of me transporting illegal merchandise through five states? Even if it is legal here? I haven't told anybody. I'll break it to 'em later, when it's too late to care."

"You could have told me, you know," said Nick. "My car and all."

"Would you have let me pack it?"

"Probably not."

"Well then." He smiled and shrugged and Nick smiled back. Jim wasn't so bad, he thought. Nick never minded a good joke at his expense, so long as there was no trouble involved. He wondered if Jim felt the same. Because he intended to wait until just before they were ready to leave to break the news to him that the pistol stayed here. It was just as illegal one way as the other. There would probably be some yelling. Those earplugs might come in handy.

They heard Laura shouting for them to hurry it up. Nick closed the trunk and they moved around to the front of the car. "Just checking the spare," said Jim. "Carla says the roads get pretty rough up here. Looks fine to me, though." He glanced at Nick and smiled.

"What kind of beer d'you get?" asked Dan.

"Budweiser," said Nick. "In the bottle."

"Long neck?"

"Sure."

"Good man!" said Dan. "Let's go find Carla. I never tied one on in the country."

5:45 P.M.

Carla had spent her day alone and, for the most part, indoors. She'd gone for a short walk down to the brook around noon, giving into an irresistible impulse to have a picnic by the water. She had carried her sandwich in a brown paper bag, just like a schoolgirl. She climbed over the rocks, moving upstream, looking for just the right spot. Along the muddy banks she noticed the paw prints of some animal—probably a raccoon, she thought—leading to the water's edge, and some large boot prints, too. The boots had corrugated soles. She wondered if they belonged to the man she'd seen the day before.

She found a little glade where the stream widened and the water ran more slowly. It was possible to work her way over the rocks to a single huge stone in the center of the stream. The stone lay in brilliant sunlight, while the rest of the glade was bathed in shadow. She could sit there and eat her sandwich and listen to the water lave the rock and watch the water striders skate the placid surface. The half-hour or so she spent there was serene yet invigorating. The woods around her were a palpable presence, uniting opposites of silence and motion. All the trees and fish and insects and the birds whose calls she could hear on every side, even the water itself, presented to her eyes and ears a brilliant farrago of life and sound and movement, and yet her dominant impression was one of still, sleeplike silence; a silence alive and vibrant with energy.

It soothed her deeply. If she could feel like this all the time, so many things would be so much easier, so much clearer than they were. It was a wonderful place. She would bring them all back here tomorrow. She was sure they'd like it as much as she did.

It was hard to go back to the house. The house was fine and charming in its way, but this was what she had come here for, really; these sounds and this wild peacefulness, the cool and shadow of the forest. She supposed she would have plenty of time for these things once her guests were gone. She wondered already how she would feel about going home again, back to Manhattan. She crumpled up the brown paper bag and let it drop into the water. She watched it float slowly downstream until, a few yards from her, the water became shallower and its flow much more rapid. Soon it was only a tiny brown speck on the glistening surface of the water, and then it was gone. She climbed down off the rock and started off toward the house.

The remainder of the day she spent over her manuscript. It would be good, she thought, to get some pre-liminary work done before anybody arrived, a few notes just to set herself in motion.

She'd left both doors open so she could hear any cars go by. So far there had been only one all day, a gray pickup that rumbled up the dump road and disap-peared. One truck in how many hours? She smiled. God, she really was alone up here. She was glad the rented car was a new one and not apt to conk out on her. She'd hate to have to try hitching that road to get into town—it would be an all day proposition. But at least she'd never miss them when they arrived. In fact she'd know they were approaching five minutes before they could even see the house from the road.

It was getting on toward dusk. The wind was kicking up again outside. Leaves swirled by the window. She hoped they'd arrive soon. An hour ago she'd put a roast in the oven, thinking that it was the sort of thing she could keep warm however late they showed up. Hell of a lot better, though, she thought, if they managed it soon. Especially since she was starving again. She could just smell the roast's rich scent wafting through the room.

She returned the manuscript to its binder and put it away in the bedroom. It was going to be a lot milder tonight than last night. She decided she'd wait out front for a while. The smell of that roast was putting knots in her stomach.

She pulled on a sweater and went to the front door and stepped outside.

Something made her look down before she took a second step—and whatever it was, she was goddamn glad of it. She could not believe her eyes. Oh *Christ*, she thought. How *disgusting!* And she had damn near stepped in it too, had damn near waded right in. She stared down at the stoop, feeling revolted and slightly idiotic, like someone who has been played a very nasty trick on Halloween night.

It looked like there was a very big dog around somewhere. A very well fed dog. A dog who liked to crap on people's porches. Good God.

Then she looked a little more closely. There were two dogs, she thought—or else one very strange one, because one stool was a whole lot darker than the other. How very neat of them, she thought, to have crapped right on top of one another. How very considerate. Wonder if I can find them.

She walked out back and around the house. Nothing. If she found them she was ready to skin them alive. Where had they come from, and where had they gone? They were nowhere in sight. A pair of furtive shitters, she thought.

She went inside and looked for something to clean it up with. There was toweling by the sink left over from the cleaning yesterday. She wadded up a fistful of it, picked up a handful of stool, and dumped it in the garbage can behind the house. She had to make a second trip for the rest. Then she went inside again for a scrub pail and a brush. She filled the pail with water, added some bleach and stirred it in, then returned to the stoop.

She was on her knees, still scrubbing, when the car pulled up. The timing was okay because by then she was over her anger and indignation. It was pretty funny, actually. Jim was the first one out of the car. She stood up and he walked to her and smiled and put his arms around her. She hugged him back, the scrub brush in her hand.

"There's dogshit on the mat," she said. "Welcome to the country."

6:40 P.M.

Peters tapped Shearing on the shoulder and motioned him into his office. He took off his hat and sunglasses and put them on his desk, moved around to the other side and sat down. It felt good to sit down. "Close the door," he said.

Shearing did what he was told and stood there, waiting. Peters made a noise that was something like a groan. The big man looked tired and sour. Shearing knew the look and knew it usually meant a long day ahead. Outside on his desk a report was waiting. Three-car collision on Highway 1. Looking at Peters, he guessed he was going to be late filing.

"Well, we got it," Peters said. "I just talked to our Jane Doe. Mrs. Maureen Weinstein from Newport, Rhode Island, age forty-two if I remember rightly, out here to visit her son and daughter-in-law in St. Andrews. Car should be sitting somewhere between Lubec and Whiting, she doesn't know exactly where."

"Would that be a '78 Chevy Nova, black?"

"Yes, it would."

"Willis just reported one maybe half an hour ago, three miles north of Dead River."

"That's the car, then. Any identification?"

"Just a minute."

Shearing went out the door and back to his desk and shuffled through some papers. He returned to Peters' desk at a brisk trot.

"Checks out," he said. "Automobile is registered to Albert Weinstein, Newport, Rhode Island. Willis found no evidence of theft, though the car had been broken into. Stuff all over the front seat, purse emptied. But there was eighty-five dollars left in the wallet and a bunch of credit cards. Strange stuff, no? I thought this might be our baby when it came in."

"Okay. The problem is we still don't know exactly what we're dealing with here."

"What do you mean?"

"She says it was kids."

"Teenagers?"

"No, *kids*. Little kids, like seven eight nine ten, in there. A couple of 'em teenagers, but mostly younger. *Wild* kids, she says. Dressed in skins, Sam. Sound familiar?"

Shearing's chin dropped abruptly. "George, please, I don't need the aggravation," he said.

"I mean it, Sam. Same thing our clamdigger friend told us about six months ago. The old gentleman with the empty quart of Rock and Rye. Youngsters in furs and skins, roaming 'round the shoreline. Only he said

90

there were a couple older ones, as I recall. Adults maybe. We take a statement on that at all?"

"George, *we threw him in the tank.*"

"I figured. Anyway, our Mrs. Weinstein says there were about a dozen of 'em. Stopped the car for a little girl wandering along half-naked on the highway. They jumped her. Marks across her back made by sticks. Seems they drove her all the way from the highway to the shore, like a heifer. Says they meant to kill her and it sounds as if she was right. She figured her chances were a lot better in the sea."

"She going to make it?"

He frowned. "Minus maybe a leg or two. Doctors haven't decided yet whether the right one has to go."

Peters stood up and went to the wall map and ran his finger down the coastline. "I've been thinking," he said. "You recall that little talk we had maybe a month ago over at the Caribou? 'Bout how the missing persons stats from all along the northernmost coastline here over the past few years were just a bit higher than, say, from Jonesport on down to Bar Harbor? Just a little bit higher than you'd expect them to be? Even though you got a good deal more people to the south, bigger towns and all?"

Shearing nodded. Peters went on. "Now the fact is that most of these folks were small fishermen, lobstermen, and youngsters. And we said, well, the waters are a whole lot rougher up north here and that takes care of the first two groups; and since there's nothing whatsoever to do up here, and since the unemployment rate for kids is so high, that takes care of the third, the teenagers. We got a runaway problem. But suppose we were wrong, Sam? Suppose that's not the case at all?"

Shearing looked skeptical. "*Kids*, George?" he said.

"The drunk saw adults. Now look here. Here's Dead River, and a mile across the water you got Catbird Island, where we lost that fishing party last year. Where did that fella see the kids now?"

"Just south of Cutler."

"That's not three miles away. Suppose we got something going along that coastline."

"Like what?"

"Damned if I know. But I've been racking my brain all day now, trying to remember what the other thing was I associated with Catbird Island and that area. An hour ago I got it. Happened three years ago last July— boy by the name of Frazier. You remember?"

"Sure. Boy took a boat out there in bad weather."

"*Rough* weather, Sam. And according to the father, the boat was sound and the boy—what was he, eighteen, nineteen?—the boy was a top-notch seaman. Should have made it in fine."

"One mistake, George. That's all you need. You know that."

"That's what we said at the time. And of course that could still be the right answer, and I could be howlin' at the moon. But think how many of these missing persons stats over the years are associated with fishing or boating and it makes you wonder. They got boats down Bar Harbor way too, yet our stats are higher.

"And it occurred to me coming back from the hospital that maybe the reason we got so many more missing persons up here than we ought to have, proportional to the population that is, is that the population is so small. Along the coast or even on the island—hell, nobody goes there—folks could hide out pretty easy. And not get noticed for years, if they kept a low profile."

"Like no survivors."

"Something like that, yeah."

Shearing thought about it. Peters was making a certain amount of sense, but to put it together you had to assume a pretty flexible M.O. Of course that was possible, especially if there were a number of people involved as there seemed to be here, especially if you had kids and adults working together. Kids and adults: he wondered what *that* was about.

There were so many small boats embarking from points all along the coastline during tourist season that some could be lost without being missed at all. And there were a lot of travelers hauling back and forth to Canada along the coast road down through Maine— just like Mrs. Weinstein, some of them on very long hauls, too. If they got lost along the way it would be hard to pinpoint where, especially if you ditched the cars somehow. A lot of local kids hotrodding along the highway: they'd be easy to spot and flag down, and we'd call it runaways. And then of course there was the beach where that drunk—what was his name?—had seen them. Beach parties, necking sessions late at night. *Did kids still neck?* Whatever. Yeah, a lot of people could have disappeared that way. It was wild. But maybe.

And he had long ago learned to trust Peters' intuitions. For all George's talk about Shearing wanting his job, it was a lot less Peters' job that he wanted right now than just to work with this tired old fat man and learn from him. If there was any better cop in the state, Shearing hadn't met him. Not that he didn't want the position. He wanted it, all right. But he could wait for that, until Peters was ready.

"So then the problem is where do we look," he said. "I'd go with five square miles, from just beyond Cutler to just below Dead River, working from inland right out to the coast."

Peters nodded.

"Take a lot of men," said Shearing.

"It sure will. Better start callin' 'em in, Sam."

"Will do. We going tonight?"

"Sure. Should be a good clear night. Might as well go while we still got the sky for it. And before we need to fish somebody else out of the water."

"Fine. I'll call the wife."

"Oh, and see if you can get that drunk fella in here. What was his name?"

"Danner. Donner. Something like that. We'll find it."

"Make it fast, Sam."

"Fast is how I keep trim, George," said Shearing.

"You watch your mouth, son," said Peters.

7:30 P.M.

Marjie was in the kitchen, washing the dishes. That was exactly like her, thought Carla. Not two hours in the house and she's appropriated half the domestic chores. She looked at the remains of the roast. Not even enough for a sandwich, she thought. She dumped the scraps into the garbage and picked up a towel.

"Want some help?" she said.

"Sure," said Marjie.

She had a good little sister, she thought. And it was good having her around. She'd always found it hard to understand sisters who were always bitching at each other, who really didn't get along. Her experience was exactly the opposite. Marjie was practically the one person on earth with whom she could count on getting along. They rarely fought, and when they did it never lasted long. And there were never hard feelings afterward. She guessed there was no rivalry between them, that was part of the magic formula. She also guessed she was lucky. She glanced out the window and saw the others smoking and talking on the porch. Let them stay there awhile, she thought.

"Carla, could we talk some time?" said Marjie.

"Sure," she said. "What about?"

"Just . . . things. It's been a long time. At least it feels that way."

"Dan?"

"Among other things, yes." She paused, sliding a bowl out of the soapy water. "Ask me what I've been doing all week," she said.

"What."

"Shopping for a psychiatrist. I've seen three of them."

"And?"

"Well, it's very interesting." She looked puzzled.

"The first one was a woman. She listened to me for a half-hour and then she said she wanted to give me pills."

"What kind of pills?"

"I didn't ask. Mood elevators, antidepressants, that kind of thing. They're very quick with the pills. The second one was a man. *He* wanted to give me pills and check me into a hospital."

"A *hospital!*"

"Said I was very depressed."

"Are you?"

"A lot less than I was three months ago. Three months ago I was too depressed even to think about psychiatrists. Which makes me wonder. Because I *did* get through those three months, after all."

"Idiots!"

Marjie looked up from the dishes and smiled. "Anyhow, the third one looks much better. No pills, no hospitals. We just talked for an hour. He told me, among other things, that he thought I might be competing with you."

"Are you?"

"Probably, yes."

"What in the world for?"

"I have this feeling of futility all the time." Carla laughed. "You don't have it, do you? Nothing seems worth doing."

"Most things are worth doing," said Carla, "if you feel like doing them. Staying alive is worth doing. And you don't stay alive by doing nothing." She laughed. "You have this 'feeling of futility,' Marjie, because you don't *do* anything. That *is* futile. And boring. And in your case, a waste of some very good stuff. I'm not just talking about jobs now."

"Dan says I'm good stuff."

"Take his word for it."

"I usually don't believe him."

"That figures."

"I guess I do compete with you, and I always lose." She sighed. "How in hell did you get so together while I've been such a cipher all these years?" She dumped the last of the dishes into the rack. "What happened?"

"You're not a cipher," said Carla.

"I'm not exactly taking over General Motors, either."

"Would you *want* General Motors?" said Carla.

The back door opened and Nick, Dan, Laura, and Jim walked in. "*Hearts!*" said Nick, rubbing his hands together.

The game was always his idea, thought Carla, probably because he was so good at it. She turned to her sister and said softly, "We'll talk later." Marjie nodded.

They took their places at the table with the others. Carla served coffee and they played cards, though Laura had objected at first, whining a little about how dumb it was to sit around playing a card game their first night in the country. But she was just as tired as the rest of them, much too tired to "hit the local joints" as she'd first suggested. Laura, thought Carla, was all front. She glanced at the blond girl's breasts inside the tee shirt and thought, *In more ways than one,* ho-ho.

Outside, the women watched the card game and comprehended none of it. One of them was pudgy, pale, expressionless, with a strange slack mouth and pointed chin; dressed in what had once been a dress but now appeared to be a plain cotton sack. The other was younger, slim, and might have been attractive were it not for the unhealthy color of her skin, the long ratty hair, and the dullness of her eyes. She wore an old checked shirt that was too tight to close across the breasts, and a pair of baggy khaki pants. Of both these possessions she was quite proud, though if asked she could not have remembered why.

They watched in silence, pale as maggots in the moonlight. They saw one man shuffle the cards and deal them out, saw each of the players fan their cards and slowly begin to toss them away one at a time. All that the women saw they instantly forgot. It was as if they were waiting for something that refused to happen. They waited until they had no more patience for waiting and then as with a single mind they turned and walked away, heading for the stream.

There were crickets in the tall grass and they fell silent too as the women walked by, and there was a moment of deep quiet that surrounded the house and then passed like a hand passing through the flame of a candle. Inside there was the sound of laughter. Outside a slight chill in the air told of winter not far away, when those voices in the grass would all silence at once and leave the dark hours to the night birds and the wind.

7:50 P.M.

The women walked the half-mile to the shore, their path basked in moonlight. It was a path they knew well. For over a year the house had been empty now, and they had come to think of it as practically their own, though they were still careful not to be seen there. Two miles to the north was another house, but a family lived there all year round. They had seen the sharp axe of the man at his woodpile and the three tall strong sons at work on their automobile in the yard. There was a second house about three and a half miles southeast, but a highway ran close by and it was not safe there.

This house, though. This had long been empty. The children played here, conjuring children's magic in the attic in the dark. The younger woman nodded to herself and rubbed a dirty, callused hand across her breasts. Before long they might play here again.

They walked the path until the great dome of sky opened up before them and they saw the sea. A wide stretch of beach lay before them, still and unearthly white against the protean shifting of the waves, the sea itself a wild sluice of light and motion against the placid, withering glance of sky and moon and stars.

As other women knew friends, books, banks, husbands, they knew these—and little else. Sand and sky and sea.

At the point where the path fed into sand dunes they paused a moment, staring blankly out to sea. Out there was the island, where generations unremembered had brought the women into being. And though it was much too far away to see, their eyes found the spot on the horizon where the island would be. They felt no emotion for the place, only a connection; but the connection was strong. They blinked and stared. Small night birds pecked the sand by the shoreline. Behind them forest toads stalked moths and snails. They trudged on, their cave only a few yards away down the beach.

The damp of night had brought out the ghost crabs now. A favored game for the women was to rout them. A quick step to the right or left was enough to scatter crabs for six or seven feet around. The women liked to see their fast, skittish sideward motion. They did not try to catch them, only to scare them.

The crabs had gills and needed to keep them moist, so they burrowed deep into the wet sand during the day and hunted at night or in rainy, overcast weather. At night their pale bodies blended so well with the sand that it was only when they moved that you saw them.

OFF SEASON

Then it was as if the beach itself were alive and shifting underfoot. The women laughed and chased them, dimly imagining that the very beach was afraid of them, darting ever away.

8:05 P.M.

The man was naked when the women returned to the cave. His red shirt, tattered jeans, and heavy boots hung from a rack over the fire. The fire was made of softwoods because of the good thick smoke. He wanted to carry the scent of fire. He did not think that for months now the cave had smelled of urine, fecal matter, dampness, and rotten meat, and that he carried those scents in his very flesh now. He did not notice. He only thought that the woman in the house would have her own fire, and the smell of this one would render him undetectable as he stalked her.

The two women laughed as they entered.

"We shit the steps," said the younger one. She reached down to take his penis in her hand. She knew her prank might anger him. But in the past this had always kept him at bay. The man's penis began to swell immediately. He grinned at her and buried his left hand in her long dirty hair. He pulled her toward him, and the woman began to laugh again.

The middle and third fingers on the man's right hand were missing just above the knuckle. He moved that hand inside the open checked shirt and slid it roughly over her breasts, his thumb and forefinger lingering to pinch the long pointed nipples. Her eyes remained dull but her tongue moved out between her teeth and wagged at him provocatively. The man had waited for that.

He let got of her hair and slapped her. She fell to the ground, whimpering, and spit blood onto the dirt floor of the cave. The older woman took a step away from him. He was dangerous now. For a moment they merely glared at one another. Then both women moved quickly away, back into the cool depths of the cave, and left him alone again.

In the dim light they saw a third woman to the rear of the cave, preparing a kind of sausage for roasting. The woman was pregnant and nearing the end of her term. The swell of her belly seemed to augment her look of lazy, bovine stupidity. Like the others, she was unnaturally pale from scant exposure to the sun. Like them, her hair was long and filthy, and the bearskin she wore was stained and stiff in places with dirt, food, and ashes.

"We shit the steps," repeated the young one. Forgetting the man's anger, they both began to laugh again, and now the strangeness in the older, fat woman's mouth and jaw no longer seemed so unusual—she had no teeth. It gave her an odd, reptilian look. Her toothless gums moved endlessly, like a lizard swallowing a large fly. She knelt down beside the pregnant woman and the neck of her shapeless dress billowed open, revealing long thin pendulous breasts.

"There are others," said the younger woman, leaning back against the damp wall of the cave. "Two woman, three men. We saw through the window."

The pregnant woman nodded. None of this was her concern at the moment. The sausages were nearly ready. She had begun almost an hour ago, slicing the intestine into eighteen-inch strips, turning them inside out and then taking them to the brook for washing. When she returned to the cave she opened up the spine, shoulder, and thighbones to get to the marrow. Then with a sharp knife she minced the choicest flesh of the loin along with some of the liver and brains, two kidneys, and a few pounds of hindquarters cut close to the bone. She went to the fire and melted the bone marrow and some kidney fat, and then added the meats.

Now she was stuffing the mixture into the intestines and tying off the ends. When the man was finished with his softwood fire, she would wait for the smoke to die down and add some hardwood and then roast them for their dinner.

Tomorrow she would jerk the remainder of the kill. From the loins they would put aside steaks for supper and then slice the flesh of hams and shoulders. They would lay the slices in a pile and cut them through to strips two or three inches wide by four to six inches long. Then they would soak the strips in seawater and dry them in greenwood racks over the fire to keep the flies away. In a few days the meat would be black and dry. It would keep almost indefinitely.

Over her head the cage rattled. She paid no attention. The other two women laughed and pointed. The cage was made of metal grating and hung suspended from a heavy rope that passed through a ring secured to the roof of the cave, twenty feet above them. The rope fed down the wall and fastened to a large cleat. All this material they had found in the dumps a few miles away. There was a boy inside the cage now, perhaps fifteen years of age. He was naked and lay sprawled along its floor, long since motionless with fear. Now and then a tremor would pass through his body like an evil wind and rattle the grating. That was good. It would tenderize the boy's flesh to allow him to fear. The female had died much too quickly. And she had had some difficulty with the hindquarters as a consequence.

She watched the man remove his clothes from the rack. *Now,* she thought. Ignoring the other woman, she gathered up the food and went to the fire. "They say there are more now," she told the man.

"How many?"

"Three men. Two more women."

He looked at the boy lying in the cage, lying in his own vomit, and smiled. Soon they would fill the cage, pack it tight. The boy would have to stand. Or die. They were great warriors. Life was better now.

The man had little memory and no sense of time at all, but he could remember their cold, spare life on the island—before the men with guns had come to search for those they had taken from the boat. He did not understand guns except to know that they brought a quick death and that they terrified him. Before the men with guns, they had lived off the sea for the most part, as the old ones had taught them to do in the lean days, off crabs and clams and algae, off baited night lines and a rude gigging.

He liked gigging even now. You would dangle a long smooth hook into the water, above which you had suspended bits of bone to shine and flutter in the sun, and these would attract the fish. Then when one was near enough you gave the line a fast jerk and impaled the fish and dragged it ashore. You had to be fast and sure. Or else you could sharpen a small bone at both ends and hide it inside your bait, and when the fish swallowed the bait he also took the bone. A tug on the line and the deadly bone slipped sideways inside him. The fish died for a long time.

He smiled at the thought.

But those were meager days. He remembered the skeletal faces of the old ones—now gone—the old man and the old woman who had called him by a name. He could not recall the name. He remembered that the old woman was Ag-Ness, and that the old man had once gone nightly to light the great Light. But they both had died before it occurred to him to ask what either name or activity had signified.

He watched the woman pile hardwood on the fire and slipped the red shirt over his shoulders. The smell was good now. He liked the smell of burning.

When the men had come with guns, they had had to hide. For many days they had fasted. They had nearly starved. The men returned each day for many days, and the island was no longer safe, and finally they had fled.

At first life on the mainland was even harder. He remembered that they had lived on grubs, moths, frogs, and grasshoppers for a while. Grasshoppers were not bad after you removed the hard parts, the wings and legs. In the summertime there had been lizards and snakes and ant eggs. They found a beaver dam, and for a time they had lived on the flesh of beaver with its birdlike taste and lit their stolen lamps at night with the oil from its tail. They lived in lean-tos and slept on browse beds of pine and fir, and kept moving. Then they found the cave.

The cave was thirty feet down a seawall more than fifty feet high, approachable only via a small goat path from the shore. He had discovered it one day while searching gulls' nests for eggs. From almost any angle its entrance—the entire right side of a cleft in the rock—was obscured by overhanging rocks. It was also sheltered from the winds. A natural chimney existed in a second, smaller hole in the rock above and a few feet beyond the entrance—though they used a fire infrequently, for fear that the smoke would give them away. Best of all, the cave was huge and relatively dry even in storms. It opened up to a space about twenty-five by twenty feet; and then to a second, adjoining space off the rear, nearly half again that size. In some places it was twenty-five feet from floor to ceiling.

They slept on skins or the browse beds, huddled by the fire in very cold weather, or in the second room when the temperature was milder. The second room they used mostly for storage. They had found the town dump early on, and now the cave was a mad clutter of random forage—a small plow with a broken handle, hoes, rakes, and pitchforks with splayed or broken tines. In one corner a mound of scrap reached halfway up the wall—an old harness, shovels, pokers, buckets filled with nails and keys, irons, doorknobs, window fittings, locks, pots and pans, pieces of broken china, a doll, a gunstock, rimless wheels, tire irons, whips, buckles, belts, knives, axes. They used almost none of it and kept nearly everything.

Beyond that was another pile, all of it items of clothing they had stripped from the bodies of the dead. It, too, climbed halfway up the wall. They would select an item from the pile, wear it until it was useless, and then select another. In the meantime the clothing at the bottom of the pile grew slimy with mold, providing homes for the horde of beetles, roaches, and flies that grew fat and bold in the cave's ripe stew of refuse.

Beside this was a pile of bones, picked clean and yellowing in the damp, stale, fetid air.

And finally a pile of skins and tools for scraping and tanning. The skins varied greatly in shape and size. But many of them were long and thin and pale yellow in color.

The man considered all this with great satisfaction. He pulled on the tattered jeans and remembered what the woman had said. Now there were three and three of them. His people would fill the cage and make up for the losses of two nights before. He scowled at the thought of what the children had done. Never had the children been allowed to kill unsupervised and alone. It was wrong of them to try.

They had been punished, though, for their stupidity, and tonight they would obey. One by one they had been beaten, eldest to youngest, while the others watched, enjoying their brothers' and sisters' agonies but terrified of their own to come. Until all were bloodied.

As he put on the boots he had taken from the fat, red-faced fisherman long ago, his brothers emerged from the inner cave, four of the children following at their heels. He grunted at them in greeting and then finished strapping the boots around his ankles. He had a secret from them now. He enjoyed waiting to tell them.

The first man was huge, over six feet tall. He was completely bald, with no eyebrows below the high-domed forehead and not the slightest trace of hair on his face or naked chest. His shoulders were round, massive, with muscles that seemed to jump at the barest movement. In his neck the tendons articulated themselves like heavy fingers. His eyes were a strange light blue.

The man had selected his weapons from the inner room, and now he strapped a thick leather belt, green with mold, around his waist, and slipped one long hunting knife into either side. He patted his belly. Ready.

The man behind him was much smaller, thin and wiry, with sunken cheeks and a sparse beard. His chin was weak and his lips thick and flabby, and his mouth hung perpetually open. Like the man beside the fire, his hair was long, a bit thinner than his brother's but just as wild and oily. His own eyes were dim now. The small pig eyes could only blaze when something bled or died.

Beneath the faded gray pants he carried a razor-sharp fold-out knife, strapped next to his penis. He liked the way it felt there. Around his neck, dangling beneath the soiled blue sweatshirt, was a thin silver crucifix. The man did not know what it was; only that it set him apart from the other men, who wore nothing they did not need to wear.

He, too, had selected a pair of knives from the pile. Now he moved eagerly to the first man by the fire and handed one of the knives to him, grinning so that his face seemed to furrow and crack, revealing soft, bad teeth green with slime. Behind him the children shifted excitedly, their minds stirring with vague memories of hiding in bushes by the deserted roadside, watching these men trap and kill.

The man in red finished with his boots. "There are three men now," he said to the others, "and three women." At the sound of his voice echoing in the still air of the cave the women gathered around him. His brothers whooped with surprise and laughter.

The man nodded. He turned to the women.

"Call the children," he said. "First we eat."

The big man smiled. He pulled one of the half-cooked sausages from the fire and plunged it, steaming, into his mouth. It popped between his teeth and fat streamed down his chin onto his naked chest.

The fat woman in the dress that was nothing but a sack pushed aside the deerskin at the entrance to the cave and walked outside. The night blew softly across her scarred and sallow face. At her feet she saw a small pile of tiny bones and feathers, shaped into a pyramid.

The children.

She kicked it aside. She put her hands to her mouth and inside the cave they heard her calling. To any ears but their own it would have been the voice of a seagull, strident in the wind.

A few moments later seven children filed up the mountainside, the smaller ones crawling like foxes on all fours. Like her mother, the eldest girl among them was pregnant by one of the men or the older boys, she did not know which. She was slower than the rest and, panting, brought up the rear.

It was dark now and the moon was high and brilliant. They smelled the food inside the cave, and their bellies began to churn in hunger. There would be a feast tonight. It was a season of plenty, they had heard the elders say, and their bellies would be full to bursting for weeks to come. They scrambled greedily over the rocks, with no mind for their scrapes or bruises. They climbed toward the scent of flesh thick on the night air. Toward the kill.

11:30 P.M.

For the first time in ages Nick was jealous again. The feeling was like an old friend he hardly recognized and in whose presence he was bored and uncomfortable. Bored with himself, uncomfortable with Laura. It had always focused on Carla, his jealousy. He'd never felt it before her, and never since. But now she was in the living room getting ready to go to bed, and he felt it flare again. He could hear them arranging the pullout couch, talking and laughing. He could hear the clatter of Jim's belt buckle on the floor. There were similar sounds coming from Dan and Marjie's room, but he paid those no attention. He was not aware of them at all. His attention was where it wanted to be and all of it was focused on the living room. He removed his glasses and put them on the night table beside him.

He lay in bed watching Laura strip off her clothes and place them carefully on a chair. He felt a faint warming in his loins as her breasts fell away from the bra that disappeared as she folded and placed it neatly

115

atop the pile on the chair. There was too much dispar-
ity between Laura's style and her real inclinations.
Like she was always hiding. It bothered him.

She slipped into bed beside him and smiled. He returned the smile, listening to Carla's voice on the other
side of the wall. You gotta stop this, he thought. This is
bullshit. But he continued listening. Laura would want to
make love. He knew better than to even try while he lay
there listening to Carla. Down that road lay Limp City.

He wondered why he'd agreed to come up here in the
first place. Hadn't he anticipated something like this?
He had not. But *why not?* He damn well ought to have. I
thought we'd talked all that away, he thought, long ago.
He couldn't even remember the guy's name she'd been
seeing at the time. He only remembered the feeling.

Laura rolled over and kissed him. "I got ten dollars
says you can't go fifteen minutes after driving all day,"
she said.

He kissed her back without passion. "Let me go piss
first," he said.

He disengaged himself from her and padded over to
his bathrobe, slipped it on, and walked through the
kitchen to the bathroom. He saw a light burning behind
Dan and Marjie's door.

He purposely did not glance in the other direction,
toward the living room. He stood in front of the toilet
and flipped open his bathrobe and aimed into the bowl.

For a moment he heard something move outside
near the woodshed, a light scraping sound. Carla had
told them about the mouse in the kitchen. But it

sounded as if she had something bigger than field mice out there. Raccoons, maybe.

He heard Marjie laughing through the wall. *Marjie*. It had really been Marjie who had continued to cement their relationship together. In some ways his feelings for her were firmer and more durable, he guessed, than for her sister.

There had never been anything sexual between them for the simple reason that she and Carla were very close, and it would have been unthinkable for Marjie to make it with Carla's man. Unthinkable for Carla and Marjie, that is. He had thought about it. Marjie was very attractive. He had thought about it particularly after the breakup with Carla. But by then the basis of their relationship had already been established. He and Marjie enjoyed many of the same things and people. They went to bars together now and then, and when they'd loosened up sufficiently each went his own way, cruising. They went to horror films together—nobody else would accompany them—and she would clutch his arm during the nasty stuff.

But nothing romantic. Perhaps he suspected that some of Marjie's eccentricities—her fear of the dark, of closed-in spaces, of fast cars, and even of cheap food, her tendency to grow moody and distant for no observable reason at all—would irritate him in a lover while they only amused him in a friend. Maybe that was why he'd never made a move on her. Perhaps it was that they both knew a good thing when they saw it. Neither had many friends of the opposite sex who were not either former or potential lovers, and minus any real sexual tension, their pleasure in each other's company was special and unique. And then of course there was always the shadow of Carla.

How was Carla. What was Carla doing. It had been slow ending. And that, like most of the rest, was his fault.

Their love had broken down into a war of nerves. Carla was on the ascendant in life, with a good new job at good money. Nick, on the other hand, was faltering. He had quit a perfectly okay job in order to write and he wasn't writing. Now, a year or so later, he was making more money writing than he'd been making nine to five, but in his last days with Carla his ego needed constant attention—or rather, his cock did.

It was strange how, when there was nothing else in your life, sex was everything. Suddenly he wanted Carla twenty-four hours a day, and she of course was too busy. Probably she knew exactly what the problem was, that he was using sexual potency to compensate for another kind of impotence, and probably he was pretty repulsive. And in the long run she was dead right. They each were more vital apart. Five days after their breakup he'd started writing.

He shook it into the basin. He turned off the bathroom light and walked into the kitchen. Marjie's light was still on and—now he couldn't avoid seeing it—so was the light from the living room. Between the two rooms was his own. And Laura.

He frowned. There were too many contradictions

about Laura. Nothing matched up. She liked to act tough but in some ways she was more timorous than Marjie. She couldn't bear to take the cat to the vet. Wouldn't touch drugs or booze at a party. He knew she was in love with him but she never showed it. Not unless he pulled away from her for some reason, trying not to get involved too deeply. Then she'd break down altogether. It was a lousy situation. But because there was nothing better in his life he hadn't broken up with her. He should have. He was cheating her. Cheating her right now, thinking of Carla.

What it all came down to was that tonight, like a lot of nights, he would say he was exhausted so he wouldn't have to make love to her, so he wouldn't feel like a complete bastard screwing Laura and wishing it were Carla. It surprised him that the past was so much with him. He hadn't known. He just hadn't known it would be this way, not until the past started whispering through the wall, calling him back and telling him to stay away.

He walked through the bedroom doorway and looked at Laura and then breathed a deep sigh of relief. It was all right, he thought. She was asleep.

In the next room, Marjie got up and closed the window. For a moment she stared out into the dark.

"I'm *cold*," she said."

"You've got two blankets," said Dan.

"It's not enough." She jumped back into bed.

"What about the good clean country air?" He sat down beside her and pulled off his shoes and socks.

"The good clean country air is freezing," she said.

"Come over here and twirl on my cock," he said. "That'll warm you."

She liked it when Dan was vulgar. He was usually vulgar. He was naked when he got into bed and already hard. His body was lean and smooth-skinned and she liked that, too.

"Get rid of the nightgown," he said.

"I'm cold."

"I know you're cold. Take off the nightgown."

"I want to leave it on."

"Will you get naked, please?" He climbed on top of her.

"No!"

He dove underneath the sheets, under her nightgown. She laughed. He bit her stomach. "What I have to go through for a mediocre piece of ass," he said, his voice muffled against her belly.

"Screw you," she said. Before Dan she would never have said "Screw you" to a man. He was bringing her out, she guessed. Dan was fun. He pressed his lips against her belly and blew out hard. What sounded like a huge fart vibrated against her flesh and made her giggle. "*Shhhh*. Shut up," she said.

"You're the one laughing. Am I laughing? No, I'm trying to get laid." He rose up out of the covers and began to unbutton her nightgown. As usual his fingers were clumsy.

"No, wait," she said. "Wait! I want you to do just one thing for me. One thing!"

"Jesus. What."

"I want you to do one thing before we go to bed."

"We *are* in bed."

"You know what I mean."

"What."

"You know."

"You mean before we fuck."

"Right."

"Okay, what."

"Could you just put a few logs on the fire first? Otherwise I'm really gonna *freeze* in here. *Please?*" She gave him the little-girl routine—three quarters plea and one quarter pout. It had always worked before. It worked now.

"Yeah, I guess I could do that. Where is she keeping the firewood?"

"Right in front of the stove, I think," she said. And then coy, fully knowing she was coy, as coy as she could get, she said, "Thank you, Dan."

" 'Thank you, Dan' " he mimicked. "You really are one real cheap trick, you know that?"

She swatted him. Without bothering to put on a robe, Dan walked to the bedroom door and peered around at the darkened kitchen. Nick's door was dosed, and the lights were off in the living room. It seemed safe to step outside. In the dim light from the bedroom he tiptoed to the stove and opened the grate. There was not much left inside. There were plenty of embers, but only half a log, smoldering. Marjie was right. By morning they'd be pretty cold in there.

He reached down and took a split cedar log off the floor and stuffed it into the fire. The house was completely silent. Almost eerie, he thought. He fed another log into the stove and winced when it slid noisily against the grate. Better get this over with fast, he thought, before you wake up the joint. As carefully as he could, he separated the largest piece of wood from the rest of the pile and slowly eased it inside.

Only now he had them lying next to one another. He knew they wouldn't burn that way. *Shit shit shit,* he thought. He looked around for the poker. He found it lying propped up against the wall next to the cupboard. Again being as quiet as possible, he used the poker to angle the second log over the first and the third on top of that. Then he lay the poker down and took a deep breath and looked inside to see if they would catch.

In the silent house it sounded to him as if he'd been moving the entire kitchen around. But what could you do. The country sure was quiet. If he stayed out here very long he was sure it would get to him. The bark caught fire. That meant the logs would take. Back to Miss Marjie. He closed the grate and fastened the catch. And in that moment he heard something move swiftly across the floor.

A rush of blood pumped through his veins. With electric suddenness he knew that someone was standing directly behind him. Adrenaline pumped heat throughout his body and his skin went suddenly damp and cold. He whirled around.

"Nice ass," said Carla, smiling. She moved to the refrigerator. "Want a drink?"

"No thanks," he said. His heart was pounding. She opened the door and the light inside the refrigerator made the thin nightgown go nearly transparent. Dan watched her admiringly. Her breasts were fuller than her sister's and her hips a bit wider than Marjie's. She looked terrific standing there. "You're not so bad yourself," he said.

She poured herself some apple juice and looked down at the nightgown. "Thanks," she said, and closed the door.

He felt kind of awkward in front of her. "I'd better be getting back inside," he said. "Just wanted to throw a little more wood on the fire. God, you gave me a scare! G'night."

"'Night," she said.

He shut the door-behind him. "Your sister has good tits," he said to Marjie.

She pulled down the bedclothes and he saw that she had finally ditched the nightgown. "Better than these?" she asked.

"Different," he said.

And then he jumped her.

Carla watched the light go off behind their door. Dan was a good-looking guy, she thought. She really hadn't been kidding at all about his ass. It pleased her that Marjie had good taste—at least physically—in men. She wondered if he'd ever amount to anything. You sound like your mother, she thought.

Their mother wouldn't have approved, exactly, of any man in the house. Writer, actor—what was Dan, a housepainter? She thought that was it. Every one of them was probably financial bad news. She thought

Jim would make it if any of them did. Trouble was, she didn't want to be around when he did. If he was already pretty egomaniacal (and he was, she decided) what was he going to be like once he was rich and famous?

But he was a hardworking boy, Jim was.

Even in bed Jim liked to do a little acting. A little light-handed Master and Slave. That was all right with her. So did she. It made a certain sense to her. In every other aspect of her life she'd become pretty forceful over the years. She took no nonsense. Not from anybody. It was not a bad game to try on the other skirt once in a while, so to speak.

Funny how people reversed roles in sex. Unless he was making love, Jim was always a bit too amiable, a bit too showy about his smile and good looks, a bit too willing to please. Carla genuinely liked him—in small enough doses—but a lot of people found him sort of irritating. Like butter wouldn't melt in his mouth, that sort of irritating.

But sexually Jim came on aggressive and even slightly cruel. She didn't think it was particularly healthy, but what the hell—it excited her. Rape fantasy, naturally. For her, next to masturbation it was the best way to fly. Suddenly she felt in a bit of a hurry to get back to bed.

She poured herself a second glass of apple juice. Let him wait, she thought. Let us both wait and work up an appetite. She thought about him lying on the pullout bed, naked on top of the covers, getting just a little bit angry over the delay. His flesh would be smooth and soft when she touched it, especially over his neck and shoulders and his small, boyish ass.

This is ridiculous! she thought. What am I standing here for? She closed the refrigerator door and paused a moment while her eyes grew accustomed to the dark. There was only a slight flickering now from the fire in the living room. It had nearly burned away.

Once again there was a moment to enjoy that incredible darkness of country nights; nights so dark they seemed to fill her with a sort of vertigo. Even with the moon out, the inside of the house was dark, with a darkness that thickened until every corner, every geometric slope of wall and furniture melted into a single sheet of opaque shadow. A Stygian darkness, she thought. She'd always liked that phrase. The darkness of dreams.

She moved toward the light. Outside she heard gulls calling. In the doorway to the living room she could see again. He was on the bed just as she had pictured him, naked and watching her. Was he smiling? She couldn't tell. It was just like Jim not to smile now.

She saw his head turn to follow her as she stooped before the fireplace and put their last piece of wood on the grate. The fire leaped to taste the dry bark and warmed her.

She turned to face him where he lay framed against the window, pale in the moonlight. She slipped the nightgown slowly off her shoulders and let it drop. She stood a moment posed against the fireplace, knowing he would like that and knowing how good she'd look, her body burnished by the same light. She felt the heat of her own narcissism flush her skin. And then another heat—his.

She moved to the bed. They said nothing. She reached for his cock and held it in her hand, warming it and feeling it throb and engorge with blood. Then she released him and climbed on top of him, beginning to ease him inside her.

"No," he said.

He lifted her up and withdrew his penis and lay there propped on one elbow. They stared at each other for a moment. Then he pushed her roughly onto her back and smiled. His hands went to her wrists, pinning them against the bed. She saw how serious his face was and she began to laugh. It was not always the same each time between them, but close enough.

The game had begun.

PART III

SEPT. 14, 1981

12:02 A.M.

Except for the room in which the man and woman had their fire, the house was dark. They knew how the moon would illuminate them should anyone glance out the window. So they kept close to the house where they could not be seen. They moved silently from front to back until they had located all the people inside. They saw two asleep in one room—Dan and Marjie—and a man, Nick, still awake in the bedroom next door. In the room with the fire the man and woman were fucking. With the fire burning, these two would be blind to them, and for them there was plenty of light. They watched. It was good to watch.

They saw the man take her nipples between thumb and forefinger and twist them, and then lift his fingers away and use only his thumbs to press the nipples back into her flesh. The man was cruel to her. Through the glass they heard her moan and saw her move over him to straddle him, putting him inside her and thrusting against him while he raised himself up, his arms around her, and bit down on the flesh of her arms, her neck, and her breasts.

Now they watched him come out of her, glistening, and roll her over on her back, spreading her legs wide and kneading the flesh of her inner thighs with his hands, and they saw her arch her back as he put first one finger inside her, and then another, and another, until she was open to all four fingers moving back and forth inside her, her hands clutching the headboard, her mouth open wide. The man's hands moved up to pin her arms above her head as he thrust himself inside her again, their bodies gleaming with sweat as they struggled in the firelight.

His mouth slack in a twisted grin, the thin man with the crucifix took his cock out as he watched them and began to masturbate against the house. Within moments he came. Beside him the man in the red shirt smiled as he saw the sperm slide down the white housepaint and fall to the ground.

And then they were ready.

Inside, Carla knew only that familiar high mix of pain and pleasure. She had come the first time with his fingers inside her, his thumb working her clitoris. And now she was almost ready again, vibratory and anticipating his every move, and the window and the cool night were far removed from her tiny world of mute sensation.

The same was true of Jim. He'd held back as long as he could or cared to. Now he began to give way within the fine warm flesh. He felt himself leap inside her.

This was what he'd driven all that way to get from her, this and nothing else, and it was worth it to him.

Their bodies tightened almost simultaneously. Carla began to shudder, her legs thrashing in waves of fever. He lowered his head to take her nipple between his teeth. He bit down. At once Carla came again, and this time he followed her immediately. His eyes squeezed shut.

The room exploded. Shattered.

Suddenly there was glass everywhere. Carla felt it spray across her breasts and stomach, splinters striking her face and falling in her hair. At the same instant Jim's mouth went slack against her. She saw a pair of arms flash out in front of her and saw something glint in the firelight. Then two more arms appeared and a broad pair of hands closed over her wrists. She screamed.

She saw Jim's head loll away from her breasts. The hands jerked her out from under him. She saw the deep red gash across the back of his neck just below the hairline and the fierce gout of blood pouring over her belly. She felt the windowpane rake across her back-bone and the next instant she was out the window and gone, his blood cold in the night air, and she was screaming again and trying to stand on legs she could barely feel in the long damp grass, staring up at the two men in the dark. She saw one of them draw back his arm and ball up his fist and she knew it could break her neck if he wanted it to. She closed her eyes and felt something strike her and then felt nothing at all.

* * *

Nick was the first one out of his room. He had not slept. He'd heard them making love. He'd heard everything. Then there was the sound of glass breaking and he thought, *What the hell?* and leaped from his bed and flung open the door. Then he hesitated, his mind reeling at the impossibility of what he saw. He watched Jim's body twitching on the bed and saw her legs slide out the window, bathed in blood. For a moment he could not understand it, any of it. It was as if he had stepped into the company of strangers, in a strange room he had never seen before, and the comedy they performed for him was awful and grotesque and impossible to comprehend.

But then he was shouting her name and racing toward the window, and he reached it in time to see the man hit her and her head roll away as she fell. He was half out the window after her when the thin, slimy thing that might have been a man whirled on him with a knife and slashed him.

He fell back against the shuddering corpse on the bed and felt his own hot blood slide down his face. He felt blank, dizzy, empty. Then suddenly Marjie was screaming beside him, and he heard Laura in her room awake and calling out to them. "What is it? What's going on? *What's out there?*" And he knew he had never heard raw panic until he heard it then.

Dan was at the front door, the poker in his hand.

He opened the door. A blast of cool air swirled through the house from the door to the open window, and he felt it like a cold hand on his naked body. Then the door was open wide and he saw something huge and snarling there in front of him; a man, stripped to the waist, his arms raised high over his head, and something glinting in each hand. Involuntarily he threw himself back. He slammed the door, locked it. He ran to the side of the house.

He peered out the kitchen window. He saw three smaller figures standing on the porch. He felt a surge of terror. *They've got us,* he thought, *we're trapped, we're dead. Oh shit!* Then almost at once he thought, *maybe not, maybe not yet.* He locked the door and fastened the latch on the window. He went to the phone. Dead, of course. He ran back toward the living room.

He saw Laura huddled in her room against the headboard of the bed, still clutching her blankets. "Come on," he shouted, "get out of there!" He went to her window and looked outside. Could they possibly be what they appeared to be? He counted them. Six. Six children. He was not crazy. They were children, all right. He could handle six children with the poker, God help him, but how many more were there? How many adults? He threw the lock on the window. Laura watched him but she refused to move when he took her arm. She knows, he thought. She smells the blood out there.

He went to the living room. Nick was on the floor, his back to the foldout bed, one side of his face horribly pale and the other covered with blood. Behind him the corpse lay quiet. Marjie stood immobile by the stairway to the attic, her hands to her mouth, her face a grimace of pain, staring horrified out the open window.

What he saw in her face made him shudder. What was she staring at? Carefully he moved in front of her, into her line of vision. The curtains fluttered in the breeze.

They had turned on the headlights in Carla's Pinto. He saw them thirty yards away, standing under a tree.

A thin man in a checked shirt and faded gray pants, and another, heavier man in red, holding Carla in his arms. She still seemed unconscious. The big man he'd seen at the door was not among them. But he saw more children there, five of them. With the six by the side of the house that made eleven. Three more smaller figures on the porch and a monster at the door. That made six adults and seventeen people altogether, and that was no odds at all.

For a moment he stood there stunned, the poker gripped tight in his hand, breathing heavily; looking around in every direction for he knew not what—for some egress to safety (he could imagine none), for some defensible position or, failing that, some idea to occur to him that would fill the void he could feel growing and spreading through his mind and urging him toward forgetfulness, emptiness, *shock*. He shook his head, forced his eyes to focus. Come on, he thought, come on. *Think*.

They would have to fortify the house immediately, barricade the doors, and find themselves some sort of defense. He could not even consider going out after Carla. That would only get them killed. There might even be more of them somewhere. His mind was working now. He looked at Jim's body on the bed. The bed was slick with blood. There was an awful lot of blood in a man. He felt a familiar churning in his stomach. He had not seen that kind of bleeding since 'Nam. I'd better get busy, he thought. He backed away silently from the window. He knelt down to Nick on the floor.

"How bad?" he said.

"Not bad," said Nick without conviction. But Dan saw the film over his eyes begin to clear and thought that maybe he was all right, after all. As gently as possible he moved Nick's hand away from the wound. He'd been lucky. The knife had caught him just under the left eye and cut him all the way to the chin. Half an inch more and he'd have lost the eye. The wound was relatively shallow except where the knife had met with the most resistance across the cheekbone and chin. The bleeding had nearly stopped. Now if he could just get the guy moving. That open window scared hell out of him.

"Nick," he said, "do you know where the tools are?"

"Where's Carla?" The voice was thick and groggy.

"Outside, Nick," he said. "Carla's outside. They've got her. We've got to fight them. Where are the tools?"

He raised his hand slowly and pointed. "I think under the sink."

"Can you stand?"

"I . . . I think so."

"Try." He turned to Marjie. "Give me a hand with him," he said. She didn't move. He said it louder. Great, he thought, they're all out on me. Marjie still stared out the window. He saw the streaks the tears had made across her cheeks. But she was finished crying now. There was something else in her eyes at once hard and terribly soft and melting. He had never seen a woman look like that. Only guys, he thought, and then only in war.

"Look," she said quietly. "Look what they are doing to her."

He went to the window. The earth, cooling, sent faint clouds of steam swirling through the headlamps of the car. He saw them clearly. They had thrown a rope over the limb of a tree. Carla's feet were tied to one end of the rope and the bigger man was hoisting her into the air. It was good she was still out, he thought. The children swarmed around her. He saw one of them spit down into her face as her legs began to rise, and another one swing a stick at her buttocks until the thin man drove him away. Marjie should not be watching this, he thought. Christ, none of us should.

"Come here," he said. It was an order.

Her voice was unnaturally quiet, on the edge of hysteria. "No," she said. "That's my *sister*."

Nick was on his feet beside them. "My glasses," he said. "I . . . I can't see. What are they doing?" Outside, the big man pulled the rope while the other wrapped the slack around the trunk of the tree.

"Get them," Dan said to him. "And you better get Laura, too."

He turned to Marjie. "Stay here," he said, "and don't move. I'll be right back. If anything comes *near* that window you call me. And you *run*, dammit!"

Nick moved into the bedroom. Dan heard him talking to Laura, and when he passed them on his way to

136

the sink he saw Nick bending over her, trying to lift her off the bed.

Nick had been right, thank God. The tools were there under the sink. Two hammers and some ten-penny nails. He took them with him into his bedroom, put them on the bed, slipped on a pair of jeans, and slid the hammers into his belt.

He walked back into the kitchen and emptied the box of nails onto the table. He glanced back into the living room. Marjie remained where he'd left her. He went to the drawer and took out the best and sharpest knife he could find and put that into his belt, too. It was eight inches of blade, a good solid pound of stainless steel.

They'd have to get out of here eventually. But first it was necessary to secure the house. If they could keep them outside long enough to create some kind of diversion toward the back, then maybe they could slip out the front door to one of the cars and drive away. If they could do it soon enough, they might even be able to help Carla. But the part of him that needed to be ruthlessly honest doubted that. He glanced again at Marjie, still staring. He had to put a stop to that. At this rate she would be useless to him, and he needed her. He needed everybody.

He went to her. "I want you to stop it," he said. "Get away from there. Please, Marjorie."

"You go to hell," she said.

Outside, Carla's hands were three feet off the ground now. Marjie saw her sister's body slowly turning, her long hair like a flame below her; and then, horribly, she saw her awaken. She stared hard, as if willing her to safety. She saw her sister's arms flailing uselessly and imagined she heard her whimpering and heard their laughter.

She watched the thin one stoop slightly and take a handful of Carla's hair and pull her slowly backward, walking backward himself and pulling her hair until she screamed in pain and he could pull her back no farther. He released her so that she swung toward them in the house, and Marjie imagined the rope cutting cruelly into her ankles. Then, on the backswing, she saw him grab Carla again, around the neck this time, and jerk her to a stop. A second scream died in her throat.

In her heart Marjie slaughtered the man.

Dan was watching too, and now he felt half frozen and knew he had begun to tremble. It was no damn good, this watching. And that window was still wide open. He shook himself free. He put his hands on Marjie's shoulders. She whirled on him.

"Let go!" she screamed. She pushed him away and lunged toward the window. "You bastards!" she screamed at them. "You stinking evil *bastards!*" All at once she terrified him. She was on the bed, leaning nearly out the window.

His hands went to her shoulders and he pulled her roughly inside. He spun her around. She was still screaming. The palm of his hand whipped twice across her face. She collapsed, sobbing.

"I'm sorry," he whispered.

And in the silence that followed he heard someone laughing, just outside the front door. The big man.

So he hasn't gone away, he thought. And had he taken just a few steps toward her he could have pulled Marjie out the window just like they'd done to her sister, and she'd be up there among them right now. My God, he thought, that close.

Something churned violently inside him, galvanizing him into action. He felt himself fill with an icy calm. He turned to her.

"You can't help her," he said. "Nobody can. But you can help us. And if you don't they'll kill you, too."

She stared up at him and heard the flat, hard sound of his voice, and then she nodded.

"We'll do what we can," he said.

Nick and Laura emerged from the bedroom. Laura looked bad. Her lips were pale and trembling. She held a white robe closed tight around her. Her eyes flickered, wary, uncertain. On the other hand, Nick seemed pretty well recovered. He was dressed and wearing his glasses, and he led Laura slowly through the kitchen to where they stood near the doorway to the living room.

At first Laura appeared not to see them. In the next instant her eyes fixed on the figure sprawled on the bed. Her mouth flew open. For a moment there was no sound. Then she screamed. A high, keening wail. She fought her way out of Nick's arms and ran back into the bedroom. The door slammed shut. Nick turned to follow.

"Let her stay," said Dan. "I think she's safe enough in there for the time being. But you'd better open the door, just in case."

Nick opened the door and they looked inside. Laura stood bolt upright in the corner behind the door, away from the window. Her eyes were blank and stared straight ahead at the wall.

"That'll do," said Dan.

He knew Marjie was going to vomit as soon as he turned back to look at her. Nick saw it too and tried to reach her, but they were too late. She turned away from them and sunk to her knees, pulse pounding and pale as death, and vomited into the thin nightgown covering her lap. She felt Dan's hands on her but she could not move. Then someone was lifting her up and carrying her into the bedroom.

Dan pulled the nightgown off her and threw it into a corner. He had to move quickly now. There would be only the two of them, and it would have to do. He handed one of the hammers to Nick. "Isn't there an axe around here somewhere?" he said.

"In the woodshed, dammit," said Nick.

"Then get another knife out of the drawer," he said. "In case they try to get in. I'm taking the door off this bedroom."

He worked on the hinges with the hammer. They slipped out easily. He carried the door into the living room, scooping up a handful of nails on the way. He called to Nick. "Give me a hand."

Nick came running. Dan saw that he'd found a knife. His eyes had gone bright with excitement. "Where are Jim's things?" he said.

"In here, I guess. I don't know. Why?"

"There's a flight bag," Nick said. "Jim has a gun."

"A gun?"

"A pistol, yeah. Big one. In a blue flight bag."

"Jesus Christ, let's find the fucker," said Dan.

They searched the room. They found his suitcase by the fireplace but the bag was not with it. "Shit," said Nick. "He *must* have brought it in with him. It was in the trunk."

"Maybe in the kitchen. We'll find it. I don't want this window open, though. Give me a hand a minute."

Nick held the door against the windowpane while Dan nailed it down, all the time thinking of the man outside. The big one. The one with the knives and the wicked laugh. Every second he thought, Now he'll come. Now I'm in for it. He braced himself against what the weight of the man would do to him. He thought he heard him laughing once, a low evil chuckle, but he couldn't be sure it wasn't just his imagination. Nothing came to crash against the window. Nothing stirred outside. Why don't they come? he thought. Why didn't they attack? The big man could have forced his way past him when he'd first opened the door. What were they up to, dammit? He slammed the last nail home.

That would do, he thought. Now for the other windows. And the gun.

Outside, Carla swung slowly from the heavy rope, lost in nightmare.

She shivered uncontrollably, her body laved in sweat, Jim's blood still slimy across her stomach and thighs. The cool night air was a vicious wind, biting deep into her fevered flesh. The wound along her backbone where they'd dragged her over the windowpane was closed now and she felt no pain. The pain was in her feet, starved for blood, and in her choked and swollen ankles. Her tongue felt thick, her lips cracked and dry. She forced her eyes to focus.

A group of ragged children were building something out of leaves and sticks and old rotted wood a few yards away. A thin gaunt man with a leering smile poked her in the ribs with his forefinger and placed a large metal bucket—the kind you could bathe in— beneath her. Next to him, a man in a bright red shirt drove two pegs into the ground with a wooden hammer, one on either side of her about four feet apart. There was something familiar about the shirt. She noticed that the man's right hand was missing its middle and third fingers. Then she remembered a man in a red shirt waving to her from down by the brook. Was it yesterday?

She watched, uncomprehending, while the man tied long leather thongs to each peg and then drove the pegs deeper into the hard earth. He stood up and ran a line to her left wrist and tied it tight. She tried to swing away from him but it was no good. Her strength was gone. He laughed at her. Now she felt a pressure in her fingertips and knew that in a few minutes they would give her pain. He ran the second thong to her right wrist and tied it. So that now she would not even be able to move back and forth on the rope anymore. She looked down into the bucket. A darkness filled with tiny motes of light began to close in on her.

Dimly she heard the hammer pounding inside the house but she could not understand what that sound meant, could not connect it to anything. She heard herself sobbing and felt tears roll across her forehead. Yet even that felt very far away. She knew she was failing and tried desperately to cling to consciousness, to ward off shock. Something would save her if she kept awake and sane. There would be some opportunity. She shook her head. She saw the thin man reach into his pants, withdraw the knife, and open it. She tried to move against the ropes, and for a moment the pain broke through and rocketed her to clarity.

She remembered Jim's body sprawled against her, the heat of his bright blood, the precise angle of his head as he tumbled away. It horrified her to know that she did not care about him, that she only cared about what was happening to her now, about Carla living, about not dying the way she had seen him die. She did not want that, she would not accept it. She would struggle against this black thing settling like a pair of wings over her that kept urging her toward sleep and carelessness. She moved her head forward and looked up, disbelievingly, at her own helpless flesh.

In the glare of the headlights she saw herself pale and trembling, her feet together and arms spread wide in some inverted parody of crucifixion. She looked up at the flesh that men had touched and she had touched, now thrust upward to the peaceful, starry sky, and knew in that moment that conscious or unconscious they were going to kill her, that there was nothing she could do or say that would change that. They were go-

ing to cut her with the knife, and she would die with
her blood pouring into the bucket and that would be
the end of her, of the good smooth flesh, of the good
mind that now at its own loss and dissolution was filled
with horror and the startled will to live, live, and live.
It astonished her.

She was still looking upward when the knife descended and then moved up again, burned over her clitoris, and moved slowly and carefully over her belly,
between her breasts and finally, to her neck, where it
slashed with a neat butcher's skill the anterior jugular
and, moments later, ended her.

The pail began to fill. The children lit the fire. The
thin man moved closer, peering down over her body. In
a slow, deliberate motion he reached into the chest and
touched the heart. It was still warm, still beating. He
severed the veins and arteries with the knife and lifted
the muscle into the light, and still it beat, steaming in
the cool air. For the man this moment was the nexus of
all mystery and wonder, the closest thing he knew to
worship. He stared until finally the heart was still. His
eyes, usually dull, filled with a fine cool light. He bit
deep into its naked fiber and grunted his approval.

"I've looked everywhere," said Nick. "It's not here."
Dan was kneeling on the floor, knocking the legs off
the chairs in the kitchen. The seats would work well
over the windows. He looked up at Nick and saw the
fear and frustration grinding at him. That man is about
to cry, he thought.

"Don't worry about it," he said. "If we know where

it *isn't* then we know where it *is*. In the trunk. We'll find a way to get it out of there. Meantime, boil some water. All you can make."

"Huh?"

Dan smiled coldly. "Ever scald yourself with hot water?"

In a moment Nick smiled, too. "I can go you one better," he said. "There's butter in the refrigerator. About two pounds, I think."

"Great. Do that up too."

He opened the potbellied stove and piled the broken chair legs inside. He left the grate open so he could see when they began to burn. With the varnish on them it shouldn't take long. Then he'd heat the poker. There were six chairs, one for each remaining window with the exception of the big one in the kitchen. He went to work on the last of them while Nick put a match to each of the burners on the stove. Nick filled three pans with water and a fourth with the butter from the refrigerator. He opened one of the cabinets and found a bottle of vegetable oil, nearly full, and emptied that in with the butter. Then he threw the burners up to high and waited.

"Get that other door off," Dan said to him.

Laura sat huddled behind the door. She gave a start when Nick walked in. "I've got to take this," he said. She made no response. Where in hell is she gone to? he wondered. Her eyes looked cold and dead. Her breath came in shallow gasps. God, he thought, I don't even feel sorry for her.

He recalled his last image of Carla, dangling by a rope from the tree. Since then he had not dared to look.

He did not want to know she was dead. That would hurt, he thought. That would hurt a lot. He felt a rush of anger. I'm so goddamned worried about my own skin . . . , he thought, and left the thought unfinished. He used the hammer to slam the door free of its hinges. Laura started again and folded her arms over her breasts.

"Bring it out here," Dan said. "Hurry."

Nick turned to Laura. "You'll be all right," he said. "I promise." She stared at him and said nothing. He picked up the door.

As he passed Marjie's room he saw her standing in the doorway, stark naked, watching Dan nail the seat of a chair over the far kitchen window. He smelled the acrid scent of vomit behind her. She seemed hardly to notice him.

For a moment everything seemed utterly unreal—this woman who had been his friend and secretly even more perhaps, standing pale and naked before him; while behind him Laura sat trembling in a corner and somewhere to his right a man he hardly knew lay dead and bloodless on his bed; while outside on a hill a group of maniacs tortured and maybe murdered a woman he had loved these many years; and he himself boarded up doors and windows and burned fat somehow to protect them from the same thing or worse. Less than half an hour ago he had been sleeping—or trying to sleep—in a peaceful little house in the Maine woods. He had risen to shattered glass and screams, and now he and Dan were fighting for their lives. All this passed through his mind in perhaps a quarter of a second as he carried the door to the big kitchen window over the sink, feeling a deep sense of strangeness and sadness. All this and the thought of death, violent death. His own. And he wondered, How can any of this be? Why us? Why me?

"Let me help," said Marjie.

Dan glanced at her and smiled. "You'll need some clothes," he said.

She disappeared at once into the bedroom. A moment later she was back wearing shirt and jeans and helping Nick hold the door while Dan drove the nails into the wall and windowsill. She sniffed the air and frowned. "Something's burning," she said.

"Turn down the fat," said Nick.

They worked quickly, Dan thanking god there were so many good strong nails. Soon they had the last window in the kitchen secure, as well as the two remaining windows in the living room and the one in Marjie's bedroom. Dan checked the potbellied stove and saw that the fire was good and hot. He pushed the poker into the embers and left it there. "We'll need some towels or something," he said to Marjie. "Thick ones. Those pots and that poker are gonna be as hot as we can make them."

"No problem," she said. "I'll find some."

He couldn't help smiling, happy to see her back to normal again. Normal? She was better than that. She was acting more like her sister, suddenly fearless and damned resourceful. He was proud of her. Now if only Nick's woman would show a little fight. He walked into her room with the last of the seats and nails and saw that she still hadn't moved.

Outside the window, the children had been joined by the three figures he'd seen on the porch a while ago. He squinted to make them out. In the spill from the headlamps he could see one of them pretty clearly. Jesus he thought. They were women! They all were visible now. One of them was obviously pregnant, wrapped in some sort of heavy skin. Who the fuck *were* these people?

He didn't stop long to consider. He set the wood in place and tacked it down, skillfully and efficiently. He heard the glass break on the other side and guessed that they'd thrown something at the window. It startled him and made his hands shake, but he was glad they'd done it. Whatever it was they'd thrown was heavy. It stood as a kind of test. His nails had not given an inch.

He had already checked the locks on both doors and found them good and strong, as were the doors themselves. These old houses had been built to last. Whoever these people were, they'd have a much harder time getting in here than they'd planned on.

He found Nick in the kitchen, emptying the kitchen drawers onto the table and going through the silver. Most of it was dull and useless, but he'd turned up a large meat fork and a decent carving knife. Both might well be needed. He wished to Christ he had that axe out in the woodshed. But it was no good going after it now. They were pressed for time and had to discuss this situation. Who could tell what was going on out there? They had to work this out right away.

"You know that window in the attic?" he said. Nick nodded. "I figure it's just about directly over Laura's bedroom, right?"

148

Nick thought about it a moment. "You're right," he said. He had stuck his head outside and had a look around, while Carla was showing the others the pile of magazines. That was exactly where it was. *Carla,* he thought. He felt suddenly sick inside. He banished her from his mind.

"And we got a group of them standing just under the window now, right?"

"Right," Nick said, grinning. He knew what Dan had in mind. He'd been thinking about it himself.

"Now my guess is that if we toss the water on them from that height in this temperature, by the time it hits them it will be like throwing out the bath water. We'll get a little rise out of them, that's all. Whereas the oil and butter . . ."

"Will cool a lot slower. And scald hell out of them. That should get them hollering and bring the others on a run. Give us time to get to the cars."

"And the Magnum," said Dan.

They stood there smiling. Nick was not as surprised as he thought he should have been to find the thought of murder so very appealing.

"We'll only get one try," Dan said. "It better go down like clockwork. The oil isn't gonna do too much harm except to make them a lot more anxious to get in here. You have any idea where Carla keeps the keys to her car?"

"No. But I'd be willing to bet they're not in the dashboard. It's not like her to leave them."

"Let's look around, then."

"Or we could take the Dodge," he said.

Dan scowled.

"I know what you mean," Nick said. "I guess it's not all that reliable. But the gun will be in the Dodge."

"Yeah." That would mean they'd have to split up. He didn't like it but there was nothing else they could do. It just wasn't safe without the pistol. "Here's what we do then," he said. "You go for the trunk and get that gun. I'd do it myself but you know where it is and what the bag looks like. If we can find Carla's keys, I'll get her car started and get Marjie and Laura inside."

"Laura will be a problem."

"No kidding. I'll handle it." He fell silent a moment. Could he handle it? He didn't know. Walking out there with a hysterical woman on his hands, it was a rotten situation. But if they left her behind she was dead meat. These bastards were crazy. They had to stay together as much as possible.

"Let's find the damn keys," he said.

"Marjie may know where they are," Nick suggested.

"I'd just as soon not ask her. I figure the less about Carla the better, right? Let's just start with her clothes and take it from there."

It didn't take long. The keys were on a ring in the right-hand pocket of her jeans. Dan turned to Nick. "Okay," he said. "You set with the trunk key for the Dodge?"

"Right here," he said. He patted his shirt pocket. "I guess we'd better try to rouse Laura"

He started for the bedroom just as Marjie emerged from the bathroom, carrying a stack of towels. Dan selected four of them and threw the others into a corner.

GET UP TO 4 FREE BOOKS!

You can have the best fiction delivered to your door for less than what you'd pay in a bookstore or online—only $4.25 a book! Sign up for our book clubs today, and we'll send you **FREE* BOOKS** just for trying it out...**with no obligation to buy, ever!**

LEISURE HORROR BOOK CLUB

With more award-winning horror authors than any other publisher, it's easy to see why CNN.com says "Leisure Books has been leading the way in paperback horror novels." Your shipments will include authors such as RICHARD LAYMON, DOUGLAS CLEGG, JACK KETCHUM, MARY ANN MITCHELL, and many more.

LEISURE THRILLER BOOK CLUB

If you love fast-paced page-turners, you won't want to miss any of the books in Leisure's thriller line. Filled with gripping tension and edge-of-your-seat excitement, these titles feature everything from psychological suspense to legal thrillers to police procedurals and more!

As a book club member you also receive the following special benefits:

- **30% OFF all orders through our website & telecenter!**
- **Exclusive access to special discounts!**
- **Convenient home delivery and 10 days to return any books you don't want to keep.**

There is no minimum number of books to buy, and you may cancel membership at any time. See back to sign up!

*Please include $2.00 for shipping and handling.

YES!

Sign me up for the Leisure Horror Book Club and send my TWO FREE BOOKS! If I choose to stay in the club, I will pay only $8.50* each month, a savings of $5.48!

YES! ☐

Sign me up for the Leisure Thriller Book Club and send my TWO FREE BOOKS! If I choose to stay in the club, I will pay only $8.50* each month, a savings of $5.48!

NAME: _____

ADDRESS: _____

_____

TELEPHONE: _____

E-MAIL: _____

☐ **I WANT TO PAY BY CREDIT CARD.**

☐ VISA   ☐ MasterCard   ☐ DISCOVER

ACCOUNT #: _____

EXPIRATION DATE: _____

SIGNATURE: _____

Send this card along with $2.00 shipping & handling for each club you wish to join, to:

Horror/Thriller Book Clubs
20 Academy Street
Norwalk, CT 06850-4032

Or fax (must include credit card information!) to: 610.995.9274.
You can also sign up online at www.dorchesterpub.com.

*Plus $2.00 for shipping. Offer open to residents of the U.S. and Canada only.
Canadian residents please call 1.800.481.9191 for pricing information.
If under 18, a parent or guardian must sign. Terms, prices and conditions subject to change. Subscription subject
to acceptance. Dorchester Publishing reserves the right to reject any order or cancel any subscription.

"I think we'd better hold up on Laura a minute," he said. "We've got to discuss this, the three of us. It's got to be fast."

His face looked strained and anxious. "I'll be the one to go upstairs and dump the oil," he said. "Check out the front window and you'll find there's a small peephole there, so you'll be able to see them when they start to move. When they get out of your line of vision, open that door and, Marjie, get to your sister's car. Do it as quickly and quietly as you can. No slamming doors. Check to see if there are any windows open and if there are, roll them up. I'll be right behind you with Laura. Make sure you get into the backseat and close and lock both back doors. Again, be real quiet.

"Nick, get that pistol out of the trunk and head for the right front door. Got that? Right front door. I'll have it open for you and the car started and ready to go before you hit the seat. Sound good to all of you?"

Nick shrugged. "Best we got."

"We don't have much in the way of weapons so I suggest that everybody tuck a knife in their belt and carry out a pan of that water. I hope to shit that nobody gets close enough to even see, but if they do, use the water and use the knives and everything you got, because I got a feeling that if anybody fucks up he's dead and probably the rest of us with him. If anything goes wrong—*anything*—we haul ass back inside and bolt up again. Fair enough?"

Marjie nodded. "Fair enough."

"Okay. Let's go get Laura."

She was still huddled in her bedroom. She barely even knows who we are, thought Marjie. She turned to the men behind her. "Let me get some clothes on her," she said. They went back into the kitchen and left them alone together.

Marjie went through Laura's closet and took an old plaid shirt off a hanger and her jeans off the chair beside her bed. "Come on," she said gently, "put these on now." There was no response, only a faint trembling in her hand as Marjie touched it. Well, she thought, I'll have to do it for her. She looked out through a corner slit in the window and called softly to Dan and Nick. "Still out there," she said.

"Good," said Dan.

She did not look again. There was something about those children waiting for them out there, an unnatural stillness, a deadly patience, that unnerved her. She supposed the women were more dangerous, and she damn well knew the men were, but it was the children that frightened her most. Perhaps it had something to do with that old fear she had of closed-in spaces. She had the feeling that the children would fight in packs, in a swarm, and she could imagine all too vividly how they would surround her and pull her down, smothering her under their sheer weight of numbers. She turned her attention back to Laura.

She stooped and took the girl by the arm and lifted her up, and then, when she was standing, peeled the robe off her shoulders. She could not help admiring her firm, full breasts; Laura was a bit on the heavy side

152

but Marjorie had seriously underestimated her body. She and Carla were both slim and that was definitely the fashion these days, but it had not always been, and there had been times when Marjie would have given anything to trade places with a woman like Laura. Not now, though, she thought, looking into the empty green eyes. Not now by a long shot.

In a few moments she had the shirt on and buttoned and the jeans pulled over her cool, pale thighs. By the time Marjie was through, her hands were shaking. "Come with me," she said, leading Laura into the kitchen. She had a bad feeling about Laura. The girl would be pretty much defenseless out there. She hoped Dan meant to take good care of her.

As they stood in the kitchen facing each other nobody said a word for a few moments. There was nothing left to do but what they had said they would do, and now that seemed enormous and filled them with a kind of awe. They listened to the crackling fire and waited—for what, they did not know. It was possible that they were walking out there only to die the way all fools die in danger, with a plan that could snag in a thousand different ways, and with little defense should it do so. They felt the adrenaline build and sluice through them like a dangerous poison, urging them to begin, to get it over with. While fear muted their voices and tried to break their will.

If Marjie's fear had a physical aspect it was the faces of countless children. She could almost feel their hands on her and she shuddered. At the same time she thought of Carla. Was she still alive out there? What if she should call her, if she should see her sister beckon to her? Could she still go on? Nick saw himself at the window again, but this time the knife sliced him ear to ear. In his imagination his blood splattered Marjie and Dan and Laura until they stood before his dying eyes, bathed in red. And Dan stood on a hill in a jungle far away from here, looking down at the face of a man he had just blown away—and this time that phrase was coldly appropriate, because half the man's head was gone, split clean as a grapefruit. He saw half a pair of lips gape at him in dumb amazement, a single eye to register that final surprise that ended all surprises.

"It's war, isn't it," said Nick, breaking the silence.

"Yeah," said Dan. Perhaps there was something to ESP after all, he thought.

There was another, shorter silence. Then Marjie picked up a towel and folded it over. "Let's get going," she said.

"Okay," said Dan. As quickly as they had come to them, the violent images dispersed, leaving them in the grip of a powerful churn of adrenaline. The fear was not gone. But in some way it had germinated, and its offspring was a clean pure thrill of sheer excitement. Soldiers know all about it, Dan thought. Fighting for your life is a fucking ball. As long as you didn't get slaughtered. The hardest thing was keeping your head. You got to feeling that they couldn't kill you, and that was when they did.

"Okay," he said again. "I'll take our little bomb upstairs and drop it on their fucking faces. When you hear 'em holler, get the door unlocked and get those pans of water."

"What about you?" said Marjie. "How are you going to handle Laura *and* a pan of boiling water?"

"Leave the last pan on the burner in case we have to use it to get us back inside. I'll have the poker. That I can deal with." He folded a towel and draped it over the handle of the poker so that when he came downstairs he could grab it instantly.

"As soon as you see me," he said, "get out the door. That's presuming those guys on the hill move around back as fast as I think they will. If they don't move, we don't go. But I think we're dealing with a little family here. I hope they'll defend one another. Keep an eye on them through the peephole."

"You take the peephole," Nick said to Marjie. "I'll get the door and watch for Dan."

"Could we do it the other way around?" she said. She thought of Carla out there. "If I have to look at her . . ."

"Sure," said Nick. "Fine. I understand." He put his hand on her arm and she realized that he was trembling, too.

Dan took a towel off the table and moved quickly to the stove. He picked up the pot of oil and turned off the burner. The oil was dark and bubbling. He headed for the stairs. At the stairway he stopped and turned around and saw them watching him. "You guys?" he said softly. For a moment he said nothing. Then he said, "Good luck." Marjie managed to raise a smile for him. Silently he climbed the stairs.

The attic was cold. He hesitated, waiting until he could make out the shape of the window across the room in the dark. He wanted the room dark. If he turned on the light those bastards below them might notice, and he didn't want them looking up at him. Not until he was ready. He crossed slowly to the window, found the latch, and gently pushed it open. He looked outside. Two of the women and a few of the children were directly below. The window was small. There would barely be room, but he'd manage.

He moved the pan out the window. There was just enough space to extend his arm fully and get his head through there. He paused a moment, calculating, making sure. He had a sudden urge to laugh as he watched them down below. For chrissakes get yourself under control, he told himself. This has got to be good. *Perfect*. In another moment he felt fine again. He took a deep breath and turned over the pan. He moved his arm side to side so the oil would spread and at the same time said, *"Hey assholes,"* just loud enough for them to hear. He saw their heads turn upward and stare at him, stare up into the falling oil. He felt a moment of glee and triumph, and dropped the pan at the nearest woman.

As he pulled his head inside he could already hear them screaming.

1:15 A.M.

Four hours beating the bush with over twenty men and they didn't have a thing. Peters had expected as much. He made a beeline for the coffee urn and drew himself a cup; black, no sugar. He shouldn't even be drinking the stuff, he thought. This goddam diet was going to kill him. That is, if the winter didn't do it first. Here it was only early September and he could already feel it in the air. Every winter for three years running now he'd caught himself a cold that had lasted straight through to February. Doc Linden told him it was the extra weight that made him susceptible, the weight and the bad food and the long hours. Bunch of bullshit. Doctors knew less about the common cold than he knew about these weird kids out there.

The coffee warmed him, though. The station house was going to be ice cold again this year, he thought. He'd dig that space heater out of the cellar and put it in his office—that would help some. He walked past the rows of desks and into the glass-enclosed office cubicle. Shearing was waiting for him with an old man in a dirty blue parka who smelled of cheap whiskey. Peters recognized him immediately.

"Danner or Donner?" he said.

"Donner," said Shearing. "Paul Michael Donner. Age: sixty-two. Height: five-two. Weight: one sixty-five. Occupation: fisherman. Present state of intoxication: minimal." Donner smiled at that one and nodded at Peters. "Mr. Donner here says he knows exactly where he saw them, George," said Shearing.

"That so?"

"Absolutely, Officer." The old man blinked at him excitedly—or was that some sort of tic? "I wouldn't forget them folks too quick. Most fucked-up thing I ever saw, drunk or sober. And that night I was pretty sober, too, though I don't expect you to believe me on that exactly."

"We're willing to tonight, Mr. Donner," said Peters. "And if we had you wrong at the time, we're very sorry, aren't we, Sam?"

"Only human, Mr. Donner," said Shearing.

"True enough, son," said Donner, "and that's why I'm willin' to help you. Because I'm not at all sure about them other folks. And by the way, call me Paulie, okay?"

"Sure, Paulie," said Peters. "Care for a cup of coffee?"

"I'd appreciate that."

"Sam, get Paulie here a cup of coffee, will you?"

"Black, no sugar," said Donner.

"You on a diet too, Paulie?" Peters asked.

"Hell, no. Only I got a sensitive stomach. Doesn't take to milk and sugar. Black coffee's a lot like whiskey, you know? All devil and no trimmin's. Always liked my sins pure and take it as it comes."

Peters smiled. Donner was a likable old wreck. Funny thing about drunks. Get them halfway sober and they were smarter than half the professors, and a lot more amiable, too. He suspected he'd be able to rely on Donner's information, give or take a little.

"So where were you that night, Paulie?"

"Like I said at the time, me and a buddy of mine had been doin' a little drinkin' down by the shoreline, just up a ways from Dead River. It was a nice night, summertime then you know, so we just sat ourselves down and pretty soon my buddy was sound asleep. And me, I was about five minutes more finishing that pint, and you know how it is, I started lookin' around for more. So I thought I'd take a walk down to . . . what's the package store in Dead River, son?"

"Banyan's."

"Banyan's. Figured he'd be open. So I'm walking down the beach a ways, figuring to hit the cutoff to the old dump road in a few yards or so—which is where we had the pickup waitin'—and then I'd drive to Banyan's and make my purchase and get right back there. And hell, my buddy wouldn't even know I'd gone.

"Well, I'm walking kind of slow and all, and then all of a sudden I hear all this laughin' up ahead, gigglin' you know, like the kind of noise little girls make, and I stop and look around and I see a whole pack of 'em

fussin' around along the dunes up ahead to my right.
And there's somethin' about it I don't like. I don't
know what it is, but there's somethin' about all that
laughin' that I don't trust the sound of, you know? So I
kind of edge over a bit and stand by the rocks for a few
minutes, figuring they'll be gone before too long, and
then I start to see what they're doin' up there.

"They got this dog on the end of a rope, see, and
they're pullin' on the rope and kicking the poor damn
animal fit to beat the band, and laughing all the while
like it's great fun. And I could tell they'd been at it for
some time already because that dog, he isn't even saying nothing, not barkin' or even whimpering anymore.
They got that animal completely beat. Hell, I can see
its poor old bug eyes starin' up at them like it would
just like to lay down and die right there, only they
damn well wouldn't let it.

"Well shit, I wasn't gonna do nothing. That dog was
a pretty good size. I didn't want 'em comin' after me,
Lord no!" The old man paused and licked his lips.
Shearing entered the room and handed him a cup of
coffee.

"You hear all this already, Sam?" Peters asked.

"Sure did."

"Go on, Paulie."

"Well, I just hunkered down to wait 'em out. And
pretty soon there wasn't nothing they could do to make
that dog stand up anymore. The way they'd been
kickin' at it I figure it was anybody's guess whether the
legs busted first or the ribs did. So then one of them,

kind of a big boy, just picked up the dog and walked into the water with it and floated it out to sea. He came by pretty close to me and that was when I had my best look at 'em."

"What did he look like?"

"Looked crazy. I mean his face looked crazy, *loony;* wild. And I swear to you that the sonofabitch was wearing somethin' strung together out of coonskins. They all had skins of some sort—bear, deer, whatever. 'Cept I recall one little guy in a pair of work pants a mile too big for him. Never saw such a goddamn thing in my life. And this kid who walked by me, he had a smile on him that I never want to see again as long as I live. Real grown-up smile, and mean from start to finish. Boy walked right by me. And then the women came by."

"Women?"

"Yeah. Two of them. Dressed in rags. Cast-off kind of stuff, you know? Nothing matched up with anything else. One of 'em even had on two different kinds of shoes, for chrissakes!"

"You're a pretty good observer, Paulie."

"You ever try to scout a school of fish from the deck of a charter?"

"So go on. What did the women do?"

"Rounded 'em up. Headed 'em up the cliffs. Cuffed a few of 'em too, as I recall."

"The cliffs?"

"I think they live there, Officer. I think they got a cave somewhere. Like a bunch of goddamn savages."

"Why do you say that?"

161

"Well, they just up and disappeared. I saw 'em climbing and then I didn't see 'em. Just like that."

"Couldn't they have gone inland?"

"You miss my point, son. *They didn't make it to the top*. That's what I'm trying to tell ya. They walked into some kind of hole in the ground like a bunch of rats and that was the end of 'em!"

Peters sat back and took a deep breath. "Jesus jumping Christ," he said.

"You're damn tootin'," said Donner.

Peters' stomach was growling. He couldn't tell if he was hungry or if it was his ulcer kicking up again. At the moment he was banking on the ulcer. "Okay, Paulie," he said. "You've been terrific. If we need anything else from you, I suppose that Sergeant Shearing here knows where to find you?"

Donner's eyes sparkled. "Much as anybody does," he said.

"Thanks, then," Peters said. "Now you place this whole thing just a little north of the cutoff to the old dump road, right?"

"Yep."

"You're sure of that."

"Well, let me put it to you this way, boys. I haven't had a bottle anywhere *near* there since."

Peters smiled. "Thanks again, Paulie. I owe you one."

Donner got up to leave. "I'll be by one day to collect it, I guess," he said. He nodded and closed the door behind him.

Peters stared at Shearing awhile. It was only a point of reference. He was letting his mind work, and if he was seeing anything at all it was the shoreline around the dump road cutoff and a bunch of ragged crazies scuttling through the night. At last he pushed back in his chair and sighed. Shearing was still standing there, watching him. "You believe him, don't you?" said Peters.

"I guess I do, George."

"Me too, right down the line. And that makes me think we ought to consolidate this search a little."

"The cutoff, right?"

"Right. Of course we're gonna have the same problem Donner did."

"What's that?"

"It's going to be damned hard to find anything along that cliff at night."

"You think it can wait till morning?"

Peters pursed his lips and frowned. He thought about it. "I suppose it can," he said. "Matter of fact, it will have to. One thing I do want to do, though."

"What."

"Have Willis out there draw me up a list of all the residents in that area, permanent and seasonal. Have him make it for, say, five square miles back from the shoreline. Have him phone King Realty and check on new rentals. Then I'll want prowl cars covering that area all night. I want them to check out every house, without alarming anybody or waking anybody in the middle of the night. Make sure everything is normal. That will mean local boys are your best bet. They'd know who is who out there. Get 'em out of bed if you have to but make sure we get locals and not fellas from

Portland or Bangor or someplace. If they notice any-thing unusual, I want you to call me. I'm going home to get some sleep. When Burke shows up, I suggest you do the same."

"What time do we start in the morning?"

"What time is sunup?"

"Oh, 'bout seven o'clock, I guess."

"Make it seven thirty."

Shearing groaned. "That early?"

"Seems to me, Sam, that we already made one mistake in not checking out Donner's story in the first place. You want to make another? We got no idea what these people are up to, or who they are or where they come from, but I got an idea that anybody who raises kids that drown dogs and women ain't exactly friendly. So I'd like to meet 'em early in the morning, just in case anybody else meets up with 'em later in the day, if you know what I mean."

Shearing nodded. "You know what bothers me?" he said.

"What's that?"

"No men."

"Bothers me too, Sam. A lot."

"You figure there might be more than just the two women and the kids?"

"Might be."

"So how many men do you want me to put on the roster?"

Peters yawned. He stood up and put on his hat and coat. He turned to Shearing and frowned again.

"How many you got?" he said.

1:18 A.M.

The feast had nearly begun. Their kill hung from a greenwood spit over the fire. The thin man's lips were slack and moist. He had peeled away her scalp with his knife and set aside the liver and kidneys while the other man cut and trimmed the branches from a young, supple birch and whittled its tip to a point. Together they worked the spit up through the kill, trussed the arms and legs together, and slung it over the fire. Now the rich aroma made them smile. They listened to the bones crackling and exploding and the sizzle of fat, and waited.

The children had built the fire well. They stood back from the carcass, pleased with themselves, watching the eldest girl turn the spit. The child in the girl's belly moved abruptly but the girl did not notice. Behind her, two of the younger children, a boy and a girl, dipped their fingers into the pail and licked the cool blood off them. The kill was roasting evenly when they heard the others scream from behind the house.

They looked up and saw the lights go off inside and saw the big man at the front door draw his knives from his belt and run around back. The screams continued. They felt no fear, nor any real concern at the sound; only curiosity. The children were the first to move away from the fire.

The man in red commanded them to stay. They did as they were told. The thin man was already ahead of him. He put a hatchet in his belt and followed. He looked for signs of movement at the front door and windows and saw nothing. He ran to the side of the house.

As he turned the corner he saw two of the older boys kneeling on the ground, their hands covering their faces. The women were still screaming, the youngest of them—the one he liked to fuck—tearing at the front of her shirt, which he saw was wet and gleaming. She bared her breasts and he saw that she had been burned somehow. He did not understand. Neither did the other men, who looked at him for an answer. He shrugged.

He saw that the bedroom window was boarded up. *They had not come through,* he thought. *They are still inside.* If they had not tried to escape, what was this? The two children who remained unharmed were looking up at the house and pointing. The man turned and saw the open attic window. Then he saw the pan lying on the ground beside one of the women. He stooped and ran his finger along the edge. It was still warm. He put the finger in his mouth and tasted it. *Fat.* He smiled. Those inside were not stupid. The hunt was better now.

OFF SEASON

* * *

Nick watched the two men disappear behind the house just as Dan came tumbling off the staircase. A moment later Marjie thrust a towel into his hand and followed it with the handle of a pan of boiling water. Nick's throat felt pinched and dry. "They're still out there," he said. "The kids."

He felt Dan hesitate beside him. "We fucked up," he said.

"This is all we got," said Dan. "Screw 'em. Let's go." Nick glanced at Marjie. She, too, seemed to hesitate. "I said let's *go*!" Dan hissed.

He unbolted the door. His heartbeat and respiration seemed to accelerate at a rate that alarmed him. His skin was cold, his kidneys felt tight and bloated. He opened the door.

Behind him Dan pulled the red-hot poker out of the fire and took Laura by the arm, thrusting her out ahead of him. "Fast!" he said to the others, and then suddenly all four of them were out the door.

The cars stood side by side; Carla's farthest away with its low beams on, about twenty feet from the house, and Nick's old Dodge between Carla's car and the front door. Spaces juggled themselves strangely before them. In the distance they saw the fire. The fire was yards away from them but now it seemed very close by. The cars were only a few feet away, but that seemed very far. And for Nick, who needed to get from the Dodge to Carla's Pinto with the pistol and cartridges, the two cars seemed separated by a chasm.

He saw Marjie run past him and open the back door of the Pinto and slide in. By that time he was at the trunk of the Dodge and his key was in the lock, his pan of water resting on the hood of the car. He pulled the trunk open quickly and easily. His senses felt incredibly alert now. He could smell something cooking on the fire. He could hear the children running in their direction. He heard Laura protest and struggle as Dan pushed and pulled her toward the car. He heard Marjie throw the locks on the rear car doors. He heard Dan cursing.

Then he had the flight bag open and the gun in his hands. He flipped open the chamber. Empty.

His hands fumbled with the box of shells. Suddenly it seemed to leap from his hands into the trunk. There was no trunk light. My God, he thought. He reached into the darkness and for a moment panic seized him as he felt the broken end of the box. The shells were scattered throughout the trunk. His bowels fluttered. He slipped the gun into his belt and groped for the shells with both hands. He heard Dan curse again and shove Laura into the car and slam the door.

His fingers closed on a pile of cartridges. He heard Dan try the ignition and knew with a sudden sick feeling inside that they had crippled the wiring somehow, knew it even before Dan did with a kind of terrible intuition that came not of knowing cars but of knowing fate when he faced it squarely. And then in an instant he also knew what he needed to do and began to load the pistol.

He had five chambers full when they attacked him.

The first one appeared only as a shadow to his right over the hood of the Pinto. He reached for the water and heaved it in a single startled motion. It splashed over the boy's face and shoulders and sent him bellowing to the ground, the knife falling beside him. A moment later there were two more of them between him and the house, blocking his retreat and moving toward him. And then a third, a little girl. He raised the pistol.

He fired and saw the first boy's chest go black and the bullet's impact slam him hard against the house. There was an incredible, painful roaring in his ears and he remembered what Jim had said about the earplugs. He squeezed the trigger again and hit upon the empty chamber.

Behind him the trunk slammed shut and he whirled, sensing rather than seeing the boy who lunged at his neck over the rear of the car. The boy's blade whistled past him, missing him by inches. Nick raised the gun again. But before he had a chance to fire the boy screeched and fell, clutching the back of his neck. Nick saw Dan behind him, the poker steaming in his hand. He smelled the scent of burning flesh and hair. Then he felt a knife bite deep into his thigh and he screamed.

He whirled again and pointed the gun directly into the face of the little girl who still tugged downward on the blade that was too big for her, thrusting and turning it inside him, grinning up into his face with an awful inhuman glee. At the same instant he saw another boy beside him raise his knife. The gun exploded in his hands and the girl's head was suddenly gone and Nick was bathed in flecks of brain and blood and bone. At the same time the boy's sharp blade descended toward his chest.

Marjie had Laura by the collar and pushed her screaming through the front door. The girl tumbled to the floor and lay there sobbing a moment and then began to crawl toward the back of the house. In the dark Marjie ran for the stove where the final pan of water sat simmering. She picked it up and the handle burned her but she felt no pain, only a fear that ground her teeth together and made her grim and silent. She stood there inside the door in a fierce eternity of waiting, resisting with all her power the urge to slam the door and race howling into the attic; resisting at the same time another urge that wanted her to dash outside and cut away at them with her own pathetic knife in some suicidal frenzy of revenge.

She saw Nick's gun go off against the girl and saw the boy's knife slash across his chest and then heard the crack of metal against bone as Dan's poker crashed down on the boy's skull. Blood poured from the boy's mouth and eyes as he slid away. She saw Dan pull the poker free and shove Nick ahead of him toward the doorway. She stepped out to help him. She saw Dan's eyes dart suddenly to the left as Nick fell in front of her and saw Dan open his mouth to warn her, but by then it was too late. Something hit Dan from behind and at the same instant the huge man roared beside her.

His hand closed over her wrist. She looked into his

eyes and his face was terrible, his teeth all black and foul, his scent the scent of blood. His fingers curled deep into her flesh. She imagined those hands on Carla and brought the heavy pot around.

The boiling water splashed uselessly behind him, but the base of the pot caught him squarely on the ear, burning him, hitting him hard. He howled and released her, lost his balance a moment and tumbled heavily to the ground. At the same moment Nick lurched toward her. She hauled him inside and in an instant she saw that the wound across his chest was not deep. She pulled the knife out of his thigh. His face went suddenly white and he stumbled and fell to the floor.

She looked around for Dan, the bloody knife still clutched in her hand. Her eyes seemed to locate him automatically. She felt something turn hollow in the pit of her stomach as she saw him there next to the car where they had dragged him. His poker was gone, and they were all around him. He was already screaming.

The woman behind him had her teeth buried deep in his neck, her arms around him and bare breasts against him a grim mockery of a lover's embrace. He was trying to shake her off but the children were at his legs with knives. She saw them slash the tendons behind the right knee, saw him hamstrung the way wolves brought down horses and watched him start to fall as the man in red appeared in front of him and kicked him in the stomach. He doubled over and vomited into the grass and still the woman clung to his neck, biting deeper, so that the bright-oxygenated blood poured steadily out upon the ground in front of them.

She tore the pistol from Nick's hand and fired. The first bullet missed, and the man in red had time to move away from her. At the sound of gunfire Dan moved in her direction and for a moment their eyes met and she saw what was in them. She fired again. The second bullet passed through Dan's right lung and the woman's stomach and pitched them into a heap together beside the car.

Marjie stood motionless, pointing the gun and blinking. *I killed him,* she thought, oh my God. There was perhaps a single second of utter silence, as wild and terrible as the fighting. The look on his face froze forever in her memory. It played over and over in front of her eyes like a loop of film and culminated each time in explosion and silence, leaving her trembling. The gun was hot and massive in her hand. Her eyes brimmed with tears.

The huge man beside her began to rise in the shadows.

She slammed the door shut and, with a sob, thrust the bolt home.

Her attackers backed away slowly, stunned by the violence done to them. These people were not hunters; they had not expected guns. Somewhere in the amphibian murk of the big man's mind he regretted the time wasted seeing to the women behind the house. Now the best of the women was dead and three of the children were dead and there was only the single man that the gun had killed and the woman on the spit to lay his people's spirits.

He thought of the spirits, angry, maleficent, and powerful, and a chill scuttled like a crab through his body.

The wounded women and children began to whimper. He motioned them back to the fire.

The carcass was nearly burned on one side. This, too, was bad. It was the flesh of the dead that gave them power. He gestured to the kill and they understood him. He picked up a hatchet and hacked off one of the legs. Holding it sizzling and dripping fat in front of him, he walked back to the house.

The thin man brushed away his tears of rage and severed the head with his knife. He cracked it open on a nearby outcrop of rock. He scooped out the brains and with the brains in one hand and the head in the other, followed his brother. One by one the others followed suit, stripping the flesh from loin and breast and returning to the front of the house. There they stopped and waited for the man in red to join them, holding the flesh high so that those inside could see what they had done and fear them.

The man in the red shirt walked empty-handed from the fire to the body that lay sprawled beside the car and separated it from the body of his woman. He dragged the man in front of the car so that all could see in the headlights, and laid it on its back. The bullet wound was long and wide. With his knife he slit the man open from vent to sternum and, bending over, buried his face in the liver. He looked up, his face smeared with blood, and saw that the others had also begun to eat.

When the liver was half finished he pulled out the

slippery pile of intestine and with one hand worked its contents down and away from him, while with the other he fed the long gray tube into his mouth and chewed. He smiled when he heard them screaming inside, and knew they had seen him, feeding like a wolf on their friend. The thin man joined him, then, slitting the man's pants from the bottom to the top of the leg, and began tearing at his inner thighs. Around them the dark venous blood oozed into a slowly spreading pool. The thin man gestured to the eldest woman and the pregnant girl to come nearer.

He opened his knife and sliced off the penis and testicles and handed the penis to the girl and the testicles to the toothless woman. The girl ate with quick, bird-like movements, her head darting forward to her fingers like a bird pecking seeds on the ground.

He watched the door and window for signs of movement, for the gun, ready to spring away at any moment. He saw nothing. After a while he relaxed. Only the sound of someone sobbing reached his ears through the thick haze of pleasure and the good salt taste of blood.

It was Marjie who screamed, gazing out the window and seeing what they had done to her lover and her sister. The rest of what they heard outside was Laura's ghostly keening wail as she pressed herself to the back wall and hugged her knees like a child, the wail turning to tears, having seen nothing and knowing all that she needed to know. For Marjie it was the end of something, and the beginning of something else. The beginning of acceptance, physical and mental which included the sudden numbness in the lips, the ringing in her ears that was only partly gunfire—acceptance of the fact that the death that was spread around her like a plague and that had come to her sister in such horrible fashion could come to her as well within the instant. It was cold and final, this feeling, a push into icy waters, but it made her clear-headed and sane where Laura was not, awakened part of her that loved life and would not retreat from death, because retreat was death now.

She saw that Laura was doomed and felt a surprising contempt for her—Carla had fought, Dan had fought. If she would not, to hell with her. She turned to Nick on the floor.

"How bad is it?" she said.

Nick grinned. It was not a good grin. "I heard that one before," he said. "Last time it was Dan who asked me."

"Dan's dead," she said.

"I know."

"I shot him. I don't think I meant to hit him. I think I only meant to hit the woman." She felt the tears returning.

"It's all right. Marjie."

"They were . . . slaughtering him. Like an animal."

"It's all right."

"Do you think you can stand?"

"I think so. Sure." She helped him to his feet. "Thank god it was only that little girl on the knife and not one of the others," he said. He winced trying to walk with her. "Did you see her? Did you see her face when I . . ."

"I saw it," she said.

"We've got to think how to get out of here." His voice sounded flat, like her own. They had arrived at the same place, then, she thought. It was not a good place, not a place she wished to be, but it might help them to survive. "How many times did you fire?" he asked her.

"Twice."

"There's one cartridge left then. I loaded five." He smiled humorlessly. "Not even enough for us to—"

"I wouldn't, anyway," she said.

He nodded. "Neither would I. Is there anything else in the house? Something we can hurt them with?"

"Not much. The shovel by the fireplace. A couple knives—I can't believe they'd do us much good. An axe in the woodshed, but damned if I'm going out after it."

"Nothing in the attic?"

"I don't know."

"Your legs are better than mine," he said. "Go look. And leave me the gun just in case."

She took the stairs two at a time, stood on the landing, and turned on the light. Nothing, she thought. Some milk crates, magazines, an old dresser and an old mattress. Then she saw the scythe. Maybe this, she thought. Then something else occurred to her. She ran back down the stairs to tell Nick. He was watching them through the peephole. His face was white.

"They're not human," he said. "Not even close."

She ignored that. "Listen," she said. "I think we can barricade ourselves into the attic. The door's not as strong as this one, but there's a big heavy dresser up there and a mattress. Suppose we nailed the door shut and put the mattress in front of it, and the dresser in front of that? We might keep them out. At least for a while. Somebody's bound to see that fire eventually."

"Show me," he said.

They went upstairs, Nick leaning heavily on the banister. Ordinarily, the leg wound would have laid him up for a week. Every time he put the foot down it felt like somebody was slapping him with a trip-hammer. He'd have to keep moving or it would stiffen on him. But he was going to have to keep moving anyway if he was going to stay alive.

They made it to the landing. Nick went to the dresser and gave it a push. Marjie was right. It was some kind of hard, heavy wood. Oak or something. The mattress was double-bed size and it occurred to him that that was why it was up here—there were no double beds down below anymore. The attic door was not too strong but the dresser and mattress together would make a pretty good defense. It could be done.

"Only one thing I don't like," he said, "and that's putting our backs to the wall this way. If they do get in here the only way out is through that window. That's maybe fifteen feet to the ground and I don't even know if I fit through. At least down below we've got two doors and plenty of windows."

"Yes, but that's just the problem, isn't it. Plenty of ways for them to get in and only two of us to keep them out once they start trying. And they will start trying. We wouldn't have a prayer."

"Probably not."

"This way there's only one place to fortify."

He walked to the window and looked outside. "Jesus, I hate that jump," he said.

"It's our only alternative. Unless you want to run for it."

He frowned. "Laura can't run," he said.

"To hell with Laura," she said. Her voice was like a slap in the face. For an instant the change in her astonished him. Was this the same girl who worried about fast cars and needed aisle seats in movie theaters? Carla was always the tough one. Marjie was the one who needed protection. But maybe they both were tough; they were sisters, after all. And maybe now he was the one who needed protection.

"To tell you the truth," he said. "I'm not sure I can run, either."

"You'll do it if you have to, Nick."

He thought about it. "No," he said. "I don't want to do that. Even if we got by them we wouldn't know where to run to."

"The woods."

"They know the woods. We don't."

"We could still hide out there. We could split up if we had to."

"I don't like it," he said. "But I don't like this, either."

"They could burn us out pretty easy up here."

178

"They could burn us out downstairs, too."

"Yes, but there's only one way *out* of here!"

"That again."

"Yes, dammit! They could burn the house down and wait for us to come flying out the window one at a time. They could stand down there and watch us break our asses and then pick up the pieces and carry us home like toys for the kids. Down there, at least we can—"

Below them, Laura screamed. They broke for the stairs.

They heard the pounding simultaneously and it shot through them like bolts of lightning followed by unrelenting thunder. Nick felt the whole house quiver. The stairs seemed to tremble beneath him. His wounded leg forgotten, he was downstairs in an instant, pistol in his hand, with Marjie right behind him.

Outside, it seemed they were everywhere at once.

Someone was working on the back door with what was probably the axe from the woodshed. There were others at the bedroom windows. In front of him the front door seemed likely to burst open at any minute under the force of something large and powerful. Nick bet he knew who that one was. The latch held, but he wouldn't give a cent for it holding too much longer.

One of them was edging a crowbar or something through the peephole in the kitchen window. The poker, he thought. Dan's poker. He heard the sound of wood splintering behind him and saw the back door giving way under the axe. It would not be long now.

For an instant he searched around in confusion, trying to determine if there was any defense they could

make, if there was any way out of this except to retreat
back up the stairs to the attic. Again the front door
crashed and trembled under a terrific blow and something told him it would not stand another. He saw a
glint of steel through the deepening gash in the back
door and then all indecision vanished.

"Get Laura," he said, and ran for the stairs. "Hurry!"

He hit the landing on a run, bent low, and scurried to
the mattress. He dragged it swiftly beside the doorway
and left it there, careful to leave enough space so he'd
be able to close the door. Then he moved the dresser. It
was a two-man job to move that dresser but there was a
ferocious power in him now and no pain anywhere,
and all he could think was that he was damned if he
would let them kill him now. His muscles strained and
bunched together and the dresser's massive claw feet
screeched against the rough wooden floor. He set it in
the doorway with just enough room for entry. If the
women didn't make it in time he would push the fucking thing down on the sons of bitches and bust some
heads. He snatched the pistol off the floor and for the
first time noticed the scythe on the wall. He grabbed it
too, and then leaped to the stairway.

Marjie had Laura on her feet and moving through
the living room just as the kitchen door gave way behind them and crashed against the table, and the huge
bald man fell inside. The children scrambled in around
him. They saw her before the big man even got to his
knees. They shouted and started after her.

Marjie had the girl by one arm and her short-cropped hair and dragged her to the stairs, but it was too slow, *too slow,* and so she screamed at her, "*Move! Move you bitch!*" as she saw the children running toward them. But the girl would not move any faster and only stared around her, wide-eyed in horror. And then suddenly the children were there, blocking her path, and she remembered what the children had done to Dan and Nick and her dream of them pulling her down was unbearably vivid. The man was up off his knees and coming toward her too, arms reaching out, while the others poured in through the open door, holding knives and grinning, howling like animals and grinning, and she released Laura with a cry and plunged toward the stairs. *Die then,* you dumb-assed bitch, she thought, but don't let them get me. Please, God.

Her foot twisted under her and she fell against the stairs. Tiny sharp-nailed fingers curled around her ankle. She shook herself free as the gun exploded above her, and she saw the big man stagger and stare, clutching at the hand that Nick's lucky wild shot had blown clean away. Then Nick was pushing her past him into the attic.

The big man stumbled back through the doorway into the kitchen, his wound spraying the walls and molding with blood as the shattered wrist waved small dizzy circles above his head. At last he fell to his knees, groaning, and clutched at the kitchen table for support. His blood formed a pool there and drifted slowly toward its edges. The children swarmed up the stairs. From where she lay sprawled on the attic floor she heard Nick's empty pistol thump against the wall and realized he was still standing there in the doorway. *No!* she thought. *No! Get inside!* But she could not speak. She turned and saw him in the doorway with scythe in hand, saw him swing it once and then watched in horror as the spout of bright blood shot up high into the air and then down the stairwell, a child's head turning grotesquely, falling behind it.

She heard them howl in anger and surprise and saw the children stumble as the boy's body tumbled down the stairs. She heard Laura scream, a scream of the lost and damned. And then Nick was inside with her at last, the bloody scythe tossed to the floor, and he was throwing the bolt and shoving the mattress against the door, and she rose heavily to her feet to help him push the dresser into place and make them safe again.

The room seemed to close up tight around her. Outside they pounded on the door.

At the foot of the stairs Laura stood blinking at the object that had rolled down to stop at her feet. It seemed almost her mirror image—the open mouth, the wide eyes, the lips specked with blood and foam. She stared and sank into the dream that had protected her, which was punctuated by her own distant screams yet which was still unreal to her and never really threatening. The living room was unfamiliar now. She had never seen these stairs before and never these people who rushed to climb them, shouting and pushing when they reached the door. She was alone with a group of strangers engaged in some wild, inexplicable pursuit the object of which was unclear. She knew there was nothing behind the door. She did not know how she knew that, only that it was true. Nothing but some old magazines and papers and a dusty, empty attic.

So that their strange arterial flow through the house and up the stairs and into the attic could have no meaning except to disgorge them again, through the top of the house perhaps, through the tiny window, like water spilling onto the ground through a fire hose.

She laughed. It was like that game they'd played back in high school, Chinese Fire Drill. They would pull up to a red light and open the car doors and run around the car once or even twice if they could before the light changed back to green, and then they'd have to get back in the car through the same door they got out of and drive away. She saw these strange people in a never-ending spill through the front door into the kitchen and into the living room and then up the stairs to the attic, flowing around the house in a bright painted stream and back again like Little Black Sambo's tigers turning to butter—soon they would not be people at all but a fast-moving stream flowing in a perfect crimson circle through and around the house, while she stood just outside the circle, safe, and watched them with eyes wide because even though it was a dream it was also a miracle, funny but mostly just amazing that people could be shepherded into a stream of fluid and then be people not at all anymore.

She sat down next to her mirror image on the floor and reached carefully for the eyes, and as she pushed the eyelids gently down, her own eyelids fluttered and closed. Now she could picture herself seated at the bottom of the stairs, and although it was very dark she saw living shapes glide by.

The stream was moving more quietly now, and she wondered if it would be safe for her to step in. It was not nearly so exciting as it had been a moment ago when the stream was . . . well, *flooding,* as if they'd just had a rainstorm or a flash flood, but she thought it would feel very good to step in now, it would be cool and refreshing and not at all frightening as, she now admitted to herself, the more rapid flow had been. She would try.

She lowered her left hand into the stream. Would the living things—they were fishes, weren't they?—would the living things bother her? She thought not. She slid inside. She was surprised at how warm it was, not cool at all, and how good the waters tasted on her dry, parched lips. She took a deep breath and opened her eyes.

The child's head lay face upward in her lap.

She knew it was the child now and not the mirror because the mirror's eyes would have been open like her own. She stared at it hard to make sure. She began to cry. The stream was gone. There was only howling pandemonium on the stairs and the salty taste the stream had left in her mouth. She cradled the head to her breast and did not feel the steady drool of dark blood that spread over her shirt and down across her belly like a purulent sore.

Between her and the open front door there stood

only two small ragged girls, staring down at her. Yet it did not occur to her to run, to leave the house. There really was no need. She closed her eyes again as the little girls advanced on her and tried to count the fishes.

On the stairway the two men broke through the thinly paneled door to the attic. They could hear moaning from below as the women bound the big man's wrist to staunch the flow of blood. The children pressed close to them on the narrow staircase, anxious to get inside. The thin man put his arm through the hole in the door and slipped the bolt. He turned the knob and pushed. The door would not budge. He glanced angrily at his brother. They pushed the children aside and moved a few steps down the staircase and then hurled themselves forward against the door, the greater bulk of the man in red nearest the doorknob. They smiled to see it give an inch or two. They stepped back to try again.

Inside the attic Nick swore and pushed hard against the dresser. It angered him to know that they'd delayed too long, so that there had been no time to go for the hammer and nails in order to secure the door. His fault. He heard them break through the panel. Even with all his own weight and Marjie's against the dresser they would not be able to hold them back for more than a few minutes. They'd have to jump.

He wondered if all of them were in the house now. What if they were waiting down below? Below the window? He felt the dresser move back toward them as the men slammed against the door. "It's no good," he said.

She nodded. He was so close to her he could smell her sweat and feel her breath on his cheek. He glanced over to the window. "You first," he said.

She looked at him. She was flushed and frightened.

"How do I . . . ?"

"The roof is directly over your head. There's about a foot of overhang. Reach up until you've got it and then pull your legs out, nice and slow, and let yourself fall straight down. Try it any other way and you'll break your neck. Don't let go until you've stopped swinging, until your legs are still and you're just hanging there clear of the house. Try to keep your knees bent a little to break the fall."

He saw the look of hopelessness pass over her face. There was one other possibility but there was no point mentioning it to her. She was simply not strong enough. But it did give Nick an option if it turned out he needed one.

"Marjie," he said. "Do it. Don't be afraid. You can make it. I swear you can. I think we've got them all inside. When you get out, head for the woods and watch for me. Stay low. Then get to me if you can; if you can't, if anything happens to me, just run like hell. Just remember to keep your knees bent while you fall. No broken legs, please." He saw her smile slightly. That was better.

"Now hurry," he said. She stood away from the dresser, and Nick felt the sharp impact as outside they rammed the door again.

"One more thing," he said. She turned and he saw that she was close to tears. As it dawned on him what he was going to say to her, so was he. "You're all that's left now," he said, "and I love the hell out of you. Always have. You and Carla together. *Be safe,* Marjie." He felt her lips brush his own and then she was at the window.

He watched her edge her head and then her right arm out the window and then the left arm and shoulder, then reach up for the roof. He saw the thin arms strain as she pulled herself outward inch by inch, resting first on her buttocks, then her thighs and then, agonizingly, on her calves—until her knees cleared the top of the window and finally she had one foot on the windowsill and then the other. She stood poised there a moment and he saw her ease her weight down over the ball of her foot to her toes, scraping them slowly and carefully along the sill and then down the side of the house. He essayed a grim smile. She was handling this sensibly and cool-headedly. She was a damn fine smart woman. If any of them deserved to get out of this alive, she did.

He saw her swing free of the window and heard her gasp with the sheer effort of hanging on. In a moment her body was steady. Then suddenly she was gone.

For Marjie the fall seemed to last forever. She tried to breathe but it was impossible—it was as if she'd forgotten how. Her lungs seemed to want to expel air even though she'd commanded them to draw it in. She knew she was not falling right, that her balance was slightly off somehow. Images slammed home through her mind with a physical force. *Falling on her back; the sickening snap. Falling face down, arms ludicrously, uselessly splayed in front of her. Falling headfirst onto macadam she knew was not there, bleeding in a crumpled heap.*

The house seemed to move closer and closer to her, as if it were the old house falling and not she, or as if it toppled along with her and would fall directly over her where she landed, crushing her. She saw those grubby little children standing over her broken, crippled body.

Were her knees bent as Nick had said they should be? It was hard to tell. She felt that any voluntary movement on her part now would destroy her precarious balance and send her tumbling head over heels to the ground. She had bent her legs as she let go of the roof: she knew that. She would have to trust to luck that they'd stayed that way. In her imagination she saw Nick following her down, falling into a slippery pile of gore that had once been her body. All this she saw in less than a second before she hit the ground.

Then there was a jarring in her ankles and a sudden sharp pain in both feet and her knees slammed hard against her chin, drawing blood from somewhere inside her mouth. At the same time her buttocks came down with shuddering force, her lungs yielded their contents in an audible rush, leaving her gasping for breath, and small dancing lights in a wall of solid darkness fell like a sudden screen before her eyes. She had the beginnings of a tremendous headache. But she was down. She was alive and knew she was unbroken. She felt a moment of wild elation.

Then just as her vision cleared, she sensed the children around her.

Nick had seen them seconds earlier, and he was nearly on the roof by now. The roof was his option. The hard part had been getting out the window. For a terrible instant it had seemed that his right shoulder would never fit through. He brought his elbow down across his stomach and forced the shoulder downward and in as far as possible, and then found the widest angle to the window and slipped the shoulder through. His wounded leg was throbbing miserably. Ignoring it, he reached up for the shingle roof and heaved himself up and out until he was standing on the windowsill. Then he hauled himself up to the roof—thanking God for the chinning bars at the West Side Y. As it was, he'd barely made it. Six months ago he wouldn't have had a prayer. Beneath him he heard them break through the door and push over the dresser. He flattened himself against the roof and peered over the side. Marjie seemed unhurt. She was standing, turning, looking for a way out. Nick could see there was none. There were children all around her, brandishing sticks and knives. He felt a sudden sickness spread throughout his belly. He saw one of the men lean out the window, look down, and then pull back again. He heard them run across the room to the stairs.

Soon they appeared below with the other children and the big man who was without a left hand now, thanks to him, and the two remaining women, leading Laura between them. It surprised him to see Laura still alive. So maybe there was a chance, he thought. Maybe they wouldn't kill them. Maybe he could do something.

He saw Marjie's eyes go to the window and, risking discovery, he waved at her. He needed her to know he was there and alive, that if possible he would help her. He saw her nod once to him and then glance down again. If she kept her head, he might be able to get her away from them somehow. He slid back a few inches into the darkness and waited.

It was obvious that they thought that he'd escaped them. There was a lot of unintelligible shouting going on at first and then the two men—the two *whole* men, he thought with satisfaction—edged slowly into the scrub. He could hear them running and then stopping to listen, running again, fanning outward through the brush. He was damn glad he was not out there. They were in their element out there in the woods.

The others waited. In a while one of the men—the thin one with the scruffy beard—returned alone. He guessed they were leaving the other man behind to search for him. Laura had fallen to her knees in some kind of stupor, and he saw the man lift her roughly to her feet and turn her away from him, then push both girls in the direction of the fire on the hill. They've had enough for one night, he thought. They're going home. That gives us time.

He knew it depended on him now. He felt his responsibility like a physical weight. Yet for a moment he could think of nothing to do. Without the cars or the phone they were still completely isolated. By the time he found another house, Marjie and Laura might be dead. How much time, he thought, before they killed them? How much have I got?

No answers came to him. He felt himself give way to self-pity and despair. They had attacked and nearly broken him, just as by now they'd attacked every woman he'd ever loved. The one he'd loved the best of all lay dead out there, and she had suffered horribly before she died. He could not let that happen to Marjie. He remembered with a kind of amazement his crazy stand on the attic stairs, and all at once he knew what he would do. He pushed his glasses up over the bridge of his nose and, motionless, he waited.

His senses felt keen and alert. He barely turned to watch them as they moved past the fire. Only enough to allow his eyes to trace their route over the hill and determine in what direction they were going. He heard Marjie cry out as she passed the charred corpse of her sister. Then there was silence.

When they were almost out of sight he lowered himself slowly over the shingles to the side of the house opposite them, and when he reached the aluminum gutter, dropped silently to the ground, trying to dismiss as best he could the shock of pain that coursed through his leg muscles and sent a quick spasm sliding through his cheek. He worked his way carefully to the front of the house, watching for the man in red, and saw that at least for now, he was alone. He went inside.

Glancing over heaps of wreckage his eyes scanned the floor for the pistol, praying that they'd left it behind. The pistol meant everything now. He found it in the living room, lying beside the attic steps, and remembered being angry and thinking how useless the pistol was and tossing it at one of the women, cursing himself for dumping the cartridges into the trunk. But that was the good thing about machines—you could always get them working again.

He pulled open the chamber and tried the trigger. It seemed fine, unharmed by the fall. He put it into his belt and moved silently into the kitchen. As gently as possible, so as to make no sound, he opened each of the drawers, looking for a flashlight. He found one and tried it. On the dim side but it would do. He left the drawers open and tiptoed to the door. He looked around. The way was clear.

While he walked to the car he fished the keys out of his pocket and found the one for the trunk. He opened it quickly and switched on the flashlight, holding the beam close to the base of the compartment so there would be no spill. He gathered up every cartridge he could find and then killed the beam and moved back against the house, into the shadows. He loaded the pistol and put all the spare cartridges into one pocket and the keys into the other.

He decided to take the long route around the fire, keeping in the shadows. He'd noticed this afternoon that there was a trail back there that led down to the stream, and he thought they would probably keep to that, at least for a little while. And they'd be moving relatively slowly, with Laura half-comatose, holding them back. Thanks, Laura, he thought.

By his reckoning there were seven kids left and two of the women and the three men, one of the men somewhere behind him in the woods and another badly hurt—minus a good left hand and a couple quarts of blood from the look of the living room. He could take out the two men and the women and two of the kids if he was lucky and fast enough and made every shot pay, and as long as the third didn't come climbing up his asshole he just might pull it off.

For a moment he wished he'd brought the poker or the axe in the woodshed. But the axe is no longer in the woodshed, he thought. They have it now. They've got it all—all but this, he thought, his hand on the pistol. Those last five kids were still going to be a problem, no question about it. But if he was good and fast he could blow hell out of every last one of them. And that was what he intended to do.

The first one dead would be for Carla. He pulled the pistol out of his belt and moved off into the woods, nearly invisible, wrapped in the cool cerements of darkness.

3:30 A.M.

State Trooper Dale Willis got out of his car, propped his big feet in front of him, and leaned against the door. He lit a smoke. He just did not feel comfortable sitting in the car, no way. Whatever had gone on here was finished—or that was how it looked, anyway—and Peters was on his way over with Sam Shearing. But Jesus! The place was a sight, and it had not been over long. He felt better standing outside. You never knew.

That thing back there on the fire. It was hard to believe it was even human. He knew damn well it was, but that didn't make it any easier to accept. Some things were just beyond acceptance. Death was like that, especially this kind of death. *Death and taxes,* he thought. He remembered a teacher back in grade school who used to give them that inevitable-as-death-and-taxes routine. What they didn't know back in grade school was enough to make you shit turquoise.

One thing for sure, they didn't know about this. He glanced over at the fire.

Come on baby light my fire.

You sick bastard.

It had been the smoke from the smoldering fire that first brought him around. Then he'd seen the auto lights burning and the house all lit up like a Christmas tree. Then he saw the rest of it. He'd missed the action by no more than half an hour. Some action, he thought. Whoever was responsible—well, he didn't want to meet those guys stretched out in an automobile, that was for sure.

Willis had seen corpses before—the highway was full of them. Burned, crushed. Hell, he'd even seen one guy with the dead limb of a tree poked right through his windshield and into the center of his forehead. But a survey of this place was like a little stroll through hell. That charred mess by the fire. Some guy with his intestines spilled out all over the walkway. Another guy lying in bed with his throat slit, starkos. Somebody's goddamn fist lying in a corner.

And then the kids. One of them with his head about fifteen feet from his body. Another one, outside, with no head left at all. That one looked like a heavy-caliber bullet. So did the woman, if you could call that thing that stunk like last week's empty milk carton a woman. Willis shook his head. What you had here was a fucking battlefield next to a bunker. Somebody around here was as crazy as a whore in the Vatican.

He'd known the old Parks place since he was a kid.

OFF SEASON

Old Man Parks would have slipped a disk if somebody'd told him that something like this had happened
even in the city, in New York or someplace, much less
here on his own land. Good for him he was safely
tucked under ground ten years now. He had all the pure
moral strength in the world, old Parks did, and he'd
brought up Joe and Hanna pretty much the same way
he'd been raised by his father before him. You didn't
cuss, you didn't drink, and you didn't whack the wife.

Of course Hanna'd been slapped around some by that
character Bailey she'd married, but as far as anybody
knew she'd never slapped back. The old man would have
killed her if she had. And then Hanna and Phil Bailey had
a couple of kids, who lived in Portland and never even
used the place nowadays, only rented it out when they
could, and Willis couldn't help but feel that somehow
that had led to this, to death and slaughter in the drive-
way. The new age. In three generations you could slip the
tether of the past with no more trouble than it took to
drink a Pepsi. Some folks could, anyway. Those who had
the money. He tossed the cigarette away and lit another.

He saw the headlights rake the trees and heard Peters' heavy Chrysler rumbling over the old dirt road.
The boss is gonna have himself a time over this one, he
thought. Better get to looking busy. He walked to the
open trunk of the Dodge and threw his flashlight beam
inside. Look but don't touch, he told himself. You lay a
finger on anything here, and Peters will see you get
your head shaved for it.

When Peters' car pulled into the drive, Willis looked

up and clicked off the flashlight and walked to the car. Sam Shearing was looking real tired in the driver's seat. Funny how Peters always seemed to have so much energy. He was strictly heart-attack city with all that weight on him and had a mild coronary to his credit already—everybody knew that—but the old bastard never let up. Well, good for him. He smiled.

"Rough night, George," he said. "*Real* rough. You gotta *see* this place!"

Peters got out of the car. "What we got here, Dale?" he said. Willis had a closer look at him. He looks okay, he thought, he really does. And you can bet they got him out of bed on this one.

"Hell, the place is lousy with bodies," he said.

"What kind of bodies?"

"You name it, George, we got 'em. They had a helluva weenie roast out back there. Not what you'd want to see at the ball park, either."

"Kids?"

"Yeah, I think we found some of those kids you been looking for. Sure do."

They walked to the house, Willis leading at a brisk pace. Peters stood in front of the black Dodge and looked around. They had kids, all right. One with his head split open, one with his head—or was it *her* head?—pretty near gone. "Jesus," he said.

"There's more inside," said Willis.

Peters turned to Shearing, who looked wide awake now but not much the better for it. "Sam," he said, "I want you to get me a couple more cars out here. And get me the coroner, too. Anybody left alive in there,

Willis?" The question was pro forma; he already knew the answer to that one.

"Not a soul. You still might want the ambulance, though."

"Why's that?"

"There's somebody walking 'round minus a hand. Don't know where the fellow is but the hand's on the floor. Big damn ugly thing, too."

"Okay. Get the ambulance too, Sam. And tell 'em back at the station to find out who rents this place and who they rented it to. How many occupants. Names. Descriptions. And get me a tracer on these license plate numbers here. This one's a rental. Find out who rented it and when. And I want all this stuff *yesterday*, understand?"

"You got it," Shearing said.

"Let's have a look," said Peters. He and Willis stepped inside.

Twenty minutes later they were through. Peters had seen quite enough of the house by then so Willis led him up the hill to the smoldering fire.

As far as Peters was concerned, it was worse looking at the thing on the spit than at all the others put together. He had never had much stomach for burn wounds, and this was the worst he'd ever seen. This was not burn wounds, this—as Willis said—was barbecue. There were bones and half-eaten bits of flesh scattered all around the front of the house, and now he was looking at where it all had come from. The roast. There was no way to tell if it was a man or a woman. It was enough to know it was human. His most outlandish hunch about Donner's story and Mrs. Weinstein's story was confirmed and then some. At the time, he'd thought his imagination was getting a bit frisky, that he was seeing ghosts and monsters where there were only idiots and crazies, routine human evil. But here it was, grisly beyond belief. And now he wondered if he hadn't underestimated them.

He knew two things now that he hadn't known twenty-four hours ago. One made him sick, the other made him scared. The first was that they killed and ate their victims. The second was that they had menfolk.

The hand on the floor belonged to a male Caucasian of darned-near enormous proportions. It was filthy and it was the hand of a workingman, scarred on the back and callused on the front. It did not belong to any of the discovered victims. Both the male with his throat slit on the bed and the man out front had smooth, tender hands. City hands. This one was used to wood and dirt and stones. Just like the woman's had been. And God help him, just like the kids'.

Peters watched Willis pour some tap water over the last few burning embers. They left the human carcass hanging from the spit exactly as they'd found it, for the photographer. Tonight, thought Peters, the photographer was going to be a busy man.

"How far to the ocean from here, Willis?" he asked.

"Oh, 'bout two miles. As I recall, there's a path or two leads you right down there. You follow this one here to the brook and then there's another a couple yards downstream, takes you right to the shoreline. Used to come down here to bait our hooks when we

was kids, then walk over and do some surf fishin'.
Never got much, though."

"Any caves or anything down that way?"

"I don't really remember, George. Might be."

From where he stood at the top of the hill, Peters
saw headlights in the distance. It had taken them long
enough to get here. He saw Shearing approaching on
the run. Shearing was always running someplace,
thought Peters. 'Course, part of that was Peters' fault.
But it keeps a man trim, all that running. He envied
Shearing his youth and strength.

"I think I've got what we need," said Shearing.

"What's that?"

"The station says the house was rented through
King Realty. We woke up Mrs. King and she says that
her client was a Miss Carla Spencer, New York City.
No other clients involved. No males. But Mrs. King
says she knows Miss Spencer has a sister and that she
mentioned something about her coming up to visit
sometime. She couldn't say when she was expected."

"Damn," said Peters. "I was afraid of that."

"Of what?" asked Shearing.

"New York plates on one car, local rental on the
other. Three victims, counting this one here. Two of
the victims males. This one possibly male, possibly female. Suppose we say it's female. What's that suggest
to you boys?"

"Suggests another woman," said Shearing. He consulted his notes. "Rental on the Pinto is to Miss Carla
Spencer, New York City. That means the black Dodge
was company. Probably the sister, with two male

friends. That means there's at least one more woman around here someplace. Maybe Carla Spencer, maybe the sister."

"So we've got another potential victim out there," said Willis. "Somebody they took along for the ride. *Hot* damn."

"That's right," said Peters. "At least one. For all we know there could be half a dozen of them. As soon as the coroner and backup make it up the hill, let's go through the house for sets of identification. That should give us some idea."

He watched a pair of headlights swing around a turn. That would be them. He frowned and let loose a sigh. It was a heavy man's sigh, half wheeze. "Problem is," he said, "we still don't know how many of these sons of bitches are out there, do we? I know I gotta go after 'em, but I didn't know whether I'm after ducks or dynamite, so to speak." He thought for a moment, watching the headlights draw closer. "So I got a suggestion to make," he said. "See how it sits with you. I suggest we take us an army in there. I suggest we get every car up here we can lay our hands on."

"That's damned good," said Willis, grinning. "That sounds just fine to me."

Shearing nodded. "I agree."

The relief in the air was nearly palpable. Both these guys were scared. Well, Peters had seen the bodies. So was he. Only now he had to give them another scare.

"There's something else that you are not gonna like, though," he said.

"What's that?" said Willis.

"I have to play it rough on this. We got a trail here that's gonna cool down fast. So I'm giving you both exactly ten minutes to get those cars up here. And if they're *not* here in ten minutes—say they're here in eleven—neither one of you boys is gonna be around to greet 'em. Because I'm going to have to sit here by the car and wait for 'em and the two of you will have to start out after these folks all by yourselves. We got no time to waste."

"*Jesus,* George," said Shearing.

"Move," said Peters. He had to teach that boy not to whine. Very important in a policemen. "Move and kick ass if you have to, but get them up here. Fast." He wished briefly but passionately for a drink, and not a beer, either. He glanced at the thing on the spit.

"Before these folks decide on breakfast."

4:08 A.M.

There was no doubt that the last man would be found.
Their firstborn—the man in red—was a good hunter.
All the same, the cave was in a state of turmoil unusual
even for them. None of them could remember when a
hunt had failed, and now within three nights two had
failed one after the other. In the minds of all except the
very youngest was the dim fear of discovery, of disaster. Yet mingling with and overwhelming this fear was
the sheer excitement of having killed and hunted. Eyes
that were flat and colorless sparkled in the light from
the fire. Mouths that never smiled, smiled now, and not
one among them gave any real thought to their losses.

Near the fire the pregnant woman and a girl-child
nursed the big man's arm, binding the wrist tight a few
inches below the elbow and wrapping it in skin. The
man was weak from loss of blood, his great bulk tossing and feverish in a dazed half-sleep. A few feet away
a small boy watched them for a few moments, then
turned to piss against the side of the cave.

All the children had cuts and bruises and some had bad burns from the boiling oil and water. But they gave them no attention. The children were used to pain.

Their legs and arms were already covered with older scabs and sores; a few more meant nothing to them. Much more annoying were the lice and other insects that infested their hair and clothes, but even these were forgotten now. Back near the cage a boy and girl chased a rat into the dark second room with long birch sticks. The pregnant girl walked past them carrying a pail of water. She set it down in front of the fire, where the fat woman in the plain cotton shift crouched low, licking her lips like a coiled snake. The woman was hungry again. She would make soup. She waited for the girl to return with more water and wished she would hurry.

When the girl did return, the woman rose heavily and stretched and padded off to find the hands and feet of the kill they had butchered that afternoon—of the girl they had found with the boy in the cage—and then had wrapped in hide and left in a pile against the cool rear wall of the cave. She gathered them up eagerly along with a jar of wheat grains and on a whim chose a long rib and the shaved, split, eyeless head as well. She slung the pot over the fire and emptied a pail of water into the pot, and then another. She threw in half a jar of wheat grains. Then she added the meats.

She watched with pleasure as the water began to boil. They had hunted every animal but there was no flesh like man's, she thought. It was sweet and more subtle than game. Delicate streaks of fat ran through even the leanest meat. If you placed a piece of venison or bear in a pot to boil, it would lie at the bottom like a stone. But man's flesh had life. It would bounce and swirl inside the pot. The other was just meat, just a meal. Her toothless gums worked rapidly from side to side and her fat stomach rumbled in anticipation.

The pregnant girl wandered back to the cage. Three of the children were amusing themselves by poking sticks through the open spaces in the bottom of the cage at the bare feet of the two new captive women. The eldest boy, a year younger than the girl, stood beside the cage and watched them closely. The girl smiled at him but he did not return the smile.

The children had cut the right foot of the blonde woman. There was blood on the bottom of the cage. But watching did not interest her much. She scowled at the children and chased them away. The big boy laughed beside her.

The girl looked at him with a sudden interest and then reached up quickly and thrust both hands into the cage. Startled, Laura tried to pull away but the girl was much too fast for her. With one hand she gripped her ankle and squeezed while she ran the other hand roughly over the bleeding sole of her foot. Then just as suddenly she let go. She looked at the boy again and smiled, holding out her hand palm upward so he could see the rich smear of blood. He moved closer.

She lifted the skin she wore over her head and dropped it to the ground, then wiped the blood over her naked breasts and belly. The boy's eyes went wide. He reached for her but she laughed and stepped away. He followed her. He pushed her to the wall and pressed himself hard against her, heedless of the unborn infant inside her. He reached down to free his penis from the stained white pants, and while he was doing so, the girl moved her left hand with a pickpocket's delicacy to the bulge in his back pocket, where she knew he kept the knife.

When she saw his pants fall about his ankles, she laughed and pressed closer to the boy, flipped open the knife behind his back and then stabbed him lightly in the buttocks. He jumped away and howled. She laughed again, dropped the knife, and went to him. She reached both hands around him and rubbed the slowly bleeding wound until her hands were slick with blood. Then she stepped back and held her hands up to him to show him what she'd done. The boy's face lost its angry, confused expression and he smiled. His penis was hard again as she reached down for it and covered it with blood. Then she lay down on the floor of the cave. She spread her legs for him and waited.

They moved together quickly and almost silently, without expression. Behind her two of the children watched them, and, although they were much too small, threw off their clothes and imitated their positions on the floor and the noises they made and the odd, jerky way they had of moving their hips. In another part of the cave, a little boy squatted to defecate. The boy and girl who were chasing the rat caught it crouching under a pile of clothing and stomped it quickly to death.

OFF SEASON

* * *

Marjie watched it all; nothing they did escaped her notice. What she saw frightened and sickened her, but she would need to understand them if she were to have any hope of getting free; she knew that. It was like watching another species entirely, a pack of wild animals.

Behind her, in the second cave, she could see the piles of implements and bones, and the pale yellowing skins. She recognized the bones and skins as human. At the entrance to the room a long row of human skulls gleamed in the half-light, mounted on poles thrust from neck to cranium. One of the skulls was new and still moist. On the ground beside them lay a great many more skulls, these sawn off just below the eye sockets and fastened with rawhide for use as drinking cups. She wondered just how many they had killed.

She noticed their ornaments—the beads and colored stones for the women, the leather fringes. Knotted into the fringes was what might have been human hair. One of the girl children wore a necklace. *Finger bones,* Marjie thought.

She watched the thin man eyeing the couple rutting on the floor of the cave. Around his neck was a silver crucifix. It was the only ornamentation she saw on him. The women wore gull feathers and porcupine quills in their hair. Both men and boys were painted with coal dust, vermilion, ochre, ashes, and berry juice thickened with fat.

They wore the smell of fat and decay like a second skin. The odor was everywhere, in their browse beds and in the stolen clothing, in the very walls of the cave itself.

She had smelled something like it once before. It was on a car trip to Florida she and Carla had taken with their parents when they were teenagers. They had been visiting friends for the day and were on their way back to the motel, driving a narrow two-lane blacktop that skirted the Everglades. It was Carla who spotted the vultures up ahead on the side of the road, and Carla who wanted to stop. Her parents made a fuss and refused at first, but even then Carla was used to getting what she wanted. The vultures were feeding on the carcass of a dog. Marjie surprised everybody by deciding to get out of the car with her. Her parents had made them promise not to get too close—though they couldn't have walked far from the car if they'd wanted to.

Even yards away, the stink was immense and awful, a salty unspeakable tang in the air that spoke of years and years of dried and matted blood, of old rotten meat; the dark breath of corruption. Somehow she'd known instinctively that it was the birds and not their prey who bore this horrible, foul odor, and that they bore it for a lifetime. And it was the stench and not those tiny alien eyes—terrible enough in themselves—which drove them back inside the air-conditioned automobile. It was the unmistakable smell of the carrion-eater, the very reek of death.

And now, inside the cage suspended above the floor of the cave, she smelled it again. From where she sat she could see the stewpot, a set of disembodied fingers turning slowly. She would not call these people human, she refused to think of them that way. They were what they smelled like: vultures. They intended to make a grisly meal of her. Just as they'd made of Carla. Just as they planned to do with this strange, sad boy sprawled on the bottom of the cage.

Marjie had touched him, then shook him, and gotten no response whatsoever. He seemed worse off than Laura. The children had not even bothered trying to rouse him with their sticks. She wondered how long the boy had been here, what miserable sights had been presented to those blankly staring green-blue eyes. Had he watched them butcher others? She didn't doubt that he had. There would be no help from him or from Laura. Only Nick. Only Nick waving from the rooftop, safe, Nick who would follow her. If he could.

That man in the woods, she thought. The man in red. Nick might not make it. He might not live to follow her. She had to consider that. What then? *Please,* she thought, let him follow. Her fingers clutched the bars of the cage. Her knuckles went white. The thin man was staring at her from where he sat against the wall. The couple on the floor had finished with one another. How long, she wondered, before they start on us. How long do I have, how much time?

Her answer came swiftly.

4:12 A.M.

Nick lay on his stomach behind the sand dune and waited. He heard the roar of rushing water behind him as the tide spilled through the channel. He parted the tall grass with the barrel of the .44. Amid the shrubs and grass and hard-hack, he was only a shadow. The sand made his chest and leg wounds itch, though the anger he felt was not for the wounds but for himself. He had lost them.

He'd expected some sort of house, he guessed, not this long empty stretch of sand and rock. There was only one thing to do now, and that was to wait here where the path through the woods led onto the beach and hope that the man behind him was not too long in giving up his search. If the man passed by, Nick would follow him, and a lot more closely this time. He just hoped the only access route was the one he'd come by. He cursed himself for thinking it would be so much easier to find them than it was, for coming down off the roof so slowly. His little excess of caution may have already cost them their lives.

He tried to shake off the sense of bitterness and frustration, the anxiety that unnerved him. It was calm he needed now, calm and alertness. Anxiety would only screw him up and fog his senses. It was just possible that he'd hear them or see a light somewhere if he was calm and easy enough, and then he wouldn't have to wait for the man at all. He didn't like the waiting. He was primed for another fight. *Shithead,* he thought, you should never have let them out of your sight. Never. And his fears for them rushed him all at once.

But for now he'd have to wait, and it seemed to him that there was probably a better way to do it. He turned over slowly and lay quietly on his back, astonished at the huge bowl of stars that appeared before him. It was a beautiful night and he'd never noticed. The depth and clarity of a night sky like this had never failed to touch him, and even now for a moment, on the worst night of his life, a little of the serene indifference and loss of will that always accompanied his gazing at such a sky sounded in him briefly, and then disappeared.

Great night for terror, he thought, and moved his head back a few inches so he could see the path again. He felt a little better now. His heartbeat and respiration felt regular and even. And though he saw the path upside down now, his field of vision was much greater than before—as wide as possible, actually. He'd only to adjust his glasses. That was pretty good. By moving his head a few inches he could keep an eye on the path and those areas to both right and left of it; and then by moving again slightly he could look down over his body right to the shoreline, making it impossible for anyone to approach him from behind. Much better, he thought. I'm actually doing this right. He wondered if they taught this position in the army. Dan would have known. But Dan was gone.

He parted the grass with his gun again so he'd have an unobstructed view of the path, found himself a comfortable position, and relaxed as best he could. No telling how long this will take, he thought. The air was damp, chilly, filled with a tight salt spray. If the man was too long in coming, he was going to have one hell of a stiff neck. But it was a lot better than getting his throat cut from behind. These guys were pretty good in the dark. He wondered how long they hung around the house, checking the place out before making their move. He'd bet it was a while, and of course nobody'd heard or seen a thing. The dark would be this man's natural ally. Like most predators. He remembered Jim's naked body on the couch, the shards of glass glittering along his chest.

He glanced down past his feet in front of him again. His eyes flashed. Suddenly he felt as if he'd been stuck by a cattle prod. His body recoiled and threw him back six inches in the grass. There the man was, framed against the shoreline and the sea, a big dark silhouette in the moonlight, moving slowly past him only two or three yards away. Nick felt damned lucky.

He'd been stupid again. There was a second path through the woods—of course there was. They lived somewhere around here, didn't they? They were

215

killers. If there hadn't been a second route they'd have made one. They were not about to get trapped into a single line of retreat. He was one very lucky sonofabitch. *I'd have missed him,* he thought. On my belly I'd have missed him completely. Turning over was absolutely inspired. *Even luckier that he missed me.*

He drew the gun slowly down beside him, relying no further on chance. At any moment he half expected to see the man bolt in his direction, knife flashing. All at once he was miserably cold. The damp sea air seemed to creep up his spine and over his thighs. He felt his penis retracting, his skin tighten. And then a moment later the man was only a tall figure on the beach, walking the hard wet sand at the tideline, all the threat out of him; and Nick rose up into a crouch and scrambled through the grass and shrubs to the high ground at the base of the cliff and, invisible in the darkness, followed him.

4:15 A.M.

He keeps it in his pants, thought Marjie, *right next to his cock. How fucking sick.* She heard the soft snap as the blade of the knife slid into place and saw the long broad glint of steel. He walked over to the cage, looking up at them, grinning stupidly. I knew it, she thought. You had only to see the way he'd been watching the couple fucking on the floor. The couple were finished now. They sat together beside the cage, picking one another over for lice, squashing them with their fingers.

The boy lay to the left of her, his legs pulled up tight to his chest, his long dark hair hiding his face. Marjie could not even tell if he was awake. Laura saw the man approach them and moved closer to her side. Marjie slipped her arm around Laura's waist, again a little surprised to find how strong and firm the flesh was, at the tightness of the skin over her rib cage. Nordic, she thought. Big-boned. Now there was a bad joke for you.

She watched the thin man wind the rope off the big metal cleat and then begin to lower it hand over hand, the knife held pirate fashion between his teeth. She was so struck by the incongruity of the weapon that she had to stifle a laugh that she knew was mostly hysteria. A boy-scout knife. It should be flint, she thought, or stone—not polished steel. The man had long, thin fingers. He stunk like a Bowery drunk. She felt her stomach turn in disgust.

He lowered the cage and she realized how strong the lean wiry body was. She noticed the tendons in his arms and neck. Laura was trembling now. The cage came to rest on the cave floor and the boy stirred a little. Marjie had never seen catatonia but she imagined that if this was not it, it was very close. The boy seemed to have reached a place where he had no nerves left at all. He was lucky in a way. She would envy him, she thought, just as soon as she was convinced that there was no hope anymore. If it came to that. She was not convinced quite yet. Not quite.

The man left them a moment and went to the fire, and she saw that the others, most of whom had settled down and seemed, from above, to be sleeping, were in fact wide awake and watching him intently. Did they never sleep? It was nearly morning, damn them. Only the big man by the fire had his eyes closed. There would be no hope of escape, of getting beyond him somehow and out of the cave, if they were still awake. She knew he'd open the cage door soon now. It was pretty obvious what he was after.

He returned from the fire with a torch in hand. He paused a moment, staring at them openmouthed and slack-jawed and empty-eyed, and then thrust the torch inside the cage, giggling like a little girl as they jumped away. He wiped his lips with the back of the hand that held the knife, and his eyes darted back and forth from one woman to the other. He did not even glance at the boy. I was right, then, thought Marjie. He's picking himself a whore for the night. A whore or a victim. Or both.

She fixed her eyes on his with a pure effort of will and glared at him, trying to tough it out. I bet I'm pretty convincing, she thought. The contempt was there in gross. She thought that in over thirty years, she'd never seen anybody so worthy of it. The tiny pig eyes, the loose wet lips that never seemed to close, the weak chin, the thick dark cover of grime and the stink of him. A jellyfish, she thought. A roach.

She knew she'd worked herself up to looking hard and ugly now. In fact she was counting on it. Once, long ago, the same expression she knew she wore now had startled her in a mirror. It was the night she threw Gordon out for good. Is that me? she'd thought. I look like a bitter old hag. I look like I hate the world. And she did. Now she looked like that and with a much better reason. She thought of Carla and felt a surge of rage. She used the rage, keeping it under control, pouring it into her face and body. If that look in his eyes was only murder, then trying to face him down like this was an awful miscalculation. But she did not think it was murder. She thought it was cunt. Well, fuck him, she thought. I'm sorry, Laura, but here we go again. If it's me or you, I'm damned if it's me.

He put down the torch and reached into his pocket.

She heard the rattle of metal. Then the keys were in his hands. He fumbled at them like a nervous adolescent. He glanced down at both women again, and Marjie felt a sudden chill at knowing that he'd chosen between them. His eyes gave away everything. Even though he'd chosen as she thought he would, she felt no relief. Instead it filled her with remorse and horror. Oh my God, Laura, she thought, are you in for it. Are you in for it now. The key turned in the lock. And Marjie found herself wishing for a forgiveness she knew she'd never find. The fear of dying, she thought, makes you very unfair.

He threw the door open and reached inside. He tittered as his fingers closed over Laura's wrist. He jerked the girl toward him, out of the cage and into his arms, and it was as if she'd come suddenly to life. Her eyes went wild and seemed to fix for a moment on the blade he held between his teeth. Her head wrenched backward and she screamed. "*Shut up!*" he said, slushing his words over the knife, and slapped her. The slap was effective. It stopped the scream. And for a few seconds they simply stared at each other, the man grinning at her and holding her tightly with both arms around her waist while Laura's eyes seemed to grow wider and wider, focused entirely on the knife and the evil, smirking mouth.

I have to watch, thought Marjie. Tonight, tomorrow, it could be me. I need to know what he does to her. And maybe that will stop him from doing the same to me, from killing me. She realized that for the past few seconds she had not even dared to breathe. The man and woman now stood before her as if suspended in time, and somehow she joined them in a strange deep empathy, deeper than any she'd ever known before. Like Laura, she barely moved. She could almost feel his arms around her, her hands against his chest, could almost smell the foulness of his breath. Then as quickly as it had come, the feeling was gone and she felt released from them. Something had warned her away. Something told her that Laura was as good as dead.

For Laura, those few moments brought back a measure of self-consciousness she had not known since she watched the grim warfare on the attic stairs. It was the touch of him that shocked her, the force of their contact, and she knew him for the enemy now—not just a cruel phantom presence who frightened her with fire but a flesh-and-blood man who had murdered Jim and Dan and Carla. In a few seconds everything that she had seen throughout the night but had remained unwilling to accept washed over her all at once, in all its alien horror.

She saw Carla's body blackened by fire, the children attacking Nick (was Nick alive?), and the woman's teeth in Dan's neck as he fell backward through the doorway in a blast of gunfire. She heard gunfire again and saw a hand fall to the floor and then another object, a head, a child's head, which she had held in her lap and . . .

Suddenly it was not a nameless, sightless fear that held her in thrall, but the fear of her own death so close at hand that she could smell and taste it. It was the sud-

den clarity of that fear which froze her now. She stared
at the knife and saw the man's cloudy yellow teeth and
knew them to be the shepherds of her own annihila-
tion. She felt his cock growing against her hip, his
powerful embrace, his body slick with sweat.

In her retreat from reality she might have survived
him. She might have succumbed to him passively, feeling nothing, knowing nothing, whimpering quietly in
the clutch of demons. Her sanity betrayed her instead
and delivered her up to him whole, sentient, and
strong. She could not bear him. She screamed.

"Said shut up," he snarled, and slapped her again.
But now she could not stop screaming. There was too
much racing through her memory now, too many ter-
rors past and present. It was as if her voice was not
hers anymore but came from someone who had lain
hidden deep inside her, and now the one within was out
of control with terror. Her breath came in sharp gasps.
She saw that behind him some of the others were on
their feet and angry.

"Shut her up," said the toothless fat woman.

The man who had lost his hand awakened and sat up
suddenly. "*Kill her!*" he said.

For a moment the thin man was confused. He kept
slapping the woman but it did no good. What was
wrong with her? His brother was annoyed with him.
She kept screaming and the screams got louder and
louder. His hand moved instinctively to the knife.

"Use . . ." Beside him the pregnant girl hunted for
the word. "Use . . . *tape*."

Tape. He saw it in his mind. He pushed the woman

to her knees. He ran quickly into the second room and then had to run back out again because it was dark in there and he had no light. He snatched up the torch. The girl was still screaming. "*Shut*—" he said and hit the top of her head with his fist. She bit her tongue and drew blood but kept up her miserable noises, screaming and crying. He went for the tape.

"Please, Laura," Marjie whispered when he was gone. "*Please*. You've got to be quiet! You've got to control it." But she did not seem to hear. The man returned with a roll of heavy silver electrician's tape. Laura was on her knees now, sobbing. Disgusted, he tore off a piece of tape and palmed it, slapping it across her mouth and then smoothing it down with the side of his hand like a man using a trowel on wet cement. His erection was gone. He looked at her face, wet with snot and tears. He no longer wanted the woman. He disliked the noises she made—mewling noises, whimpering noises, and because she had to breathe through her nose now, great heavy snufflings of mucus. The man decided he did not like her much. He decided to kill.

The idea excited him. His body began to twitch. He removed the knife from between his teeth and placed it on the ground in front of him, then put the roll of tape in his mouth for the moment. His knee in her back, he reached around her and pulled both her arms out behind her and held them together with one hand while he taped the wrists together with the other. She did not resist him. She was still sobbing weakly. He wrapped the wrists tight.

He slid his fingers into her short-cut hair and pulled her head backward until her back was arched and her forehead pressed up against his cock. He felt it start to rise again. He pinched her nostrils together so she could not breathe, and then when he saw the fear in her eyes and she began to struggle, he released them. He heard her gasp for breath. Giggling, he pinched the nostrils again. This time he did not let go.

Fifteen seconds passed. He could see her trying to stay calm, assuming he would release her as he had before, and then he saw the doubt and then the terror. Her face flushed red. She began to pitch furiously from side to side, trying to throw him, tossing her head against the hand clutching her hair. He held on. She tried to fall face forward but he would not let her. Behind the tape he heard her scream and moan. He felt her weaken. Then after a while she stopped struggling and hung limp in his arms. He lifted her eyelids and checked the pupils. She was still alive.

He released her for a moment and tore off another long, wide piece of tape. He looked back at her lying in a heap on the wet floor and saw that her chest was moving. There was a brief choking sound, then coughing, and then she was breathing regularly again. He grinned and palmed the tape. He reached into her hair again and heard her try to scream. The scream resonated in her nostrils and then a moment later became shrill and far away as he clamped his hand over her face and pushed the tape into her nostrils, then wiped it smooth over her nose and cheeks with his thumb and forefinger, sealing her off.

This time her struggle was tremendous, filled with the power of her blind panic. She tried to stand up but he pulled her back by the hair and pushed down across her shoulders with his free hand. She heaved herself forward and at the same time kicked backward with her legs, pushing them out behind her and scraping them across the floor. Marjie saw the toenails break away. She kicked at him and tried to turn over on her back but he held on tight, on his knees now beside her. Her legs were still free of him so she thrashed and kicked at him wildly. Marjie watched him frown and pull back hard on her hair. Then Laura caught him slightly off balance and managed to get over on her side, facing the cage. Simultaneously Marjie saw the terrible fear and plea in her eyes and saw him release her hair and reach for the knife.

He lifted the knife over his head and brought it down hard in the middle of her back. Marjie heard her muted scream and saw the eyes squint shut in pain. But something had happened, something had gone wrong for the man and she heard him mutter something fierce and crazy and she saw him work the knife loose and raise it again. Laura struggled even harder now. The knife flashed again and Marjie heard the blade scrape sickeningly against bone. He can't kill her, she thought. He's hitting her in the backbone, the blade can't get through

He stabbed her again and there was the same awful sound and she saw him struggling to free the knife. The man was screeching himself now, some wild and unintelligible babble of frustration. He stabbed her a fourth time. This time the blade bit deep into her side. Marjie saw the dark cloth of Laura's shirt begin to glisten. Laura lurched over on her back and lashed out at him with her knee, still screaming behind the gag. She missed his head by inches. He stabbed her in the stomach.

She rolled over, trying to slide out of the way of the knife, but he stabbed her in the back again and this time the wound was clean. Still the girl wouldn't die. She tried to push forward with her legs but she slipped and then rolled over on her side. She tried to ward him off with her legs but the awesome reserve of desperate strength that had animated her was fading rapidly. He slashed her calf and she pulled her legs back away from him.

That was the end. The man leaped on top of her and with one hand grabbed her chin and lifted it and with the other slid his knife into her throat just above the collarbone. There was a spray of bright blood and Marjie closed her eyes.

And yet, amazingly, when she opened them again, Laura still lived. There was movement in her eyes. She could see her shallow breathing. The man was gone. He had removed the tape from her mouth and nose. He had disappeared into the inner room of the cave again, and when he returned, there was a hatchet in his hand.

4:17 A.M.

Moving among the great flat slabs of granite, Nick followed the man at a careful distance. He'd found himself a weapon—a good one, a short sturdy piece of smooth driftwood about three feet long and maybe two inches thick. Just about the size of the riot stick which, he remembered, had nearly split open his skull years ago on Moratorium Day in Boston. He had hated cops then. He was wishing for them now. There was every reason to believe the stick would be necessary. There would be only six bullets in the pistol when he broke in on them, and even if every shot found its mark he was still going to come up short. The idea scared hell out of him. It repeated itself interminably in his brain: *Not enough. Not enough. I can't get all of them.* It was going to be hand-to-hand combat with a tribe of loonies.

I have to try, he thought. No way to stop now. He had seen what they could do to a woman, and to leave Marjie to that would mean he would despise himself the rest of his life. Like it or not, he was not capable of

abandoning her. What if it had only been Laura? he
thought. Would I still be here? He didn't know. He
doubted it. It was Marjie. He felt responsible for her. If
his sense of responsibility had always been hard on
him, it had never been so hard on him as now. He felt
alternately terrorized and oddly elated; he was going
into combat again. He had won the first time—or at
least not lost—and he would win again.

He had totaled an automobile a few years ago, he remembered. It had been a hot sunny day and the roads
were slick from a recent shower. A Volkswagen tried to
pass him and went into a skid, its rear end fishtailing
into his left front bumper and forcing him over an em-
bankment. There was a moment that had remained
clear in his mind ever since, when he was falling
through the air while the car did its own flip and
slammed down hard, roof first. He did not think about
the steel-reinforced doors then, though it was the doors
that saved his ass and kept him from being crushed inside. He only kept thinking that somehow he was going to get through this and in good shape at that. He'd
known he would be all right.

And that was exactly what had happened. He'd
walked away without a scratch. People he'd told about
it kept saying it was a miracle but he didn't think so. It
seemed to him it was the precognition itself that had
saved him, which had allowed him to relax and fall in
time with the heartbeat of the incident, and which had
precluded the panic that might have killed him. He had
a similar feeling now, a mix of fear and excitement
with optimism as its base, a feeling that whatever the

odds, things would be all right. Something told him he wasn't going to die tonight. He only hoped that it wasn't something that came to everybody on the edge of disaster, that it really meant what it appeared to mean. He hoped, for instance, that John Kennedy hadn't felt similarly on his way to the hospital, with half his brains shot the hell away.

He watched the man walk ahead of him by the shoreline. He shook the driftwood a few times, getting a feel for its weight. He thought, *This is for you, you big drooling eight-fingered bastard. You go first if I can help it at all. This is for wanting to eat me, you sick fuck. This one's for Carla.*

Strong but careful, he stayed low and moved along the rocks.

4:20 A.M.

No wonder they bitch about the police, Peters thought. How long had it taken them? A half-hour to assemble. A hell of a long time, considering how fast things were going tonight. He'd been so nervy by the end of it that he'd half considered sending Willis and Shearing on ahead the way he'd promised he would do. But he was too good a cop for that. It wasn't their fault. They were good boys, and he needed cops, not heroes and dead men tonight. I got enough of those right here, he thought.

The ambulance had arrived and the photographers were already working. Peters and Shearing stood by the embers of the fire and watched a much smaller man—in clean white shirt and tie at this hour of the morning, for God's sake—photograph the coal-black remains of what had once been a human being. Behind them a dozen men stood ready, armed with shotguns. Peters carried his own sawed-off pump, the one he kept in the car for special occasions. He guessed this was as special as it got. He spotted Willis amid a second group of men down by the house.

"Willis!" he yelled. "Come on, son, haul it up here!" His voice was a little hoarse. Willis motioned to the other men and they arrived on the double. Another dozen or so. Peters counted them. Yeah, another dozen.

"Sorry, George," said Willis. "Mott wanted the info on their automobiles."

"Let him get what he needs off the radio," said Peters. "We got a good deal of work to do here. You say there's two paths that lead down to the beach?"

"That's right. At least, two that I know of. They branch off this one a couple hundred yards down. One of them isn't used too much as I recall."

"Rough?"

"Pretty rough."

"You remember it well?"

"I think so."

"Okay," said Peters. "We'll take the nice clean highway, me and Shearing. I don't want to get lost on the way. You take your group and head on through the rough stuff. With a little luck we'll meet down there, right?"

"I'm going to come in behind you if I remember correctly," said Willis. "Should take maybe five minutes more my way."

"You'll just have to walk a bit faster then. Okay?"

"Okay." Willis smiled.

Peters hoped he wouldn't go eager on him. "I want you to be real careful. If you see anything you follow it, you don't mow it down. You shoot only if you have to. We've got IDs on two more women and I don't want to spook them into harming them. Also, it would be nice to get them resting real quiet at home if we can. And remember, there could be a whole trainload of 'em out there. So watch your step."

"Will do."

He turned to Shearing. "You ready for this, Sam?"

"Do you ever get ready?"

Peters smiled. "No, I don't think so. Tell you what, though. Do me a favor and run over there and tell that ambulance to hang around till we get back. We're gonna move, so you catch up with us fast as you can. And don't take any shit from them, either. If I get back and they're not waiting here to greet us tell 'em I am ready to take a ruler to their asses and kick in anything over one and a half inches. Got that?"

"Sure, George."

"Let's go, boys," he said.

He turned away and they began to move along the narrow path. They kept their flashlights on their belts. The moon was bright enough. By the time they were out of sight of the house, Shearing had already joined them.

"*Go screw yourself,*" he said. "That's their message. 'Tell George to go screw himself.' But they're staying."

"They'd better," Peters said. He shook his head. "'Screw yourself,' huh? That's real nice. Old fat cop risks his tail in the woods at night and that's what his colleagues give him. I tell you, Sam, civilization stinks."

"I wouldn't know," said Shearing. "Never seen it." They fell quiet then. Their eyes searched the empty path ahead of them.

4:22 A.M.

The man in the red hunter's shirt walked the beach in a kind of stupor, unaware that he was followed. Not only had he lost his prey but there had never been any trace of him at all in the woods. That could only mean one thing; that he was still somewhere in the house. The man did not know how that could be, but he could reach no other conclusion.

So he had doubled back as quickly as possible only to find the house aswarm with new activity. He had not seen the man he was hunting but he supposed he was there among the others. The others had guns.

He knew that they would have to leave the cave now and go north, deeper into the woods. It fell to him to tell them, and this depressed him. They would say it was his fault. He was the eldest and they would blame him for the failure of the hunt, for his failure to find the man. It made him angry that they would think this of him. His anger fell over him like a blanket and he could think of nothing else. It dulled his senses. It prevented him from hearing the man he hunted moving clumsily along behind him near the rocks.

Hunting him.

4:25 A.M.

She didn't know if Laura was still alive. She knew she had no right to be. She'd watched as long as it was possible to watch, and Laura was still living when she could bear no more of it, when there was nothing left in her stomach to get rid of.

She had seen the man toss a pail of foul-smelling water in her face, saw the eyes flutter. He took another torch from the fire to replace the one that had burned away, and propped it against the wall. She had watched with dumb horror while the man bent over her and used the knife to cut away her jeans and strip the bloody shirt from her body. She tried not to look at Laura but only at the man. He arranged her arm out along the floor like a piece of kindling, and it was a moment before she realized what he meant to do to her. By then it was too late; by then the hatchet had severed her arm at the elbow.

That time when she vomited, there was still something left inside her.

She heard a loud hissing sound and an awful stench

filled the room. Trembling, she turned back to look at him again and saw that he had seared her wound with the torch to close it up. He was sitting cross-legged on the floor, drinking her blood from a bowl. Steam rose from the blood-slick floor and from the black, gleaming wound. She may have vomited then too, but now she could not remember. Laura's eyes were open, flickering, watching him through some horrible last effort of will. Perhaps she feels nothing by now, thought Marjie, knows nothing—perhaps she's in shock. Then the man threw down the empty bowl and extended her remaining arm along the floor, and Laura's eyes went bright with knowledge and terror, and Marjie knew that shock had not spared her.

She had to look away as the hatchet fell. She moved back into the cage nearer the boy and put her hands to her ears against the sounds he made—and against the splashing sounds, the hiss of fire and blood with its attendant reek of burning flesh, the low moans, the terrible thump of metal against bone, the sounds of breakage, and the liquid sounds which perhaps were worst of all.

He was keeping her alive as long as he could, and she participated in her torture by her body's blind attempt to survive it. Didn't she know that it was better to be dead now? What awful fraud animated her? Her will to live was as cruel as he was. Marjie could only pray that when her own time came she would . . . what?

She dismissed the thought. It was evil, stupid. Laura had no choice, she understood that. When her own time came, neither would she. *If it came,* she added. And there was the proof of it, she thought. She did not believe that they could kill her. Reduced to cinders, she still would want to live. She thought of her sister.

It seemed to go on forever. Then at last there was a silence and she turned back to them because she knew that she owed it to herself and even to Laura somehow to see what he had done, to witness his crime. Yet it took all her courage to do so. When it was accomplished, when she opened her eyes again, it seemed she had used up the last of her courage, that there was a gaping hole where her defiance had been.

An uncontrollable shudder possessed her now. She did not know when it had begun. It seemed to drain her like a tap on a dying battery. She opened her eyes and saw that both Laura's arms were gone at the elbow, and both legs at the knee. He had piled them beside her like firewood. And still Laura lived, her glazed eyes still blinked and stared, her chest rose and fell in an irregular broken tremor.

Her mouth was open wide. He had impaled her tongue—the offending member with which she had cried out to him before—on a fish hook. And now he was pulling on it, slowly, grinning with an imbecile's ripe pleasure as blood trickled down her chin and dripped across her breasts.

He reached into his pocket and she saw the knife again. He moved the blade into place and pulled the tongue out further. He sliced the tongue carefully along its base and pulled it free. He held it a moment dangling from the hook as though admiring it, opened his mouth and pulled it away with his teeth. He knelt down in front of Laura so he was certain she could see and with both hands fed the tongue into his mouth and began to chew.

It was then that she vowed to kill him if she could.

A few moments later, she heard his key at the lock.

There was no room for anger. Her terror admitted nothing else; it was deep and rapacious. She found herself clinging to the boy's arm so ferociously that she made him cry out.

He tried to pull away. "No," she said, "you have to stay, you have to help me!" She knew that somewhere in her mind she was confusing him with Nick—Nick who had not appeared, who had deserted her, who was still hiding on the rooftop. Oh, help me please, she thought. She was calling to anyone, to everyone—but there was only this boy here with his calm dead eyes.

The cage door opened. Her eyes quickly searched the room but she saw nothing to help her, so her eyes registered nothing. She took no notice of the children huddled by the fire or of the two women, standing watching her. She did not see that Laura was dead now at last, her bowels lying beside her, spilling from the deep rictus in her side. She did not notice that the man was covered with blood now. He was only a shadow reaching out to her from the wide expanse of empty space, empty because it held no help for her and help was all she cared to see.

She held tightly to the boy and tried to wish the man away. He did not go away.

His long thin fingers closed over her forearm and pulled her slowly, almost gently, from the cage. It was a hard, callused hand, slick with dark blood. She tried to cling to the boy but he shook her free with something strangely like irritation, as if she'd interrupted him somehow, and he returned at once to his place in the shadows toward the back of the cage. Her hands went to the bars but there was no real power in them and he pulled her away like a baby from a crib. Tears blinded her eyes and flowed across her cheeks yet she made no sound. For a moment the cave seemed unnaturally quiet. Remembering how Laura had cried, she willed herself to stop.

Don't fight him, she thought. Careful, careful now.

He stood her up against the wall opposite the broken carcass of her friend. She still refused to see it. He stared at her. The quiet deepened. He reached down between her legs. She turned her eyes to the dark ceiling and tried not to feel it, tried to feel nothing, yet he made her skin crawl, her nipples stiffen. Please be careful, she thought.

His hands moved over her body, describing a trail of loathing. She tried to stand firm and not to move away from his touch, to give him no reason to harm her. Then he slapped her lightly on the back of the head.

The sudden impact made her jump. He liked that. He laughed and slapped her again. Against her wishes she felt her anger returning. Oh no, she thought, take it easy; please don't fight him.

He slapped her a third time and now she heard the women laugh too as she stumbled against him. He pushed her back against the wall, his hands on her breasts. Then he began to poke her in the ribs and belly. She put up her hands to fend him off and he slapped them away and poked her, hard this time, just below the rib cage. She stifled a cry of pain. She heard their laughter like the cawing of blackbirds, mocking her.

In front of her the man jumped back and clapped his hands with glee. He slapped her across the ear, and she winced and fell away from him. He poked her breasts, her stomach. He put his hand between her legs and clutched at her, dragging her painfully toward him, then released her and slapped her hard across the face. She fell back against the wall and when she gasped for breath, he broke into a roar of gibbering laughter. Something in her cracked beneath the strain and mockery. Her anger rose swiftly, unrestrained.

She balled up a fist and hit him.

It felt wonderful.

She was not a big woman but there was all the force of her body behind the blow. Her fist caught him just behind the ear and staggered him. He stared at her uncomprehendingly. Behind them she heard the women and children howl with laughter. This time not at her. She took a step forward and hit him again. She caught him square on the ear and the man began to yowl.

And then suddenly she was raging out of control. The blows came furiously. Her face hard and empty, her eyes cold and shining, she kept moving in on him, cutting off his amazed retreat, hitting him in the face and head, heedless of the pain in her own hands. She could do little to hurt him seriously, but the attack confused and astonished him, and instinctively he raised his arms in front of his face to protect himself. That made the women laugh all the harder. Marjie felt a momentary rush of triumph. *Kill him,* she thought, *Jesus fucking kill him*. Wild, joyful, nearing exhaustion, she pressed her attack. The blows kept falling. But she began to know frustration, too, as she began to tire. She had not really hurt him. What would happen when he . . . ?

The man ducked a blow and stepped backward and reached into his pocket, smiling. He pulled out the knife.

It was not even open yet, but to Marjie, seeing the knife in his hand was like seeing a snake coiled to strike. She froze. Instantly a wave of exhaustion swept through her body, nearly toppling her against him. She felt dizzy and miserably, shamefully weak.

She backed slowly away. "No," she said. "Please, whatever you want. Anything. I'm sorry. I swear it. Please, whatever you want. Please."

He advanced on her. She could not tell what he was thinking or what he would do. She could not take her eyes off the knife. She felt the wall of the cave at her back again. He walked toward her. He still had not opened the knife . . .

The man was not really angry. It amused him that she had tried to fight. All the same, he would have to show her, show all of them. He was not to be laughed at. He moved close to her and tapped her on the head with the heavy handle of the knife. He tapped her lightly but it would hurt. He laughed. He would have fun with her awhile. He tapped her again on the top of her head.

He tossed the knife from one hand to the other and back again, to confuse her, so she would not know where the blow was coming from. Then he hit her hard on the ear—where she had hit him, of course—and heard her cry out, and saw the trickle of blood roll down the side of her neck.

He pushed her back against the wall and held the knife in front of her face as he opened it. He opened it slowly, giving her fear time to grow. He watched with pleasure as terror transformed her face and made her soft to him. He turned the bloodstained blade delicately in his hand, only inches from her soft white cheek.

He wondered if he should cut her now . . .

She wanted to speak to him, to calm him, but it was impossible for her. Her voice was gone in what felt like a high wind, a continual struggle for breath. Her body shivered uncontrollably. He held the knife between two fingers and pointed it at her. He moved it up to a level directly between her eyes and then began to move it slowly forward. She pressed her head back to the wall and watched with an irresistible fascination as the blade advanced on her. Oh, please, please, she wanted to say, but only closed her eyes as the point of the blade touched the bridge of her nose and then suddenly withdrew, sliding a terrible thin line of fiery pain across her forehead.

Then he was staring down at her body, his smile vanished, his face dark and serious. His hands went to her shirt, and in a single motion that jolted her back against the wall he tore it open. Beneath the shirt her breasts were naked. She wiped the blood from her eyes and looked down and saw that the tip of his knife was only inches from her stomach, moving forward in the same, slow glide as before.

She stared up into the darkness. If she had to die this way, she didn't want to see it. When it came she did not want to watch and know, the way Laura had known, that the life was pouring out of her. She braced herself against the wall. She felt the cold tip of the knife press against her lightly, just above the navel.

She withdrew, moving back as close as possible to the wall until there was nowhere left to go and she had to suck in her stomach when she felt it again, and still the blade advanced, pressing forward. She felt her flesh retreat and tighten against the slow, even pressure, the growing ache, and then the sudden shock of agony as the tip of the knife invaded her soft flesh. In the cool air of the cave her body felt moist and she knew she was bleeding. The knife stopped but did not withdraw, and her flesh closed over it.

She could hardly feel her legs now. Her mouth filled with bile. Her head began to reel and her eyelids fluttered uncontrollably. Suddenly she could picture herself falling against the knife. *Don't move!* something screamed inside her. *For the love of God stand up!* But her legs would not listen, her legs were giving way and she began to shake with the effort of standing.

The knife withdrew. She started again and groaned as she felt it flick across the nipples of both her breasts. Then they too were wet with blood.

And then his mouth was on her, sucking at the wound in her stomach while his hands pulled off her jeans and pushed them to the ground. She was naked now, naked and beslimed with his lips. It felt evil to be naked in front of him, evil and sick and frightening. Then his mouth deserted her too and his hands were at her shoulders, forcing her to her knees. Weak as she was, she fell gladly.

She tasted blood on her lips and felt it flow from her nostrils as he began slapping her again around the face and ears. Suddenly she was impossibly tired. Her hatred of him remained, a thick knot inside her, but her strength and resistance were gone. In her imagination she tore him limb from limb, but had there been a gun in her hand she'd have had no strength to pull the trigger. The anger burned dull and sullen and useless. She was about to die. Yet all she wished for was a single moment of a power sufficient to kill him. Was this how Laura had felt? A single moment. She tried to summon it.

He lifted her chin and pushed back her head so that now she had to look at him. She saw the pleasure in his eyes and the wide, voluptuous smile. He pressed the point of his knife to her lips and she parted them so he would not cut her. Steel grated against her teeth. She parted them too. She had never felt so helpless in her life. It was too easy to imagine the knife emerging from the back of her throat, the swift wash of blood, her body going suddenly limp, her eyes glazed and dead. One move and . . .

The knife probed the inside of her mouth, passed over her tongue, described an icy circle around it.

At once she understood. She tasted the bitter steel and the salt taste of blood as the knife moved round and round her tongue. He laughed and nodded and there was no mistaking his meaning. He withdrew the knife and then released her.

So that's the end of it, she thought. She watched

him pull off the filthy jeans and saw his cock leap free. She thought, *I'll be good, then*. It was not entirely resignation.

He moved in close and reached into her hair, pulling back her head with an exaggerated slowness, enjoying her helplessness. She opened her mouth and took him inside her.

He was eager and ready and she went to him as she was supposed to—as a lover, with all her skill, with fear and daring in place of passion, and she pleased him. It didn't take her long. In a few moments she felt the sweat begin to break over his body and heard his idiot moan and felt the cock jump between her lips.

In her mind two thoughts blended and began to weld together into a single construct. Her hatred of him was one: that ran deep and thrilling. The other was a vast new sense of her own evil—of the awful place she had been brought to by these people, where there was no love or tenderness but only gruesome death and an appetite that never sated itself, which fed upon itself and drew all who came upon it into the same dark circle of self-destruction. She envisioned a night littered with corpses; the house a vague necropolis of strange dead children and friends and a sister she had loved; this filthy kennel the end of the journey of a lifetime. Whatever she did now, whatever happened to her, would not matter. Nick would not find her. No one would. What she had to do now was dictated from the start, when she had seen her sister die. It was very simple, actually.

He began to come. She waited until she felt the first warm jet of him at the back of her throat. Had she believed in god she might have felt grateful then—she had prayed for a moment of power over him and it had been granted her. She closed her eyes and felt her hatred in her jaw like a clenched fist. *It is not killing him,* she thought, as she brought her teeth together, *but it will do.*

Then suddenly she was on her feet, feeling his warm blood splash her legs and naked thighs while he screeched and released her hair and tried to halt the pumping gout of blood. She reared back and spit away the stinking stump. He howled like a mutilated animal. She loved the sound. She loved the cooling gore across her thighs. And then in an instant she was rushing toward the entrance to the cave, her mouth an angry, wild grin, unmindful of the women who seemed to rise up out of nowhere to clutch at her, unmindful even of the huge bald man who was weak from loss of blood and unable to stop her.

She thrust them all aside with a preternatural power, tossed a child against the cave wall with such violence that she heard its skull pop and split open like a melon. She heard herself wail with all the mad joy of a warrior delighting in his fallen enemies. And she *was* delighted, at last to have hurt him and to be free. Arms wide, she ran toward the entrance, past the fire that licked at her shins, past all the half-human vitriol and garbage sprawled stunned around her.

She saw the moonlight peeking through the entranceway and raced toward the clean scent of the sea that at once assailed her nostrils through the heavy reek of smoke and gore. I did it, she exulted, I got him!

She tore away the skin at the mouth of the cave and hurtled forward into the night.

The man in red was walking slowly up the pathway to the cave when he heard the screams inside. They were not the screams of his captives, of the boy or of the women, but of his people. The loudest, the worst—the one that froze him there—was his brother. He had never heard anyone scream like that before but he knew his brother's voice. There were ghosts angry in the night tonight. The hunt had gone bad, and they all would pay now.

He hesitated in fear of what he heard inside. But the screams continued. They pressed him on, despite his fear—their urgency a dim call to the depths of his compassionless soul, reaching to a common heritage of blood and violence; a summons to be answered. Grim, silent, joyless, he walked on.

In her rush to freedom she did not see him. For a moment the clean fresh air embraced her like a gentle lover. Then his hands were on her and she was struggling against hard male flesh, tearing with bleeding fingernails at the red shirt he wore, and all her new-found strength could not save her.

That Nick, following behind, had seen them from the rocks below she could not know, nor that he was racing toward them up the rockface. For Marjie everything crumbled in an instant. The momentary power in her fled, routed forever. Her body went limp against him as he carried her inside and tossed her down by the fire.

She was lost, used up, vanished. The strength she had called upon could never be summoned again. The struggle was over. The struggle but not the nightmare . . .

In moments the children were upon her like flies at an open carcass. She began to scream, a high thin wail that could not even begin to express the pain and despair, the thousand tortured nerve ends that tore and broke under their weight and beneath their jaws. They went at her like wolves, gouging flesh from her cheeks and arms and shoulders, ripping wildly at her breasts and thighs. In mindless astonishment she saw them in the act of eating her alive. She saw them tear a nipple from her breast, and they were still on her when she heard the gunfire.

It was a tableau Nick had never dared imagine as he ran up the narrow path to the cave. But in an instant his eyes took it in. The man in the red shirt whirling on him in front of the fire. The two women flanking him—the pregnant one standing beside a blood-splattered child whose head lolled off to one shoulder at an unnatural angle. To the rear, the boy in the cage looking up at them in wide-eyed surprise and the thin man on his knees, screaming and clutching his genitals. The third man, a huge one, looking bloodless and reaching toward something—some weapon, Nick was sure—on the floor. And finally the pack of howling malefic children who slavered like beasts over something that rolled and thrashed in front of him in frantic desperation. *Marjie*. He took it all in within a second and immediately began to kill.

His first bullet went wild, careening harmlessly off the walls of the cave behind the man in red. In the enclosed space the explosion was tremendous, and the man was startled and slow to respond, amazed to find Nick here inside the cave, firing a gun. In the time it took him to recover, Nick aimed again and fired. The second bullet caught the man full in the chest and pitched him backward into the fire. He was dead before he landed. Thick dark smoke and sparks filled the air and the red hunter's shirt began to turn black. The man's legs and arms began to jerk spasmodically. The stewpot spilled its contents on the earthen floor.

The big boy hissed and darted away, back into the cave, and the other children followed. Nick could barely see them through the heavy smoke. He saw Marjie stir below him and heard her moan. She was alive, then. Thank God.

He swung the driftwood at the women on either side of him, driving them back. He saw the huge hairless man lumber toward him through the smoke, his wrist wrapped in skins, some kind of club raised high above his head. Nick fired once and saw the man stagger, what was left of his shattered hand reaching instinctively for his belly. He lurched forward again, and Nick fired at him a second time and saw half of his neck disappear and a huge whale spout of gore shower the room as the head toppled sideways to his shoulder like a fallen tree. The man fell to his knees and then tumbled forward. His club rolled over the embers of the fire and stopped at Nick's feet. He saw what the weapon had been. A human arm.

Then, suddenly, the children poured out at him past the now-dense clouds of smoke. His peripheral vision registered that the women beside him were moving too. He dropped into a low crouch and hurled himself against the nearest one, the fat one, and drove his elbow hard into the soft pillow of her stomach. He heard her grunt and heard something metal—a knife—rattle to the ground. At the same instant he fired at the children but there was too much smoke in his eyes and too much motion and the bullet went wild. Before he could squeeze off another round they were on him, their jaws working like the mandibles of hungry insects.

Suddenly he was aswarm with them. He felt a set of small sharp teeth at each leg. Another at his hip. A fourth child slammed into his back at his gun-hand shoulder and began to claw at his neck. He felt a moment of pure panic. Then he saw the biggest boy leap at him from amid the smoke and he pulled the Magnum around and fired, catching the boy in midair, his knife poised to strike. The blast jolted the boy backward as though pulled from behind by a rope. The knife fell spinning against Nick's chest. He lurched forward and doubled over at the waist and shook off the clawing thing—a girl—at his shoulder.

He screamed in agony as yet another girl found his leg wound with her teeth, and thrust the pistol down at her. He pulled the trigger but the chamber was empty. He tried again. He screamed again as he felt the pregnant woman behind him bite deep into the arm in which he held the driftwood, biting him just above the elbow. He swung the arm up and rammed her hard but she would not let go. He swung the gun barrel around and slammed it into her face. She fell backward, blood streaming from her mouth and nose. The little girl at his leg wound bit harder, jaws working cruelly from side to side, trying to reach the bone.

He brought the gun around again and slashed twice at her skull with all his power. His second blow broke the child's neck at the shoulder. A bubble of dark blood burst across her lips and she crumbled to the floor. But the leg was finished now. It buckled and he fell to one knee.

The boy at his hip released him with a snarl (he's been biting my belt, the crazy bastard! Nick thought wildly) and threw his arm over Nick's neck, his other hand raking Nick's face with his long filthy fingernails, clawing for his eyes. Nick hit him with the pistol, but the boy was wild now with the rich scent of blood and the blow did nothing to stop him. He scraped at Nick again and tore open his cheek. Nick hit him a second time and watched, stunned, as the blood welled up along the side of his head and the boy simply shook himself like a wet dog and growled and reached for him again.

For a terrible moment Nick imagined he would have to go on killing the boy forever, that he would never stop. He shifted to one side and slashed at him with the driftwood again and again, hitting him across the shoulders and head, and still the boy clung to him and clawed at him, even after Nick saw his collarbone protruding through the back of his neck. Nick lashed out blindly until finally the boy lay still, his head a muculent pool of blood and slime.

And then there was silence. It confused him. There ought to have been more of them. How many had he killed? Five? There were more children. Another man. The two women. Had he killed the women? He didn't think so. The silence glided over him like a net. He rubbed his smoke-filled eyes and peered beyond the billowing fire and saw Marjie trying to rise up on one elbow. Behind the veil of smoke he saw the naked boy standing alone at the cage door, his black eyes seeming to gaze in Nick's direction. Who was he? Nick knew he could not be one of them.

Then he saw the thin, gaunt man gripping the cage and trying to rise. Someone had wounded him. Who? When? Through the violence of his own pain he realized that the man was badly hurt, that it would be some time before he was dangerous again. But where were the others?

The right lens of his glasses was broken. It was amazing he had them at all. He pushed them up on his nose and turned his head to look behind him. There was nothing there. No one. He looked at the body of the boy he had shot, twisted and sprawled behind the fire, at the half-naked bald man crumbled beside him, at the two children he had beaten to death, at the dark body sputtering on the fire. Dead. All dead. And miraculously, the others had vanished. His sigh of relief rattled hideously in his throat. He turned to attend to Marjie.

It was hard to know where or how to touch her. Her body was covered with blood, and Nick could tell that most of it was her own. She was still trying to sit up.

"No," he said, "stay there. It's over now. Please, don't move. I'll find something to cover you with, and then we'll see about getting you out of here." His voice seemed strangely high-pitched to him. His teeth chattered and he quivered uncontrollably.

He stood up slowly and found that, as long as he moved very carefully, the leg would support him. He picked up the driftwood and the empty pistol just in case. He walked to the cage and saw what was left of Laura in a pile against the wall. He turned quickly away before the dead fish-eye stare and the open black mouth made him puke.

The wounded man was still trying to haul himself up on the bars of the cage. Nick smiled grimly and rapped him hard across the knuckles with the driftwood. The man groaned and slid heavily to the ground.

At his approach the naked boy stared at him fearfully and faded back into the cage. Nick supposed that was security for him now. He wondered how long the boy had been here and what the boy had seen. He could think of nothing to say that might make him feel that it was over now, so he passed him by without acknowledgment.

He found Marjie's torn shirt and jeans and guessed that they were cleaner than anything else the place had to offer. He knew he should cover her somehow and keep her warm to ward off shock. He noticed the entrance to the second cave. It worried him. Could someone still be hiding there? He realized now that this was where the children had disappeared to earlier. Could they have done so again?

He peered inside and heard something scurry away in the dark. A breath of chill rolled down his spine. He listened a moment and heard nothing more. Aside from the rats, it was empty. He gathered up Marjie's clothes and limped back to the entranceway.

He gazed down at her a moment and then began to dress her carefully. Her wounds were frightening. It would still be rough getting her out of here alive. He handled her tenderly.

"Easy, Marjie," he said. "Easy, honey."

She closed her eyes. He wondered if she even knew who he was.

And then he heard the gunfire.

4:50 A.M.

They'd heard the first reports from Nick's pistol just as they were coming off the path to the beach. Peters motioned for the men to stop, though it wasn't necessary. The gunfire had stopped them all cold. Now what the hell kind of party we got here? Peters thought. There was no mistaking the sound of a Magnum once you'd owned one. Firearms, he thought. I hope Willis is real close by.

Two more shots sounded in the still night air. Not far away, he thought. "Let's go," he said to Shearing. "I can't exactly run but I can take a poke at trotting."

"I think that was a Magnum," said Shearing.

"I damn well know it was," said Peters. "Which is one more reason you'll have to hang around and wait till I retire. I'm too damned good for you." They headed out across the hard-packed sand at the shoreline.

By the time they heard the third pair of shots, Peters was already breathing hard, his men at some pains to stay behind him. Anxious young fellows, thought Peters. But then the young are always anxious. And of course these boys smelled blood in the air. He couldn't say he didn't himself. Guns. He didn't like that development one bit.

"You boys see any hardware pointed at you, you be sure and blow it to hell." He was panting now. "We can figure out how and why at our leisure."

He tried to put on a little more speed. He wondered where the hell Willis was. This running was doing his heart no good at all, and Willis was fifteen years his junior. Willis should be doing the running. Probably that path was worse than he'd thought.

"Sam," he said, "I'm slowing you down. Go on up ahead and let the old man bring up the rear. But watch yourself, will you?"

"Okay," said Shearing. But there wasn't much time for him to fall behind. They had only gotten a short distance ahead of him when they saw the smoke, just a few yards away up the side of the rockface. Shearing was first to notice it and he stopped the others. "That would be it," he said.

"Yes it would," said Peters. And now he could smell it, too, and he knew immediately that it was not wholly wood smoke. It seemed inconceivable to him that he should have this stink in his nostrils twice in one night but there you had it, pure fact. Goes with the job, he thought, and tried to shrug off his repulsion. "Easy now," he said quietly.

They moved off the shoreline and crossed the fine white sand to the cliffs. The curl of smoke was just above them now. Almost at once Shearing heard a man's voice, a faraway cry of agony. He turned to Peters. "I heard it, too," Peters said. "Let's get the hell up there."

"Find the path," said Shearing. "Spread out."

They turned on their flashlights and Shearing found it immediately.

"Here we go," he said. The men grouped around him. Peters thought it best to let him lead the way. It looked like a steep climb from where he stood and it was probably better to have a younger man up front. A younger man, he thought. Same old bullshit, but there was no getting around it, he wasn't as fast as he used to be. And Shearing was a good man, even if he was too damn skinny for his own good and even if he did hover over Peters like a buzzard sometimes, watching for an opening, a chance to prove himself. Well, he had one now, by God. Sam would be fast, though, thought Peters, and he'd be careful.

At least they knew now that there was somebody alive up there. Or had been up until that scream. What the scream was about he didn't like to guess.

"You get to it, son," he said to Shearing. Shearing smiled. Peters would remember that smile later. It was an excited smile, the kind you saw on a good man about to show you what it was that made him good. They started up the mountain.

It was the pregnant woman who led them down the path, her nose still dripping blood from the blow from Nick's pistol. They had fled the gun. All the men were dead now except for the one the woman had rendered useless, and the intruder had fought like a demon. So they had fled. As the woman left the cave, she found two of the children already ahead of her. She called them to a halt. She was leader now, and an idea was slowly forming in her. It went like this: *they had to leave the cave sometime.*

The women and children would wait for them down below. She knew the man was wounded, and as for the woman—she thought that the woman must be nearly dead. So the two of them would leave the cave eventually and die together on the beach. It was good that way. They would surprise them; as they came down the narrow path the children would attack them. The man would not have time to use the gun. They would gather rocks and smash them to pieces. They would sleep outside that night and feed on the flesh of the man and woman until dawn came. Then they would return to the cave. The man and woman would die in the moonlight where the gun did not roar and split the shadows.

She whispered some of this to the fat woman and the children as they descended the cliff to the beach. By the time they were nearly at the bottom, the young pregnant girl was laughing, merry with the prospect of a clever kill. The woman had to make her stop laughing and restrain the children from running noisily ahead of her. She was leader now. She told them to keep quiet or she would send them to where their brothers and sisters had gone, skinned and jointed. Her plan was a good one. Perhaps she would not even kill the man right away. The man was strong and their own men were dead, and many of the children were dead. She knew ways to make a man fuck her even if he hated her. When the time came, she would decide.

Peters guessed later that the woman was as surprised as they were.

Had it not been a woman, and looking the way she did, they might have reacted a split second sooner. Shearing had barely moved when she walked right into him. None of them had ever seen anything like her, half-naked and maybe eight months gone, covered with filth and grime, bleeding from the nose and smelling like a herd of cattle. Peters thought he'd smelled her even before he saw her. And he knew for a fact that he'd never heard her at all. Where the knife had come from none of them could say.

It was obvious they were in for bad trouble, packed together the way they were, waiting to begin to climb. There was no room to maneuver, and the woman was fast. He saw the wildness in her eyes and saw the knife and tried to step back to give them room up front and to raise his weapon, stumbling against Daniels right behind him in the process, but Shearing never even got his safety off. She cut his throat from ear to ear and never made a sound.

His body fell forward against her instead of backward into Peters, and dying that way, Peters guessed, Shearing saved his life. Because the little pump moved up fast then and before she could move again, Peters blew off the top of her head. The woman went down like a cardboard duck in a shooting gallery. The others were right behind her.

Peters saw them scatter off the path, leaping down over both sides of the rockface into the sand. And for a moment he felt like he was in some crazy Western movie with them all huddled tightly together like the last survivors at a wagon-train massacre, shotguns pointed every which way while the strange mad bastards turned and ran at them as if there were hordes of them and not just three kids and a woman against twelve armed men.

He'd never seen anything so fast or so audacious. They haven't got a prayer, he thought, but nobody seems to know that, and nobody seems to care. Like rats, he thought. Except that they were not cornered, there was the whole wide beach to run to (though he'd have cut them down in a second if they tried to run. But how could they know that? And why not quit now? Give it up?). In an instant all this flooded through his mind and Peters' final thought before the fat woman planted her blade into young Parsons' shoulder was that he'd never known the human animal to react this way, and he'd never been so terribly frightened of anything in his life.

It began and ended in less than three minutes. Suddenly the knife was up and then down and Parsons screamed and Kunstler stepped forward and took her out with both barrels at point-blank range, nearly cutting the woman in half. By the time anybody took the little girl seriously, she had launched herself at Caggiano and had most of his throat torn open with her teeth. Peters was first to react. He put the barrel of the pump to her left eye so there was no question of his missing and pulled the trigger. Her jaws were still in Caggiano's neck when they pulled her off him. The rest of her head was gone.

It was then, Peters thought later, that some furious kind of panic seized them, because there was no real reason to kill all the others. Maybe it was seeing what the little girl had done to Caggiano and maybe it was all of it, the whole craziness of the attack in the first place (these were *kids*, weren't they?) but something wild and treacherous passed between them and suddenly it was a different ball game altogether, suddenly there were no sane heads left among them, Peters' included.

The girl—who was maybe eleven and pregnant, as the woman had been—was holding onto Charlie Daniels' leg and trying her damnedest to bite him while Daniels screeched like a woman and started dancing to shake her off, like he'd just been bitten by a snake. They could have maybe pulled the girl away. Instead Sorenson broke her back with the butt end of his shotgun and then broke it again for good measure when she was face down in the sand.

The boy had his legs wrapped around Beard's middle and his teeth were tearing away at his shirt and then they heard Beard howling as the kid ripped past the shirt into his chest. Probably they could have pulled him off, too, but it was . . . Peters didn't know exactly how to put it . . . *loathsome*. Like the kid was some kind of huge leech. Sucking at him. And then with his teeth still in him, the boy began reaching for

Beard's eyes with those dirty little fingers, poking at him, trying to stab him blind. It was an ungodly thing to watch that hand scraping and darting at him, and Parsons, who had been a buddy of Beard's pretty much all his life, must have gone a little bananas then because he grabbed the kid's arm and twisted it back until all of them heard it snap and the boy howled in pain and tumbled free, and then when Parsons had him squirming on the ground, he just put the barrel of the shotgun into the boy's mouth and pulled the trigger.

They did not stop to think what had happened to them or what they'd done—that it was more an execution than a police action. None of them did. Not even Peters. The fear was full and churning in them, and they raced up the hill to where the smoke was still drifting out of the entrance to the cave and that was where they found the rest of them and where they found the girl.

I knew there were men somewhere! thought Peters. It did not occur to him to notice that one of them was still wearing glasses. Nor did he recall that the scream they'd heard below had also been a man's. He was busy. Being scared. Killing.

Nick bent low over her body. He'd been trying to get Marjie to her feet ever since the shooting started but she was in too much pain, and no matter how he did it he seemed to hurt her more. It looked like they had broken one of her legs because the first time she'd put any weight on it, she'd fainted. With his own leg the

way it was, there was no possibility of carrying her. He
had her awake again now but he was thinking that it
was probably better just to leave her here, now that he
knew there were people outside who had come to help
them. He was thinking that the man back on the floor
by the cage didn't look quite so harmless anymore, but
he thought he could handle him. He had just lowered
Marjie gently to the ground when the police broke in
on them.

He whirled when he heard them because for all he
knew *they* were back again, and he knew instantly he'd
made a mistake; recognized the fear in their faces and
saw that they were ready to shoot him. So he threw out
his hands to show them that they were empty and to
wave them away, and he opened his mouth to tell them
No, he was not one of them but the words dried up in
his throat when he saw the fat man's eyes and he
tossed himself to one side and never even heard the
explosion.

Peters saw the glasses fly and something in him that
did not exactly register the word *glasses* did register
that something was not right somehow, but the man
had turned on him and his hands had gone out, *not up*;
and there was no question about the other man, who
looked wounded bad but who suddenly bolted toward
them in a low crouch, sporting a black-handled knife.

The moment Peters saw the knife he fired. It was
odd, though, that even before he fired he seemed to see
the blood there. Or maybe it was the bloodstain he

fired *at,* maybe it was already there, between his legs. It all happened much too fast to say. But in any case Peters hit what he aimed at. The man fell face down, his legs jerking back as if somebody had pulled a rug out from under him. When they turned him over there was nothing left at all below the belly except a pair of legs. He wasn't quite dead.

Later, Peters felt worst about the boy—even worse than about the one the girl called Nick. But again, they were all unglued by then and with damn good reason, though at the time he seemed to know that there was something wrong about the boy, that the look in his eyes did not exactly jibe with the bloodlust frenzy he'd seen below.

But God knows the boy was strange enough, walking toward them, naked, with his arms held out in front of him, walking in that slow, dreamlike glide. And when Peters told him to stop he didn't stop or even hesitate at all, and by then they were taking no chances. It was impossible to say who killed him. Six shotguns opened up on him at once, and what was left of him was not going to fill up a good-sized shopping bag.

But Peters felt bad, real bad, about the boy. The boy was going to haunt him for a long, long time.

When it was over, Willis and the rest of his party came jostling in behind them. Willis took a look around and whistled softly. "What the hell is this?" he said.

"This?" said Peters. "*This is where I get off.*"

And Willis seemed to know what he meant by that.

5:35 A.M.

The last of the bastards died on the way up the hill to the Hallan place, where the prowl cars waited. Peters thought that a normal man wouldn't even have gone that long. In the end he pointed his face to the sea and vomited up a little blood, and they carried him into the clearing, pale as a ghost. Peters couldn't say it made him sorry. The ambulance was there. It didn't do Caggiano any good, though. He was dead before they left the beach.

As for the girl—well, they'd just have to wait and see. It seemed to Peters that she was pretty bad. She was going to lose the little finger on her right hand. It was bit clean through. Compound fracture of the right leg. And one of her breasts was a terrible mess. Running a pretty strong fever, too. Still, she might make it. It all depended on how tough she was. She didn't look tough. Skinny little thing.

That made him think of Shearing. He guessed it would be Willis who told the wife and kids. Probably it ought to be me, he thought, but I'm afraid I'm not up to that. She said that guy Nick had saved her life, he thought. Cried like a baby. And I killed him. Then she said that the kid was wrong, too. My God. Twenty-three years and nothing, absolutely nothing, to mar the record. Oh, there were a few things you had to do that didn't make you feel so good, sure, but nothing like this. An innocent boy dead, and a man who must have walked through hell and back. Because we fucked up, he thought.

Sam Shearing had been a very nice man. Caggiano he didn't know too well, but Shearing, he had been really fine. Even out here they could breed them special sometimes. I need some sleep, he thought. I got to make up the reports. How in the name of god am I gonna be able to do that? How did you write up putting a shotgun to a kid's nose and blowing her head off? How did you deal rationally with any of it? Savages on the coast of Maine, Governor. Wiped 'em out to a man. And then some. Jesus.

He took a last look at the girl in back of the ambulance and then got into the prowl car next to Willis. He didn't know how or when he was going to replace Shearing or who with. For that matter he didn't know how he'd replace himself. But Willis might do. The boy knew the lay of the land. At least, as well as anybody did.

"Get me out of here," he said.

5:40 A.M.

It was nearly dawn.

Marjorie listened to the wail of the siren. It seemed very far away to her but she knew that was not so, that it was just outside the ambulance, and that it was for her, to help her. The gunfire, she thought. It's ruined my ears. She wondered if she was going to hear again. She did not want to be deaf.

There was just a little pain now. The doctors had seen to that. Were they doctors or paramedics? Whoever they were, they had been very gentle with her, very kind, and she thanked them for that, and for getting rid of the terrible pain. It had seemed to her that all the gentleness was gone from the world (when had she felt that? before or after they had shot Nick?), but evidently that was not the case. She could see it in their faces. Even in the faces of the policemen who had carried her here. No policeman had ever looked gentle to her before. It was strange. They had killed Nick without a word and for no reason, and yet she could not hate them. Not now, at least, she thought. She was glad she could not see the house as they pulled away.

Suddenly for a moment she felt afraid again. She cleared her throat with difficulty and spoke to one of the doctors or paramedics, the young one, the one who looked the nicest. Like the siren, her voice sounded faint to her and far away. "Will I sleep now?" she said.

"Not yet," he told her. "Soon. The injections were only locals. They'll give you something stronger at the hospital, after they've had a chance to look you over."

"I don't want to sleep yet," she said. "You won't let me, will you?"

He smiled. "I promise."

She touched the man's hand. It did not seem to be a strong hand.

She turned her head a little to look out the window. From where she lay, she could see only the slowly brightening sky and the telephone wires that seemed to glide slowly along above her as they drove the smooth new tarmac. The wires were studded with wooden poles, like dark stab wounds in the flesh of morning.

AFTERWORD

by Jack Ketchum

Hope you've enjoyed your night-ride along the coast of Maine.

I've written about the hopeful genesis of this book and its somewhat dispiriting aftermath several times and discussed it at length in interviews. So I'm going to ignore the former and be brief about the latter and assume that most of you readers of this new edition are pretty much aware of the book's history and instead, get right down to the heart of the matter—*now why did that sound like a pun to me? Is Bob Bloch somewhere in the room?*—which is, I think, okay, I plunked down my bucks and not a few of them, so what's so different about this? What's the big deal? What's so all-fired unexpurgated?

It's pretty much like the paperback.

But it isn't. Not to me it isn't.

* * *

To date, I have very few regrets as a writer. I regret the last paragraph of *She Wakes* and hope to change it someday. A particularly graceless line here and there. An occasional bad edit. And that's about it except for what happened to *Off Season*.

What happened, exactly, was *negotiation*.

When Marc Jaffe at Ballantine bought the book it was on the condition that I'd be willing to rewrite. And I was. Of course I was. It was my first novel and I was delighted to have the contract. Did they think I was *crazy?* I'd rewrite in a minute. We were all very much aware that the book was over-the-top violence-wise, that it had the kind of teeth pretty much unseen before in mass-market fiction. It was just that quality that they were buying. But I knew I'd have to make some cuts.

I just wasn't prepared for them to want so many.

I remember afternoons sitting across the table from a young pretty pencil-editor whose name now escapes me. Her distaste for the book was clear but she was nice enough and she was loyal. Her firm had bought a nasty sonovabitch of a novel for which they had very high hopes for some ungodly reason and that was that. Her job was to whip this vicious shit into shape. She had a yellow legal pad in front of her with pages full of suggestions. At every session, *more* suggestions.

To some of them I'd say sure, no problem.

To others I'd just shake my head and say, *I can't do that. How can I do that? You're killing me here.*

OFF SEASON

She wasn't trying to eviscerate the book exactly but she wasn't just trimming its nails either.

What it finally came down to was a case of, *I'll give you this bludgeoning if you leave me that beheading*.

Seriously.

There were times we fought through paragraphs line by line. Word by word.

It was basically friendly fighting but frustrating. The goal was the same for each of us—to put together a book that was going to leap right off the shelves. She'd look pretty good to the corporation if it did. I'd be pulling in the bucks. But we had vastly divergent ideas as to how in hell to go about it. We were like a couple of sparring partners both training for the same title shot but using wildly different styles. She was looking to mainstream the thing up a bit. I wanted a goddamn flood-tide.

This went on for a couple of weeks.

By then my manuscript was sporting a lot of red ink. Her notepad had a lot of scratch-outs.

When it was over I went home and a few weeks later produced the version of *Off Season* you've just finished reading. The original I tossed in the garbage.

Yeah, yeah, I know. You don't have to tell me. I'm an asshole. What can I say.

But then it was back to the table again. She'd consulted with Marc and they agreed that the book was *still* too severe. They wanted a book that was going to turn heads, sure, but not one likely to induce projectile vomiting.

Some of the recipes would have to go, for one thing.

273

More negotiating.

So that in the Ballantine edition you don't get to hear the pregnant woman's musings about what she's going to do tomorrow with the rest of their first, nameless kill once she finishes with her sausages.

You don't learn how to make man-meat jerky.

Which I always thought was a shame. I adapted the recipe from a book called *How to Survive in the Wilderness* and figured you never knew when it might just come in handy.

Similarly I missed the lines further on about fear as a tenderizing agent for flesh. I believe I got this from Vardis Fisher's wonderful novel *Mountain Man*, from which I liberally borrowed for the book and from which Hollywood made the movie *Jeremiah Johnson*. Supposedly it's true. Being scared shitless makes you tender.

They also objected to my boiling the shaved, split, eyeless head, suggesting I simply substitute "other cuts of meat." *Sigh*.

They didn't like the boy in the cage lying in his own vomit.

Eighty-six the vomit.

They *really* didn't like the scene where Laura gets her tongue fishhooked and then cut out and eaten. Again I disagreed. Hey, to these guys it's practically a metaphor. I particularly liked the phrase, *offending member*. She *has* been doing a lot of screaming.

They wouldn't let Marjie spit out the cock-stump either. I never did get the reasoning on that.

The way it reads in the original edition, for all we know she swallows it.

All these cuts I gave them. But where we parted ways completely and almost disastrously, this editor and I, were on a few simple lines in the last five pages or so of the manuscript. And I'm happy to say that now, finally, after all these years it's *me* who gets to make the deletions. If this isn't your first time reading the book you've probably already spotted them.

Delete from the original edition *The man Nick would probably make it. There was a hole in his chest that would take a lot of patching but he'd hit no vital organs, thank god.* Delete from the original *Nick lay unconscious beside her. "Will he be all right?" she asked.*

"He's lost a lot of blood. But yes, I think so."

"Good," she said.

Delete from the original the words *damn near* so that when Peters confesses, it's to simply say *And I killed him.*

That's right. They made me save Nick. I wanted him dead.

And that, I remember, was a tough one.

At first I flatly refused. The very suggestion pissed me off. What I was looking for with Nick, what I'd been looking for all along, was a portrait of a guy rising to levels of heroism and loyalty he'd never dreamed he had in him. And then, at the very last moment, when all this pain and effort should have paid off for him, when he *should* have been rescued, when holy smoke here comes the cavalry! the goddamn cavalry are the ones who cut him down.

Night of the Living Dead you say? Absolutely. I remember that the impact of that final scene devastated me in the movies and I wanted the very same effect on the printed page. I even cited the film to Ballantine. Neither my editor nor Marc had seen it. I might have been talking to them in Ancient Celtic. *Living Dead* was a low-budget quickie. This was gonna be a blockbuster. Just you wait.

They turned my own reasoning against me. Here's this guy, they said, he goes through hell all night. He *ought* to live.

Ought to?

The readers will want him to live.

Want him to? Sure they will. So do I. By the end of the book I practically love the guy. But who *cares* what the readers will want? For the book, this was just *right*.

Period.

Nick's death was crucial, I said, both thematically and dramatically. It's what the book is *saying*. That life's like that. That the world's like that. You make a killing on Wall Street and the next day you're hit by a crosstown bus. You fall in love and find out you've got Alzheimer's. Why does Carla—the strong sister—die horribly in the first act and Marjorie, the weak one, survive? *Who the hell knows?* Irony, chance, the sudden drop off the edge of the world, the whole vast roll and toss of circumstance, they're the whole damn point!

I pled my case.

I lost.

I figured, all right, it's your first book. Bend with the wind.

Remember, this was gonna make me rich. They promised.

Remember too, that it didn't.

By the time distributors were backing off posters and point-of-purchase displays in stores, by the time the cover was changed from a severed female arm to a single drip of blood, by the time Ballantine had backed off from all publicity and refused, first, a sale to a British imprint and then to distribute their own edition in the U.K. as planned, it was clear they were going to make no attempt to keep the book in stores here in the U.S. either. My local Barnes & Noble sold out a dozen copies in a matter of days. I never saw another there again. Ballantine were engaged in sweeping the whole nasty mess under the carpet. Phones were ringing. The CEO of Random House, their parent company, had been chided in print by the *Village Voice* for publishing violent pornography. *Off Season* had become an embarrassment.

The pretty young editor whose name I don't remember stopped returning my calls.

Marc Jaffe left the company.

I've wondered over the years what further rude noises would have been heard on Publisher's Row had they published this version.

Forget the recipes and the bit—*Bob? is that you?*—about the tongue.

For me, Nick's death makes the whole thing infinitely darker.

Just think who's left at the end of this cruel night. One woman—mutilated physically and psychologically damaged, who has found a cold tensile strength inside her but has seen and done things nobody should *ever* have to see or do. And Peters—a decent man, a cop who has killed not just one innocent civilian tonight but two for godsakes and *of* those two civilians, one has committed the kind of staggering acts of will and commitment which will weigh on Peters' heart and soul forever.

It was this bleak, nobody-wins-in-this-world notion I was after.

If Nick lives, there's hope. For all we know maybe he and Marjie will get together.

If he doesn't, she's alone.

I think that for Ballantine that was a deal-breaker. I think that for them that was intolerable.

There was one other change I made. Not for this edition but for the British paperback.

At the very end of the original Marjie's in the ambulance, shot up with painkillers and speculating through her haze on whether these people who are treating her are paramedics or doctors. *She hoped that they were doctors,* reads the line.

A few months after the book was published I got a letter from a fan who said he'd enjoyed the read immensely. Until he got to that line.

He went on to say that *he was in fact a paramedic* and in Marjie's situation she'd be far better off in the hands of a trained ambulance crew then with a bunch of doctors. I checked it out and he was right of course. *Whoops.* I hadn't done my homework. I wrote back and apologized and thanked him for bringing the error

OFF SEASON

to my attention and promised that if the book ever went into another printing anywhere I'd fix it.

In '95 the Brits at Headline came along and I did.

My editor there, Mike Bailey, laughed when I told him why I wanted the changes.

Said *certainly, send them along.*

No negotiations.

—Jack Ketchum

WINTER CHILD

By Way of Introduction

On page one hundred eighty-six of my novel, *She Wakes*, a group of seven people, a mix of locals and tourists, are sitting around a table in an outdoor taverna on the Greek island of Mykonos, drinking too much wine and nervously nibbling at mezes, discussing their . . . uh, situation.

They're waiting for the ax to fall.

Each of them has been visited and seriously terrorized by the spirit of a dead woman, the ex-lover of one of them and who's been killed, accidentally, by his hand—a strange passionate schizophrenic beauty in life, now reincarnated, appropriately enough, as the split-persona, tripartite ancient Goddess of pre–Golden Age Greece—her aspects Selene, goddess of the moon, Artemis, goddess of the hunt, and Hecate, the goddess of witches. And the dead. In fact she is in the process of raising the dead and commandeering the wild things of the island to do her bidding—though none of the people at the table have tipped to any of that yet. But they will.

The shit is about to hit the fan—both in Mykonos and on the neighboring island of Delos, the legendary birthplace of the Gods, to which they are about to flee and there, to meet their fates.

Among the group is a man named Jordan Thayer Chase, the only one who has any clue as to what might be going on here. Chase is a psychic—has been since he was a boy—and knows that for some reason he's been summoned to this place at exactly this time, for what reason he doesn't know, but understanding that quite possibly he's been led to his doom. He's accepted that. The call is that strong. . . .

Most writers like to experiment. It helps to keep the work interesting and the writing fresh. In *She Wakes*, my fourth book, I experimented with a story-within-a-story, something I'd never tried before, a short tale within the mainframe of the novel which would have a coherant beginning, middle and end, which could stand alone but would also shed some light on Chase's history and character and how he first discovered his fine and dreadful gift. I had in mind something on the order of Robert Shaw's wonderful monologue from *Jaws* the night before the film's climactic battle, the story about the fate of the crew of the U.S.S. *Indianapolis* in shark-infested seas—the dark, dark quiet before the storm.

It didn't work. I'd built up a pretty fast pace to the book by then and all the story did was slow things down. Shaw's creepy monologue had lasted only a few minutes of screen time. Chase's yarn went to almost twenty pages. I couldn't justify it. It wasn't really crucial to illuminating any of my characters' various situations, not even Chase's own. So I dumped it. I realized it couldn't possibly be of use so I never even bothered to try to cut or revise it.

I did keep it, though.

I was going through some old papers and there it was, by now completely forgotten, a sheaf of yellowing paper. I read it through and it surprised me. It still didn't work at all in terms of the book. But that didn't necessarily mean it wasn't working.

And reading it over I remembered that for years thereafter I'd retained a certain fondness for the story, a certain regret that I couldn't fit it in. That was why I'd held onto it for so long. *She Wakes* was my only supernatural novel for one thing and I liked the way the story took the reader back to the horrors of reality. In it Chase is a budding psychic, yes, but the antagonist he faces is completely possible within the real world, completely human, with no supernatural powers whatsoever. In fact—and this is the second reason I liked the piece—she's borrowed directly and quite consciously from my first novel, *Off Season*. The mute sinister little sister of my ferocious group of cannibals on the coast of Maine. The nearest town to Chase's dad's farm is Dead River, just as in *Off Season*, only here that stunted northern coastline is observed mostly in winter. The town sheriff is Sheriff Peters, a momentary appearance. The little girl in the story prefigures the sole young survivor of my initial feral clan who was to reappear, with her own brand-new family of people-eaters, in the sequel *Offspring*, written ten years after the original—though the story itself is set some thirty years before the original, some time in the early 1950s.

Confused yet? I can only beg pardon and say that sometimes the roots of what one imagines in this business are tangled even for the writer.

Anyway, for any of you readers out there who might be interested in what was left out of the original plan for *She Wakes* or are looking for more in the way of *Off Season*, I give you *Winter Child*. Hopefully it stands on its own without either book to support its claim to a few minutes of your attention. I've gone over the red-ink scratchings-out and writings-in and the many paste-ups—the thing was written on a typewriter!—to give the story a final shape, but otherwise it remains the same as it was back in 1988, for better or worse. My castaway, my orphan in the snow.

—J. K. December 1996

WINTER CHILD

The waiter brought the wine, uncorked the bottles, placed a cash-register stub under the ashtray along with the breakfast stubs and walked away.

Chase began to pour.

"I was just a boy," he said. "Seven years old. But it was the very last year of my childhood . . ."

My father was not young that winter, he was fifty-five. But he was still big and strong and probably could have remained a jack for ten more years had it not been for the injury to his back. The lumber company had reduced him to clerking, probably because he was one of the few men along the timberline in all of northern Maine who could add a six-figure column and still know birch from poplar. He wasn't happy at it though, and I think the only reason he stayed was the land.

We owned thirty-two acres, most of it rough scrub and bare mountain but some of it prime. We were alone there, he and I. My mother had died two years

287

ago in the dead of winter the same way my younger
sister June had only weeks before her, of pneumonia.
Bad lungs ran on the female side.

So there we were, just the two of us on all that land,
the nearest neighbor six miles east past Horsekill
Creek and over the hills halfway to Dead River,
halfway to the sea. And it was winter again, and we'd
survived just one other winter since my mother and
June died, and the first big snowfall reminded us hard.

If depression can kill a man then my father was in a
lot of trouble that season.

There was plenty to keep him busy. It wasn't that.
There was the job—he reported there daily after drop-
ping me off at school, or whenever he could make it in
to town in bad weather, taking the four-wheel drive
over rutted treacherous roads—there was taking care
of the two of us and our basset Betty and keeping up
after our pair of geldings. In what time was left to him
he'd go out with the shotgun for rabbit or quail, or else
you'd find him at the worktable in the barn beside the
portable heater, at what we called our shipyard.

Shipbuilding in the state had pretty much dried up
by then as the great forests had died from overharvest-
ing and underplanning but there was a time when our
tall white pine produced hundreds of masts and spars,
our oak produced ribs, our ash, fastenings, our yellow
pine, planking. During World War II Maine built sub-
marines and destroyers at the rate of one a month.

My father had become fascinated with ships as a
boy growing up in Plymouth and built models of them
in his spare time, a lifelong hobby. I'd help him now

and then. Or try to. He was good at it, meticulous and patient, and I reaped the rewards. My bedroom was full of his finished pieces. I had longships, galleys, clippers, paddlewheels. There was a model of Fulton's famous Clermont and White Star's Oceanic.

My mother used to talk about sailing away on that one.

I could stare at those shelves for hours, imagining ships at full sail or riding out the storms. And if my mother never got to sail away on one, I did, plenty of times.

But you could see there was no joy in that for him either now. He used to love to talk to me when he worked, about how one piece fitted into another just so, about how he was adapting ply to do the work of yellow pine, about joints and fittings. He'd joke about the clumsiness of his hands. His hands were far from clumsy. But now he worked in silence. His ships were at the service of some infinitely sadder impulse, far more solitary than before.

Most of the time I didn't even come around anymore.

I know that by January I was already worried about him, in the way that kids are apt to worry. I reacted badly. Insecurity made me frustrated. Frustration got me angry. I gave him a hell of a hard time. I was scared.

My father was supposed to be open, steady, easy. A rock. Not silent and withdrawn like he was now. I started sleeping badly. There was always something in the closet when I went to bed. I remember creeping up on it one night with a model Spanish galleon in my hand to impale or smash whatever was in there, then flinging the door open to stare relieved and bewildered at my usual everyday clutter.

And then in February we had the biggest blow we'd seen in years. The snow was over my head in the flatlands and over his head where it drifted by the sides of the house and the barn in bright crystal waves. It was soft and powdery so that if you tried to walk you got buried in the stuff. School was closed indefinitely. Getting to work over the roads was impossible. So my father stayed home all that week spending most of his time on a three-foot model of the battleship *Monitor,* which had defeated the Confederate *Merrimack* during the Civil War, the first successful ironclad in the U.S. Navy. Even our bitch hound Betty wouldn't go out in all that snow and normally she was game for any kind of weather. Though she was pregnant at the time, so maybe that also had something to do with it too.

It was beautiful, so much snow, and at first it made you happy just to look at it. All the familiar shapes softened, recast in white, sparkling in the sun or gleaming beneath the stars.

It was beautiful—and then it was confining.

It shrunk our world to five small rooms and a barn and a shovelled path between them. While the cold kept it from melting. And every night it would start again, to trap us further.

By the third day I think I'd gone a little crazy. I brooded and stomped around. As far as I was concerned the *Monitor* was garbage and my father was a fool for bothering with it. To me it looked like a boring flat cigar with a turret on top. I barely spoke to him. I barely touched my dinner. And just before bed I caught him glance up at me from a magazine and felt as guilty as I've ever felt in my life before or since. Because the man was clearly suffering. I'd made him suffer. As if he weren't unhappy enough that winter without my mother and sister there. One spiteful little kid, the last of his family left to him, was enough to take him all the rest of the way down to empty.

It was just what I'd wanted. And now I had it.

And now it was my turn to suffer.

I sat in bed wondering how I was going to make it up to him, trying to get up the nerve to go apologize. I thought about my mother and sister and knew he was every bit as lonely and unhappy as I was. Probably more so.

I'd been a little shit and I knew it.

I felt like crying.

I was still trying to fix the right words in my mind, to get up the courage to go out and say something when I heard a knock at the door.

Not a loud knock. Almost hesitant, soft. Polite-sounding. Which was strange because the night was absolutely wild, cold wind howling and the snow streaming by my window so that tomorrow was going to be a replay of today weather-wise, and here's this sound at the door like a neighbor come to visit on a bright sunny summer day. I heard my father get out of his armchair and cross the floor and heard the door open and than I heard his voice, excited, though I couldn't quite make out the words. I heard stamping feet and our pregnant hound Betty growling and my father shushing her and then the door slammed shut.

I sat up in bed and it was the slamming door that did it, all at once—all of a sudden I was frightened. As though whatever was out there that isolated us on that winter night was inside with us now and the closing of the door made it final. I knew instinctively that whatever it was, it was not going to go away, and that scared me too. It was the first time in my life I'd ever had the sense of something, yet I knew immediately that it was a completely true sense like any other, like sight, taste or touch, and for a moment its sudden presence in my life blinded me. In my mind I saw something dark moving along a forest floor, something that lived and belonged there, a human shape yet belonging to the forest.

Not in here.

I was just a boy. I didn't understand.

I heard my father call and walked out of my bedroom, knowing I wasn't just shaking from the cold air swirling over my feet. The dog was growling again low and steady. My father ignored her this time. He was full of purpose, eyes moving fast over the girl who stood in front of him as he brushed her down, threw a blanket over her and moved her gently toward the fire.

I'd never seen anybody so pale.

She looked to be eleven or twelve, with light brown hair and wide green eyes. She wore a dirty woolen coat over a thin white cotton blouse and a faded floral-print skirt that came down to her ankles over a pair of old galoshes that looked nearly frozen to her feet. My father positioned her so that her feet pointed away from the fire so they wouldn't warm too quickly. Her face was streaked with dirt. So were her wrists and hands.

"Turn on the stove, Jordy," he said. "Put up some water."

I did what he said while he rubbed her arms and legs. The girl just sat there silent. Then she looked at me in the kitchen by the stove as though she'd noticed me for the first time.

And I remember thinking, here is somebody who has probably almost died out there, and it astonished me, because her face betrayed nothing—no fear, no pain, and no relief. Her face was the flat even surface of a pond on a windless day. It was as though she'd been out for a stroll and was back at someplace familiar, just as expected.

When the water was warm he poured some into a bowl and used a warm wet cloth to wipe down her face and hands and told me to put the kettle back on for some tea. By then she had a little color in her face. Betty had stopped growling. She lay in the corner by the stack of firewood looking very pregnant and basset-hound mournful and somewhat uncomfortable in her skin. The girl shifted closer to the fire and sipped her tea while my father worked slowly at the galoshes, wiping them with the warm cloth and then drawing them off her bit by bit.

I listened to him asking her name, where she came from, how long she'd been out there, were her parents nearby. She never answered and after a while he stopped asking. She just looked at him calm and expressionless, shivering, glancing occasionally at me or the dog, and never uttered a sound or a cry though what my father was doing must have hurt some. Under the heavy wool socks her feet were almost blue from the cold. He kept at them with the warm wet cloth and after a while they were looking better.

We were both pretty tired by the time we saw her head start to nod and her eyes fall shut for longer and longer periods of time so it was a relief when my father picked her up and carried her into my room and put her down on my sister's bed.

"I'm going to have to get these wet clothes off," he said. "Wait outside a few minutes and I'll call you when I'm ready."

His tone was gentle and easy. Apparently I was forgiven for my bad behavior earlier. Even better, he sounded as though, for the moment at least, he'd shed his depression like a snakeskin.

When he called me back into the bedroom the girl was asleep beneath three layers of covers. He'd dressed her in a pair of my pyjamas. I didn't mind. I was only happy to have my father back again, for however long it lasted.

"They're too short," he said, "but mine'd be too long. I don't guess it matters. Lights out, okay?"

"Sure, dad."

I crawled into my bed. He leaned over and kissed me good night.

I sat a long time in the dark listening to the wind in

the birch tree just outside my window and the creaking familiar silences of the house, thinking about this strange new person asleep beside me in my dead sister's bed, almost close enough to touch.

When I woke next morning she was sitting up looking at me with those big green eyes, her lips parted a little, long thin hands folded in her lap. And at first I thought she was my sister, the posture was so much alike. Then I started fully awake. She laughed.

The laugh was coy and girlish and in some way, I don't know why, offensive to me. It sounded to me like breaking glass.

Betty chose that day to throw her litter.

I remember watching her struggle with the first one. The other two came easy but the first was hard. She whimpered and rolled her eyes, lying on the mat by the fire while my father and I waited with yet another pan of water and a washcloth. The girl watched too, sitting erect and slim and alert in a straight-backed rocking chair, wearing one of my father's old flannel shirts that came all the way down to her knees. She'd put away three eggs, six strips of bacon and four pieces of toast for breakfast and looked none the worse for having weathered the storm last night.

But she still wouldn't speak. My father'd tried to question her again at breakfast but all she did was smile and shrug and shovel away the food. Later on he took me aside.

"I think she might be slow, Jordy. It's hard to say, though. She's probably been through a lot."

"Where'd she come from?"

"Don't know."

"So what are we going to do with her?"

"The phone lines are still down. Not much we can do except keep her warm and dry and fed and see what happens once the weather breaks."

After breakfast he took us out to the barn to show us his progress on the Monitor, thinking I guess that maybe it might be of interest to her. It wasn't. In fact she seemed repulsed by the thing, as though the ship or ships in general had some bad association for her, and I remember thinking that the sea was wrong for her somehow, I remembered thinking forest, and she went over to pet and stroke the horses instead. She wasn't interested in the models in my room either. All the time she was with us she never touched them. Or in the magazines my father was handing her. Most of the time she just sat and stared, watching the fire or the dog, rocking, saying nothing.

The pups were all fine and one of them, the first-born, was really a beauty—a male with rich red-brown fur, a black mask around the eyes and a white star in the middle of his forehead. The other two were female, speckled brown and white, cute as any pup would be but more or less ordinary. The male, though, was really something. We decided we'd keep him and see what we could do about giving away the females when the time came.

Early that evening my father and I were out with the horses in the barn, my father currying them down with brisk short strokes while I cleaned and handed him the brushes. We fed them and gave them water. It was still so cold in the barn that unless my father was out there with the heater on working on the Monitor the water would ice over. So you had to change it often.

We stomped on in through the door and the first thing we heard was Betty whining. We went into the living room and there was the male pup dead on the floor in front of her, its flesh half-eaten from the back legs halfway up the belly. Betty was licking at it, looking guilty and defeated.

"Sometimes they do that, Jordy," he said. "I know it's hard. But I guess there was something wrong with him we didn't see. Dogs sense that somehow. They don't want their pups to grow up sickly."

Tears were pouring down my cheeks. My father drew me to him and hugged me and after a while I was better and he let me go and went to the kitchen for some newspapers to clean up the mess. Betty was still licking the pup's head as though she'd just given birth to him, as though that might revive him.

I turned and saw the girl standing behind me and I remember glaring at her, daring her to smile. She didn't. She just looked right through me as though I wasn't there, watching Betty lick the pup. And I didn't know if it was true or not that Betty had some sense about the pup the way my father said but I knew for sure that I had a sense about the girl and that somehow the dog would have been fine if she hadn't been there. I didn't know what she'd done, but something.

And that night I made sure she was the first of us to go to sleep.

* * *

You can get used to anything, though—even lingering distrust—especially if you're a kid. My father's heart had opened up to her and there was nothing I could do to change that. I made it clear that I neither liked nor trusted the girl but my father said give it time.

She stayed.

We tried every possible way to locate parents or relatives—flyers, radio broadcasts, newspapers. My father's company even arranged to get us a series of two-minute spots on the fledgling local TV station. When it became clear that no one was going to come forward my father instituted formal adoption proceedings, which happily for me dragged on and on. Child welfare felt they had a claim to her, especially since my father was a single parent. He found himself a lawyer he could barely afford to oppose them. Meantime we needed to give her a name.

We named her Elizabeth, after my mother.

It was not my idea. But it seemed to make him happy.

Our lives slipped slowly into a routine. My father went to work. We went to school. It was a small six-room schoolhouse and Elizabeth stood out there like a sore thumb. She never talked. She never appeared to listen. She frustrated every approach to teach her, just sat and doodled with a pencil while the lessons droned on. If you looked to see what she was drawing she tore it up. Individual attention didn't help. She just stared at Mrs. Strawn with those wide green empty eyes as though she and the teacher had come from different planets altogether. We knew she could understand language, simple commands, but she obeyed them only if she chose to—that is, unless they came directly from my father. Then she'd smile in that sly sidelong way I'd come to dislike so much and do whatever it was he asked.

I thought it strange that not one kid at school teased her. Here she was, an eleven or twelve-year-old sitting in a third grade class along with the rest of us—who actually belonged there—learning nothing, doing nothing, obviously doomed to repeat third grade while we'd move on to the fourth. Yet nobody teased her. She was pretty, god knows, probably the prettiest girl in the school with her fair skin and long shiny hair and at first I thought that was it. But there was something else about her, something that only I and the frustrated Mrs. Strawn seemed to be immune to.

I had no word for it then. Now I think it's thrall. That quality you see in a cat's eyes when it stares at you. An intelligence you can only partly understand but which drives you to try to anyway, a need to comprehend the thing.

Then summer arrived, and with my father at work I was left alone with her all day. I spent as much time outdoors as possible avoiding her. I'd roam the woods with Betty and her pups, Hester and Lily—we'd decided to keep them after the male died. They were good-sized dogs by then. We'd wade through streams, chase after squirrels or rabbits, find possum tracks and bird's nests and box turtles. I'd wait till just before dinnertime, when my father was due, to come back home. What Elizabeth did alone at the house all day I didn't know and didn't care to know. For a while I'd check my room but she never touched my things or went near my father's models. We'd come home and most of the time she'd be sitting in the shade rocking back and forth on the porch swing, knitting like an old lady.

She knitted nothing but squares of swirling forest-colors, earth and autumn leaves and summer blues and greens. My father thought they were pretty. To me they made no sense at all.

I thought she was crazy.

But that was no big deal.

It was only nights that she actually scared me.

I woke once to find her leaning over me, no more than two feet away, staring. I swear I could feel her breath on my cheek. I pushed her away hard and she smiled and went back to bed. Another night I found her standing naked by the window, looking out towards the barn. It wasn't the first time I'd seen her naked, she wasn't modest at all about dressing and bathing but something about it being dark and her at the window bothered me and I watched her for a long time.

She was thin as a whip, not an ounce of fat on her unless you counted her small breasts or her buttocks. Her eyes kept flickering in the moonlight, darting back and forth as though looking for something. Finally she turned and I closed my eyes, pretending, while she slipped on her pyjamas and crawled back into bed. Only then did I allow myself to try to fall asleep.

Then one night toward the end of summer I woke from a dream in which I was a sailor jumping off a ship onto an old rotted deck high above the sea. The dock gave way beneath my feet and plunged me down to the rocks and the swirling sea below and I woke just as I was going to hit the water. Her bed was empty. It was nearly dawn. I got up and went to the window and out there everything was silent. I walked into the living room but she wasn't there, just the dogs curled up snoring on the rug. The door to my father's room was open. I walked over and looked inside.

My father was asleep. She sat at the foot of the bed watching him, her long dark hair flowing down her naked back, both her hands in front of her between her parted legs while her hips moved slowly, rythmically, back and forth, her hands and shoulders moving down and up. I watched her, not knowing what she was doing but knowing it was wrong somehow, the nakedness, the touching. I saw the beads of sweat along her brow and hairline and the sheen across her shoulders. She tossed her hair.

Then her head snapped to the side and suddenly she was staring right at me.

Her lips pulled back in a snarl and I ran for the bedroom. I jumped up on the bed and pulled my father's long-finished and reassuringly solid-feeling model of the Monitor off the shelf behind me and held it like a club—the same way I'd held the flimsy Spanish galleon months before, afraid of the Creature in the Closet. I stood there listening to my heart pound, waiting, until finally she appeared in the doorway.

She laughed, high and girlish, mocking me, glancing at the Monitor and then back at me, moving slowly into the room, keeping her own bed between us while she pulled on her pyjamas, first the top, buttoning it, and then the bottoms. Not once taking her eyes off me. And there was no laughter in her eyes, only the grey cold of winter, and warning.

She got into bed and pretended to sleep. I looked at her face. She was still smiling.

I went to the kitchen and sat at the table and waited until I heard my father get out of bed. When he came in, yawning, surprised and amused to find me there, I was still holding onto the Monitor.

It was the first of many nights all throughout the Fall when I awoke and she was gone. But after that I always knew where she was, and only once, to reassure myself that I was in fact correct, did I ever try to find her again. She stood beside his bedside with her back to me and her long legs parted, her hands moving down in front of her just as before. I turned and went back to bed.

I worried. I worried about my father and about these visitations. You weren't supposed to creep into adults' rooms while they were sleeping and do things to your body. She wasn't hurting him, not physically, but I knew she was hurting him some other way I didn't quite understand.

I wondered what would happen when I told him. I always knew I was going to tell him. I had to. It was only a matter of how and when. But how and when were what gave me problems. He thought there was nothing wrong with her, really. She was a little strange, sure, maybe a little slow. He hadn't seen what I'd seen. And I suppose that in his way he loved her. Certainly he cared about her, had feelings for her. I was afraid of losing the happy father I'd regained and renewing my acquaintance with the unhappy one I'd lost.

I was afraid of her too. I'd changed my estimation of Elizabeth. She wasn't crazy. She was bad. Evil.

The thing in the forest.

I'd be awake when she returned from his room sometimes and I'd see the look on her face and the slow languid movement of her body and I'd wonder, what if she wants more? What if this is just the beginning? I wasn't even sure what I meant by more. But the idea kept nagging me.

I kept remembering Betty's pup.

So I put it off, over and over again, knowing it was wrong, that I was helping her in some way by not telling. I know now that I was waiting for some kind of sign. A sign that it was okay to tell him. And finally, it came.

We had only one relative nearby and that was my mother's sister Lucy who lived twenty miles away in Lubec. She was a widow fifteen years older than my mother, seventy by then, a cheerful woman who favored burgundy skirts and high-necked white cotton blouses. Her two girls lived with families of their own in Hartford and New Haven. Her husband had left her money when he died and he left her the house, a big Edwardian monstrosity which she kept neat and tidy with the aid of a full-time maid. She used only the first floor, sealing off the rest in winter to save on heating bills. Besides, she said, that much space made her lonely.

Her birthday fell on December 19th and every year around that time she got to feeling particularly lonely. She couldn't get around very much. The arthritis was so bad in her right hip that she was considering a hip replacement. She hadn't been out our way in years because the maid couldn't drive. So she asked my father if I could visit for a few days over the weekend right before Christmas. My father asked me was that okay and I agreed. I think he was relieved not to have to spend too much time there himself over the holidays because Aunt Lucy reminded him of my mother and visiting there in happier days. So I would be his ambassador. As for me, I liked Aunt Lucy, who seemed to have a joke for every occasion, and being in a town for a change—where there was a movie theatre and a bookstore, and an antique shop filled with old winches, halyards, tillers and rigging, where there was so much more going on—was a treat. I didn't mind being free of Elizabeth for a few days either.

But leaving my father bothered me.

In fact I worried so much about him being left alone with her, about what I'd seen, that on the way to Lubec I finally got up the nerve to say something.

"You mean she sleepwalks?"

"No dad, she's awake. I'm sure she's awake. She goes to your room. And she hasn't got clothes on. And she . . . does things. Down here."

He glanced at me, saw where I was touching, and

nodded. Then he looked back to the road. For a while he said nothing. He just watched the road ahead, thinking.

"I've never seen it," he said finally. Then he patted my leg. "Don't worry," he said. "I'll take care of it. I'll keep an eye on her."

That was all we said. I was relieved. Now it was up to him.

Aunt Lucy greeted us at the door and he stayed with us through coffee and Toll House cookies and then he said he had to be getting back and kissed her on the cheek and me on the forehead. We stood on the porch and watched him pull away and that was when I got my second premonition, the same as on that snowy night a year before, at the closing of the door.

It lasted only a moment. I didn't let Aunt Lucy see me crying. Maybe I should have. Maybe it would have changed things. Maybe.

That night it snowed.

It snowed every day thereafter for the next four days and nights, straight through Aunt Lucy's birthday. On the first two nights I was able to call him and he told me everything was fine and on the second night he whispered, "What we talked about, Jordy, in the car. I just wanted you to know she's sleeping soundly. No problem. But it's still real good of you to worry about your sister."

My sister!

The third night the phones went out. The storm was even worse than the year before and lines were down over half the county. I cried myself to sleep. Aunt Lucy knew something was wrong with me. She was puzzled and upset. All I could talk about was when the snow was going to let up and wanting to get home. There was no way I could tell her what was really bothering me. And no way to get out of there either.

It was at some point on the fourth day that something clicked off inside of me and I went into a kind of stony silence, speaking only when spoken to and then in a low mutter that I can hear to this day. Overnight my voice had changed, become deeper, more adult. My walk changed too, got longer, looser, somehow more focused and certain. Everybody who saw me afterwards noticed and commented on it but only Aunt Lucy knew it had started there, at her house, the fourth day of the storm.

Before we knew.

Inside I was a total blank. I can't remember actually thinking anything for the next two days until the snow finally stopped and the road-crews got to work clearing the roads. I was on the phone constantly all day long trying to get through. Nobody was answering. By three in the afternoon she'd enlisted the aid of a neighbor, Mr. Wendorf, to drive us out there in his pickup. By then she was worried too, and Wendorf, a thin balding man of about her age who had long ago worked at the phone company, spent most of his time trying to reassure us that no answer on the telephone didn't necesserily mean nobody was home, not in this kind of weather.

The house looked much the same as it had the year before—big wide drifts against the house and barn and a silent, sleek white mass that covered everything so thoroughly that trees and house and barn seemed frozen in place, so heavy that the wind could get no real purchase on it but could only skim and swirl it lightly in our faces as we walked the fifteen feet from the car to the front door through a trackless, hip-deep waste.

We knocked and Aunt Lucy shouted but there was no answer. I heard the horses snorting in the barn. No smoke came out of the chimney. The house looked dead and silent.

There was a shovel by the door. Mr. Wendorf took it and scraped enough of the stuff away so that we could swing it open. Even he looked worried by then. I wasn't. I was beyond that. I was empty.

The smell of the place hit us immediately and Aunt Lucy shoved me outside and told me to wait there while they went in. I opened the door very quietly and entered behind them. The dogs were missing. I'd seen no tracks outside around the house. We never did find them.

They walked through the living room and past the kitchen and peered in. There was nobody there. The sink was clean, the counter, bare.

Then we got to my father's bedroom and Aunt Lucy started wailing, hands to her face, moaning and wailing, and Wendorf started saying oh my god, oh lord like a mantra over and over and staring into the room while Aunt Lucy turned and ran past me and got sick all over the rug by the burnt-out fireplace.

He lay on the bed in a pair of yellow pyjamas. The pyjamas were ripped open and crusted with dried blood. His mouth was pried open, his eyes stared up at the ceiling. His arms and legs were spread wide like you do making angels in the snow. His intestines trailed out of him to the floor and then looped back up to the headboard like a long brown-grey snake. His heart lay beneath his right arm and his liver below his hand and even I could tell that both had been partially eaten, and the intestines chewed.

I took it all in. I thought about Betty's one male pup. And it was only when Wendorf tried to lead me out of there that I began to cry.

"Dogs," said Sheriff Peters late that evening. "Must have got starving hungry and gone for him. I'm sorry you had to see it, son."

But that was just for my benefit. He wasn't fooling me or anybody.

There was plenty of food in the cupboard and my father would have starved himself before he'd let the dogs go without. It was Elizabeth. There were footprints leading out the back door for maybe twenty feet or so and then they disappeared into the drifts.

I knew it was her and so did he. They searched for her for weeks but I knew they wouldn't find her—I just wondered about the fate of Betty and the pups. But the sheriff had seen what I'd seen, and he knew. He'd looked at my father's face. At his open mouth.

Spread wide by the cigar-shaped body of the Monitor.

Wherever she'd come from, she'd gone back.

It wasn't to the sea.